The Addicted Offender

Also by Judith Rumgay

CRIME, PUNISHMENT AND THE DRINKING OFFENDER

The Addicted Offender

Developments in British Policy and Practice

Judith Rumgay
Department of Social Policy
London School of Economics

First published 2000 by
PALGRAVE
Houndmills, Basingstoke, Hampshire RG21 6XS and
175 Fifth Avenue, New York, N. Y. 10010
Companies and representatives throughout the world

PALGRAVE is the new global academic imprint of
St. Martin's Press LLC Scholarly and Reference Division and
Palgrave Publishers Ltd (formerly Macmillan Press Ltd).

ISBN 0–333–75445–X hardback

This book is printed on paper suitable for recycling and
made from fully managed and sustained forest sources.

A catalogue record for this book is available
from the British Library.

Library of Congress Cataloging-in-Publication Data
Rumgay, Judith, 1952–
    The addicted offender : developments in British policy and practice /
Judith Rumgay.
       p. cm.
    Includes bibliographical references and index.
    ISBN 0–333–75445–X
       1. Drug abuse and crime. 2. Prisoners—Drug use. 3. Social work with
    narcotic addicts. 4. Social work with prisoners. 5. Drug abuse—
    –Government policy. I. Title.
    HV5801 .R83 2000
    365'.66—dc21
                                                           00–031113

10   9   8   7   6   5   4   3   2   1
09 08 07 06 05 04 03 02 01 00

Printed and bound in Great Britain by
Antony Rowe Ltd, Chippenham, Wiltshire

To the memory of my mother,
Joan Rumgay

Contents

List of Figures

List of Tables

Foreword

One of the easiest recommendations to offer public or voluntary sector bodies is for more or better partnership working. In practice setting up enduring and productive partnerships often turns out to be very hard to achieve. This is true across a broad range of public services. However, it is true with a vengeance when partners have simultaneously to bridge the divide between statutory and voluntary sectors, on the one hand, and that between different parts of the public service, on the other, such as criminal justice and health. In documenting the successes and failures of partnership ventures between probation services and substance misuse services, this book dissects partnership at its most complex.

Some of the findings to emerge are unexpected, and carry important implications for the future of probation partnership work. One might have predicted that partnership projects would founder on the rocks of conflicting ideologies. There is obvious potential for strain between the coercive and controlling functions of a criminal justice agency, and the client-focused orientation of drug and alcohol services. In fact even the least successful partnerships were able to negotiate successfully around the dilemmas of coerced treatment. Indeed the perspectives of partner agencies often turned out to be a positive asset for probation, helping officers to sustain harm reduction objectives in the face of pressures to pursue narrower correctional goals.

Another unexpected finding is that partnerships between probation and substance misuse services seemed well able to stand the strains imposed by "contract culture". The study found that relationships between partners rarely degenerated into a mechanistic interchange between "purchaser" and "provider". It argues the importance of retaining a more subtle vision of partnership in the delivery of public services, whereby alliances underpinned by shared values secure benefits for all parties.

Nevertheless several of the partnerships examined in this study met with serious difficulties. The most accessible explanations for such failures – and the ones typically offered by participants – focus on the personal inadequacies and lack of skills shown by their partners in failure. One of the strengths of this study is the way in which the analysis draws the reader back to structural problems to do with the design and management of partnership projects.

The book's conclusions are fundamentally optimistic. Partnership in this field promises more gain than pain to both probation and substance misuse agencies. It offers the probation service both a rationale for, and the means to, resist the imposition of a progressively narrowing enforcement role; and, of course, it broadens the funding base for substance misuse services. It remains to be seen, of course, whether either probation services or drug and alcohol services are quick enough on their feet to exploit these opportunities.

Professor Michael Hough
Director, Criminal Policy Research Unit
South Bank University
London

Acknowledgements

I am indebted to many people without whose help this research could not have been accomplished. Firstly, I am grateful to the Mental Health Foundation for their interest and funding, and to the Research Committee at LSE for additional support. My thanks are also due to Professor Martin Davies, University of East Anglia, and John Walters, Chief Probation Officer, Middlesex Probation Service, for their initial support for the idea. Without the enthusiasm, initiative and tireless energy of Sharon Cowan, Research Assistant to the project, the fieldwork would never have been completed. Steven Spurr's mastery of SPSS and QSR NUD*IST was a godsend.

To all those probation service managers and field staff who responded to the initial documentation search and telephone enquiries, many thanks are due for their goodwill and patience in helping to get the project off the ground. It seems impossible, however, to express adequate appreciation of the contribution of the probation service and substance misuse agency staff who participated in detailed interviews about their partnership and in-house specialist projects during Phase Two. The candour and passion with which they shared their experiences testified to a belief that something should be learned from them. I hope that they are not disappointed in this hope for the research.

Finally, to the participants in the Phase Three case studies, a tremendous debt is owed for their tolerance of the researchers' presence and inquisitiveness over a substantial period of time. Their apparently dauntless enthusiasm for the research is, I hope, rewarded by the testimony to the excellence of their projects which I have tried to convey.

List of Abbreviations

AA	Alcoholics Anonymous
AGM	Annual General Meeting
AIDS	Acquired Immune Deficiency Syndrome
cond. discharge	Conditional discharge
court appear. only	Court appearance only
driving under infl.	Driving under the influence (of alcohol)
dui	Driving under the influence (of alcohol)
GP	General Practitioner
HIV	Human Immunodeficiency Virus
NACRO	National Association for the Care and Resettlement of Offenders
prison a/c	Prison after-care
prison t/c	Prison through-care
prob. order cond.	Probation order, with condition
prob. order stand.	Probation order, standard
PSR	Pre-sentence Report
PR	Public Relations
SUGS	Supervision Grants Scheme
YOI a/c	Young Offender Institution, after-care
YOI t/c	Young Offender Institution, through-care

1
The Partnership Enterprise

Concern has grown apace about the numbers of offenders with problems of substance abuse. The Advisory Council on the Misuse of Drugs, noting the evidence for a substantial involvement of drug abusers in crime and the criminal justice system, also asserted: "Evidence from several probation services suggests that drug misusers form a significant part of their caseload" (1991, p. 5). The Criminal Justice Act 1991, for the first time, made explicit provision for the treatment of offenders with drug or alcohol problems as a requirement of a probation order. Previously, such treatment was provided under the more general requirements for medical or psychiatric treatment. This explicitness in the treatment of substance misuse problems within a criminal justice framework testified to the increasing importance attached to problems of substance abuse and their relationship to offending.

Growing specificity in criminal justice, however, connected to diverse provisions in policy and legislation. The treatment and rehabilitation of addicted people have been the subjects of policy consideration in themselves (Advisory Council on the Misuse of Drugs 1982), and in relation to psychiatric (Brain Committee 1965) and community (Department of Health 1989) care, the AIDS epidemic (Advisory Council on the Misuse of Drugs 1988), criminal justice (Advisory Council on the Misuse of Drugs 1991), and health education (Department of Health and Social Security 1981). People with problems of addiction may be affected not only by criminal justice legislation but also by the NHS and Community Care Act 1990 and the Mental Health Act 1983. Whether such a multiplicity of policy and legislative connections to substance abuse has added up to a coherent set of objectives and provision is questionable. It is only comparatively recently that the multi-faceted phenomenon of substance use and misuse, and the multi-disciplinary nature of its control and treatment has been given policy recognition in a full-throated attempt to engineer a co-ordinated inter-agency strategy (Home Office 1995). Meanwhile, local statutory and non-statutory agencies have sought their own solutions to the problems on their doorsteps.

Law enforcement and harm minimisation

The discovery of the HIV virus among intravenous drug injectors profoundly influenced the direction of drugs policy during the 1980s. The Advisory Council on the Misuse of Drugs (1988) declared that the primary aim of drugs intervention should be the reduction of public health risks. It elaborated on this theme through several consequent publications which explored the potential for harm reducing practice among the various criminal justice agencies, choosing as its first focus the probation service (Advisory Council on the Misuse of Drugs 1991), perhaps because it undoubtedly represented the most receptive audience. The probation service was encouraged further down the path of harm minimisation by the Home Office Inspectorate of Probation (HM Inspectorate of Probation 1993). Even when promoting abstinence as the "ultimate goal" for drug users, the Home Office's own guidance to probation practice acknowledged that "an intermediate stage may be to reduce the damage which their continued drug misuse causes to themselves, to other individuals and to the community" (Home Office 1995).

That the probation service was amenable to the suggestion that it should embrace harm minimisation is hardly surprising. British probation officers held a long established anxiety that their role in the criminal justice system may be transformed from social work into law enforcement (Raynor 1985). Any official encouragement to step aside from the path towards correctional enforcement was bound to be seized with enthusiasm.

Nevertheless, the techniques of harm minimisation were not for the faint hearted. While emerging theoretical models of recovery from addiction (Prochaska and Diclemente 1986) offered useful tools for sympathetic and empowering counselling, new styles of adventurous practice engaged with drug users on their own territory, for the express purpose, not of stopping their activity, but of alleviating the level of risks incurred through its continuation and enhancing quality of life within deviant lifestyles (see for example O'Hare, Newcombe, Matthews, Buning and Drucker 1992). How far into that territory of illegal drug use and its associated criminality would encouragement to probation officers to support harm minimisation strategies really extend when it came to the test?

The emergence of partnership

During the latter years of the 1980s and early 1990s, government plans to reduce pressure on the prison system by expanding the community sentences (Home Office 1988; 1990a), included a wider role for the independent sector in their implementation. A strong theme developed in policy concerning the implications for the probation service of the inclusion of non-statutory organisations in the delivery of services for offenders within a new framework of punishment in the community. The new paradigm reflected the changes in the role of local authorities in the organisation and delivery of welfare services in the wake of community care legislation: "Probation officers must see themselves less as exclusive providers of services and facilities, and more as managers of supervision programmes" (Home Office 1990b). The vision of a shift in the role of the probation service, from direct service delivery to programme management, was pursued through successive documents, each reiterating the expectation that "elements of a supervision programme could and would be provided by organisations or individuals outside the probation service" (Home Office 1990c).

The move from policy intention to practical reality was initiated by the introduction of the Supervision Grants Scheme (hereafter SUGS), through which the Home Office allocated funds for initiatives by independent sector organisations in partnership with probation services. Responsibility for developing and financing the partnership enterprise was subsequently devolved to local probation services (Home Office 1992). To ensure that probation services did not default on their obligations for the furtherance of its partnership policy, the Home Office required them to submit their plans for expenditure of a minimum of five per cent of their revenue budgets on initiatives with "independent" (in effect, almost entirely voluntary) sector organisations during the period 1994–1997 (Home Office 1993a; 1993b; 1993c).

In its guidance to probation services on partnership development, the Home Office (1993c) included substance misuse treatment in a list of recommended priorities for such initiatives. This complemented the heightened attention accorded to such services which followed introduction of the provisions of the Criminal Justice Act 1991, Schedule 1A, allowing for substance misuse treatment to be a special requirement of a probation order. However, research in the early aftermath of the legislation suggested that the implementation of the new treatment requirements was geographically uneven and fraught with confusion, both as to the interpretation of their legal meaning and as to their relationship to the pre-existing general provisions which had been invoked for delivering programmes for substance misusers (Rumgay 1994). For example, one area of contention concerned the implications of explicit requirements in probation orders for the funding responsibilities for the treatment programmes. Was the Home Office signalling its readiness to fund residential rehabilitation for offenders under such compulsion? What were the responsibilities of local authorities, under community care legislation, for the costs of enforced treatment services to offenders?

Organisational decisions driven by financial strictures may have considerable impact on the avenues through which help and treatment may be offered, the forms which it may take, and the client groups to be served. For example, American services for the treatment of alcoholism were heavily influenced by financial incentives to attract clientele through the criminal justice system, and a generally more coercive and confrontational therapeutic style evolved in consequence (Weisner and Room 1984). Moreover, in the American experience of mixed provision, contractual constraints on organisational activities traditionally associated with the voluntary sector, such as campaigning and advocacy (Fielder 1992), ultimately may have broader implications for the range and choice of service available to the public. Evidence from the American experience, however, should be applied with caution to the emergent British experience (Ryan and Ward 1989), which is developing within a different professional and organisational context. American probation itself differs in fundamental respects from the British system in ways which may render superficial analogies misleading (Clear and Rumgay 1992).

Relationships between voluntary and statutory organisations are rarely straightforward, even where finance is not involved. Studies reveal the uneasy relationships which are forged, involving, for example, attempts by the statutory services to "colonise" voluntary organisations (Abrams 1981), and "blurring" of organisational identities through increasing bureaucratisation of the voluntary sector (Billis 1993). Examples of non-financial partnerships between the probation service and other organisations bear testimony to the difficulties of inter-agency collaboration, despite the good intentions which spawn such endeavours (Blagg, Pearson, Sampson, Smith and Stubbs 1998; Broad 1991; Crawford and Jones 1995). Cautionary tales may also be found in accounts of inter-agency enterprises involving the probation service and street agencies for drug misusers during the 1980s (Dorn and South 1985).

Indeed, in attempts to deliver substance misuse treatment programmes in the context of the criminal justice system, potential conflicts for prospective partners abound. Ideological contention concerning the balance between coercion, compliance and public accountability on the one hand and voluntarism, confidentiality and client-centredness on the other offer a minefield across which statutory and voluntary agencies must pick their way to reach practical solutions. Within this problematic environment of government policies and professional ideologies, voluntary substance misuse organisations naturally hesitated to enter the criminal justice arena via partnerships with probation services (Goodsir 1992; Haynes 1990; Lee and Mainwaring 1995; Padel 1990).

Moreover, it is to be remembered that the probation service has, over many years, generated its own distinctive approaches to working with alcohol- and drug-related offenders. Indeed, a focus on alcoholism distinguished even the earliest interventions of the Police Court Missionaries (McWilliams 1983). Secondments of probation officers to substance misuse agencies, particularly statutory multi-disciplinary teams, have been popular practice for several years. More recent innovations often took the form of structured programmes limited in terms of time and target group, such as educational programmes for young offenders and for drunk drivers. Such programmes have fitted well with criminal justice system demands for clear, accountable supervision strategies. The accumulated body of "in-house" experience and expertise has been a source of considerable professional satisfaction to the probation officers engaged in them (Rumgay 1998). Motivation for its preservation might well be expected to influence the development of relationships with other organisations. More broadly, the partnership enterprise was widely regarded by probation officers as a threat, both to their job security and to their professional status. The defence of professional territory provided yet another edge of controversy for agencies attempting to negotiate the pathway to partnership.

The study

A complex policy background to the development of inter-agency initiatives for substance misusing offenders has been described. This study began amid that environment of policy and legislative fragmentation, as agencies contrived local responses to substance misuse problems during a period of massive re-organisation of welfare provision and financial uncertainties. Within the ensuing negotiations of working relationships, questions of accountability for service delivery and integrity of service quality loom large. This research project set out to study the resolution of those questions, with special attention paid to particular tensions: harm minimisation versus law enforcement in drug misuse; service delivery versus case management in professional roles; voluntarism versus coercion in substance misuse treatment; and client confidentiality versus agency accountability in offender rehabilitation.

The study, which began in 1994, was conducted in three phases. In Phase One, a national mail and telephone survey of all 55 probation services in England and Wales collected relevant local policy documents and attempted to establish the scale and nature of developments in projects for addicted offenders on probation. In Phase Two, interviews with managers and practitioners from probation services and voluntary organisations involved in special projects for addicted offenders probed the detail of policy implementation. Selection of projects for interview aimed to demonstrate the diversity of approaches to coercion, confidentiality, project organisation and programme content which emerged in the telephone survey. Twenty-five partnership projects were contacted, involving 16 different probation services in England and Wales and 24 voluntary substance misuse agencies. Nine in-house specialist projects were contacted, involving seven different probation services in England and Wales. Over all, a total of 78 interviews were conducted. In Phase Three, detailed study was undertaken of three of the projects contacted in Phase Two. These projects, offering strong evidence of successful practice, were also selected for the diversity of their approaches and of the professional issues raised in service delivery. They comprised two partnership projects and one in-house specialist project. A profile of the client group for each project was constructed from a survey of case files, using data on substance misuse, and criminal and social histories. Documentation was collected which illuminated each project's development, further interviews were held with probation and substance misuse agency staff, and some observation of direct work with clients was undertaken.

Some issues arose in the course of the research which have implications for the analysis. The most significant concerns definitions of partnership and in-house specialist projects. This problem, which arose repeatedly, emanated from the tendency of probation staff to refer to any form of inter-agency activity as partnership. Nor was the term partnership confined to contacts with non-statutory organisations. It could thus embrace such diverse activities as, for example, liaison, onward referral, attendance at child protection conferences, secondment and joint programme delivery. The Home Office itself notably failed to dispel this confusion as to the form of relationship defined by the term partnership, by advising probation services in its guidance to preparation of partnership plans to review all varieties of inter-agency activity (Home Office 1993c).

To acquiesce in this broad conceptualisation would have confounded the aims of the research, by making it impossible to distinguish between collaborative projects managed in conjunction with other statutory organisations and those with voluntary agencies. It also compromised any meaningful distinction between in-house specialist projects and partnerships, since it transpired that few in-house specialist projects were fully self-contained, but rather most involved some form of inter-agency connection. The most obvious example of these confusions arose in references to secondments of probation officers to statutory substance misuse teams. Was this partnership as intended by the Home Office in its partnership initiative? Clearly not, if the partnership initiative was intended to direct funding at non-statutory agencies for provision of direct services to offenders. Indeed, it was precisely this form of relationship, in which non-statutory agencies were contracted to provide direct services, that the research set out to study. Nevertheless, the diversity of arrangements which were encountered under the umbrella term "partnership" during the research necessitated careful individual categorisation.

The research was guided in this exercise by the explicit Home Office intention to shift the role of probation officer from case worker to case manager. In order to retain this essential spirit of the partnership enterprise as intended in Home Office policy, projects were categorised according to the primary delivery of direct service by probation or substance misuse staff. Thus, dedication of probation officer time to direct service delivery identified a project as an in-house specialisation. Therefore, secondments were categorised as forms of in-house specialist project, by virtue of the dedication of probation officer time to direct service delivery, despite the existence of close working relationships with other agencies. Where the service to clients was primarily delivered by non-statutory substance misuse agency staff on behalf of the probation service, the project was identified as a partnership.

This strategy effectively distinguished between most varieties of project organisation, while capturing the sense of partnership which was intended by the Home Office. It also enabled partnerships, as thus defined, to be further categorised according to whether they were financial or non-financial arrangements. Some slight anomalies remained. Two non-financial projects involved the delivery of groupwork programmes jointly by probation officers and substance misuse agency staff. There was, therefore, an element of dedication of probation officer time. Nevertheless, these projects were categorised as partnerships since a lead role was taken by the substance misuse agency in managing the project. Two financial partnerships also involved probation officers in the joint delivery of groupwork programmes.

A further problem which arose at some locations was to define exactly how many separate projects were under discussion. This was an unforeseen problem in determining the boundaries between co-existing activities. It was never possible to establish a general principle for separating multiple activities, connected in diverse ways, into discrete projects which appeared to work satisfactorily. This was further complicated by the emergence of new information about additional activities during interviews. In the end, a more *ad hoc* approach was adopted in which projects were separated according to the perceptions of the interviewees themselves. For example, during an interview with a substance misuse agency manager about a local non-financial partnership with one probation team, it emerged that the agency was also contracted to offer a county-wide groupwork service. The probation officers had confined their remarks in interview to the non-financial project operating out of their office. This was categorised as two partnerships, on the basis of their geographical, financial and inter-professional relationship differences. However, at another interview which was thought to concern a non-financial arrangement for jointly delivered groupwork, it emerged that a more recent financial arrangement had resulted in the appointment of a new substance misuse worker to the agency whose time was dedicated to the probation service. The intention behind this appointment had been to extend the groupwork provision, and while this had not taken place, precise boundaries between the existing groupwork programme and the role of the new substance misuse worker remained unclear. Eventually, this project was re-categorised, somewhat unsatisfactorily, as a single financial partnership, based on the original intention behind the appointment, the working relationship between the two substance misuse workers, the similarity of their personal experience of the partnership enterprise and the consequent practical difficulty in ascribing their remarks entirely to one or other set of activities.

Some problems were encountered in the interviewing at certain projects. While practical hitches, such as interruptions, are only to be expected at busy agencies, on a few occasions the difficulties of the interview seemed to reflect experiences within the projects themselves. For example, after the interviewer had travelled some distance to an office for one pre-arranged appointment, the nominated probation officer declined to be interviewed. The substance misuse worker at this project subsequently described many difficulties in engaging probation officers in the partnership venture. The strangest experience of the entire research programme occurred at a project where the nominated probation officer suggested that it would be convenient to talk over lunch. The interviewer agreed, expecting to take sandwiches to a quiet office, but was instead whisked off to the local golf club, where the interview was perforce conducted in the lounge bar!

At other times, however, extensive efforts were made to accommodate the interviewer at times when a number of people connected to the project were available, and much more time was given than had been requested. On these occasions, it was clear that interviewees were justifiably proud of the fruits of their endeavours.

During the analysis of interview data it was apparent that similar issues were prompted by different questions. For example, comments about the quality of inter-professional relationships arose in response to a variety of questions, including those concerning inter-agency communication, project achievements, project difficulties, personal likes and dislikes about the project, and the most difficult action that it had been necessary to undertake. While some steps have been taken to regulate the analysis for the sake of clarity, it would have spoiled the sense and spirit of such responses simply to amalgamate them all. There is, consequently, some repetition of certain themes, which nevertheless appears to encapsulate different nuances.

Finally, some comments concerning the use of interview extracts may be of interest. As a predominantly qualitative study of inter-agency and inter-professional relationships, verbatim quotations have been used liberally, for several reasons. Firstly, telephone survey respondents were extraordinarily helpful and willing to elaborate their replies. Consequently, much greater texture was derived from their responses than might be expected in the context of a telephone interview between strangers, such that some direct presentation of their comments seemed an appropriate way to represent their perceptions. More generally, the spirit and vigour with which interviewees recounted their experiences can only be conveyed through their own words, and although some help has been provided to simplify direct speech, their passion is captured in the vernacular. At times, several different quotations are used at particular points, to exemplify a common response, to illustrate diversity, or to strengthen the emotional content of responses which is inevitably somewhat diluted by their written, rather than spoken form.

In order to allow the reader to compare the generality of responses obtained during Phase Two interviewing with the particular perceptions and experiences of participants at the three case studies of Phase Three, direct quotations from these individuals are used only in those chapters specifically concerning their projects. Their responses at Phase Two interviewing, however, have been included in the quantitative analyses of the overview chapters. It is also useful to mention at this point, that during Phase Two no interviews were conducted with staff of the substance misuse agencies participating in the in-house specialist project which later became Project B in Phase Three. The three substance misuse staff who were interviewed at in-house specialisations in Phase Two were attached to entirely different projects, and the information provided by substance misuse staff at Project B is used solely for Phase Three analysis.

Chapter 2 explores the impact of the national policy environment upon local probation services' experience. Drawing on the mail and telephone survey, it considers local strategies for the development of partnerships, early predictions of the advantages and disadvantages of partnership, and issues in the provision of substance misuse programmes. Chapter 3 describes the organisation of 25 partnership projects, focusing on the characteristics of selected partners, and the structure of the partnership arrangements. Chapter 4 explores qualitative dimensions of the partnership experience, noting the elements common to successful projects, and issues which confounded progress for problematic projects. Chapter 5 describes and analyses nine in-house specialist projects. Chapters 6, 7 and 8 each present a successful project, chosen for its distinctive approach to the delivery of services to substance misusing offenders, and illumination of important issues emerging from earlier analysis. Chapter 9 considers some notable differences between the three projects in terms of their client profiles. Chapter 10 considers the main lessons which participants at all partnership and in-house projects drew from their experiences. Finally, Chapter 11 considers the potential future of partnership in terms of the evolving role of the probation service within society.

2
The Local Context

Partnership development began amid the introduction of cash limited funding of the probation service and of new community care arrangements which had important implications for substance misuse services. The study attempted to explore the impact of this changing environment by examining local probation services' policies for partnership and for substance misuse, and early implementation issues reported in the telephone survey.

Partnership policy

Thirty-nine probation services responded to a request for policy documents concerning partnership with non-statutory organisations. In all but two instances, they provided the partnership plans submitted to the Home Office in answer to its requirement for detailed accounts of probation services' strategies for reaching the 5 per cent budgetary expenditure target. In the two remaining cases, brief formal statements of intent to foster partnership relations were received.

A question mark then arose over the precise policy status of these documents. In so far as their purpose was to satisfy a budgetary requirement, the partnership plans might more appropriately be regarded as operational, rather than policy statements. Moreover, in so far as they clearly had policy relevance, the partnership plans were remarkable for what they did *not* contain, rather than for their actual substance. Home Office guidance was echoed to a noteworthy, if not uncanny extent. There were few adventures into new territory.

Topics of particular relevance to this study concerned the definition and purpose of partnership, strategies for selection of partners and identification of substance misuse projects. Telephone survey

11

respondents augmented the documentary information in terms of local perspectives and experiences.

Defining partnership

Authors of partnership plans were keen to stress the probation service's long tradition of working collaboratively with local organisations to improve services to offenders. They described an impressive battery of co-operative inter-agency alliances, including, for example, liaison with social services and health departments, joint working, secondment of probation staff, involvement in crime prevention groups, and provision of office accommodation to voluntary organisations. Several documents contained lists of organisations with which links were identified, often in terms of onward referral by probation officers, or as recipients of community service placements. One offered staff supervision of students on placement and a teaching secondment to a university as evidence of partnership.

Worthy as these endeavours are, they do not constitute partnership as a financial relationship between probation services and non-statutory organisations for receipt of a service. Home Office guidance to the submission of partnership plans perhaps fostered confusion by requiring probation services to "embrace the full range of possibilities for partnership arrangements" (Home Office 1993c), including non-financial ones, in devising their strategy. This invitation to conceptualise partnership *both* as an all-inclusive notion of inter-agency collaboration in any form *and* within the restricted definition intended by the partnership initiative itself offered, as will be seen, a hostage to fortune.

The status of secondments of probation staff exemplifies the problem. Secondments to a variety of organisations, including (often statutory) substance misuse agencies, Training and Enterprise Councils, and local authority youth justice teams were claimed as partnerships by several probation services, some having invested heavily in these arrangements. One service alone identified 14 secondments, and while this was the extreme, others described six or seven, and one, two or three secondments within a single service were not unusual. Investment of staff resources on this scale testifies to an important value attached to such initiatives. Home Office guidance in Probation Circular 17/1993 rejected secondment of probation staff as falling within the restricted definition of financial partnership, unless the costs were fully reimbursed. Nevertheless, only one partnership plan contained a commitment to review an existing secondment to a substance misuse agency against alternative partnership arrangements, but cautioned that "local situations may mean that secondment and non-financial partnerships would be more appropriate." Conversely, another service declared an objective of taking "the opportunity of regularising current arrangements...for staff secondments": this appeared to mean that its secondments were included within its partnership budget.

In accordance with Home Office advice, plans described strategies for identifying service needs which could be addressed through partnership arrangements. These were often impressively painstaking, involving internal consultations at management and field level, and externally with sentencers and local organisations. Such endeavours, however, not only produced few, if any, surprises, but little variation on the priorities originally suggested in Home Office guidance. Yet while considerable time and effort was spent re-discovering familiar needs and priorities, relatively little attention was paid to the *form* which partnership projects established to meet them should take.

What practical forms then, might partnership take? Given the all-inclusive *principle* conveyed in the plans, a brief review of projects attempted to distil a common definition of partnership from the emerging *practical form* of financial schemes. The only common denominator which could be discerned, however, was the fact that not one service was already provided by probation staff. Nor could they be, given the nature of the services and resources involved. For example: bail support projects included placements with specially recruited families and volunteer befriending; supervision programmes included outward bound activities, drama, music, art and photographic projects; a SUGS grant established help-desks in the local courts; another founded Citizens Advice Bureau surgeries at probation offices; schemes for employment advice and training included one for assisting ex-offenders to start small businesses; volunteer recruitment and training projects included one aimed at encouraging offenders to participate in voluntary work. One probation service supported a project for furniture collection, storage and distribution; one established a drop-in centre for informal support, practical assistance and activities; one arranged a staff counselling service and anti-racism training; one engaged a consultant to advise on partnership development.

During telephone interviews, the problem of defining partnership appeared in several comments. Again, almost any informal relationship with another agency, whether statutory or voluntary, might be regarded as partnership. Ironically, however, one respondent reported that a local substance misuse agency resented being described as a partner of the probation service because its funding derived from the SUGS scheme!

Equally, one respondent asserted more than once that there were no financial partnerships within the service, despite clear evidence of SUGS schemes in the partnership plan.

> Our view is that partnerships as we are operating them are much broader than just the partnerships that emerged through the government partnership document. We've got lots and lots of local partnerships, quite often on an *ad hoc* basis, which seem to work reasonably well.

> We have actually developed quite a lot of partnerships that don't involve money at all.

The purpose of partnership

Despite these elastic definitions of partnership, plans conveyed absolute clarity as to its purpose. The point is best made in the words chosen in the plans themselves:

> [T]o acquire extra services which support and *enhance* its direct work with offenders who are supervised on behalf of the Courts or released from custody. (*emphasis added*)

> [The] Probation Service aims to develop Partnerships that will *enhance* the services offered to the Courts, offenders and the public, in line with its corporate strategy. (*emphasis added*)

> The *enhancement* of the quality, range and variety of [our] supervision of offenders, thereby increasing the Service's impact and reducing offending. (*emphasis added*)

Where the precise term "enhancement" was not used, its meaning was contained in equivalent language:

> Partnership with the voluntary sector recognises that they have expertise and resources which are complementary and additional to those provided by the Probation Service.

> Partnership arrangements will not substitute our work, rather, will supplement and compliment [*sic*] our tasks in pursuance of our corporate objectives.

Methods for operationalising enhancement were offered in telephone interviews, in terms of creating access to expertise, or developing projects jointly.

We've started the partnership model on the basis that we co-run groups, and we use them as consultants as well as making onward referrals. So we haven't passed that point where it all goes out to the voluntary agency. It is genuinely working in partnership.

The best way forward is to do joint projects rather than what is happening a lot, so far, in partnership. That is sub-contracting really.

The common sense of purpose was unmistakable: partnership would improve existing practice, but not change it. This provided a unifying rationale for the disparate varieties of partnership projects exemplified earlier. Only one partnership plan referred to the "cultural shift within the Service from caseworker to case manager as increasingly Probation Officers and their colleagues are encouraged to co-ordinate a range of opportunities to continue the level of services provided to offenders". This document, however, did not describe any partnership projects, but rather cautioned that:

> the extraction of potential partnership areas from the core functions of a probation officers [*sic*], could be seen as simplistic and isolationist. Simplistic in the fact that demarcation is difficult (where does one task actually finish and another begin?), and isolationist in that both the risk of de-skilling and/or of failing to maintain an overview of the situation. [*sic*]

Another plan contained an undertaking that the "priority of all potential projects will be determined according to its contribution to Corporate Plan objectives and the extent to which it releases Probation Service resources." Rather than replacement of probation officer activities, however, this service's existing partnerships involved advice, training and consultancy on substance misuse for probation staff, provision of a driver training track for safe driver programmes and a Citizen's Advice Bureau financial advice service. Its priorities for partnership development included volunteer recruitment and training, a psychological consultancy, accommodation provision, a support service for victims of life sentence prisoners, and links with ethnic minority groups.

One plan announced a radical enterprise: "[W]e will review all the Service's activities for their potential for contracting to another body". This service limited its definition of core responsibilities, which could only be undertaken by staff directly employed by the probation service, to the supervision of court orders and licences, and preparation of reports for courts and penal institutions, thus leaving a wide range of services, including probation hostels, probation centres and intensive supervision programmes to be defined as "add-on facilities aimed at making supervision more effective". This bold beginning unravelled as the plan progressed. Firstly, it was noted that at the end of the transitional period from the SUGS scheme, there would be a very large shortfall in monies available to sustain the funding of existing projects. Next, in its review of services, several candidates for contracting were rejected: bail information, "given the agreements that underpin it at national level and the delicacy of some of the necessary relationships with other criminal justice organisations"; interpreter services, because "we need direct control and to have interpreters working to this Service's prescriptions and requirements, uninfluenced by other considerations"; probation centres, because the "central task of Probation Centres is addressing offending behaviour" and this in itself "is core work for the Service"; intensive supervision programmes, for similar considerations; offending behaviour programmes, because "[c]onfronting offending behaviour is at the heart of the Service's work"; and residential services, because "[n]o change is required".

Clearly, probation services designed their partnership strategies with the primary purpose of protecting their traditional territory. Substitution of probation officer tasks was not an option to be entertained at more than a rhetorical level, and then only by a very small minority of services.

Paying for partnership

A few partnership plans commented on the financial constraints bearing upon the enterprise. For example, as noted earlier, one service pointed out the pending shortfall in funding for existing arrangements in the aftermath of the transition from the central SUGS scheme to a fully devolved system. Another cautioned: "The devolution of SUGS and the constraints in the cash limited grant will have a severe effect on the money available for the Service to spend on partnerships in the future and thus our primary aim is to manage our existing partnerships and protect worthwhile projects that have already been developed". A third service, which had supported several projects begun by the Urban Programme during the mid-1980s, observed: "[I]t must be recognised that the development of new projects...will only be possible by withdrawing considerable sums of money from existing projects".

This was a time of great transition in the funding of the probation service. The introduction of cash limited budgets was beginning to take effect, together with the requirement to arrange for a minimum

5 per cent expenditure on partnerships. The attempt in telephone interviews to gather impressions of the early impact of change recognised the
anxiety within probation circles that the combined impact of cash
limiting and the partnership enterprise would be to drive services into
contracting for supervision tasks at the expense of internal staffing. Four
respondents said that it was too early to comment on the impact.
Others, however, shared their initial perceptions.

Three respondents reported a substantial budget cut. However, only
one expressed the view that partnerships were evolving as a direct alternative to internal staff development. Twenty-six respondents reported
that cash limiting had no impact on partnerships, primarily because of
the effective protection of their funding through the minimum five per
cent requirement. Thus, in a number of areas, partnerships were increasing as probation services moved towards the target expenditure. Nevertheless, several respondents pointed out that the scope for partnership
development was itself constrained by overall budget strictures following the introduction of cash limiting: "So, obviously, if we are on a
reduced budget, then the five per cent is reduced as well".

An additional complication was the existence of established Home
Office partnerships via the SUGS scheme. Six respondents observed that
their substance misuse programmes were funded from this source, and
thus were protected from any immediate impact of cash limits. Two,
however, also realised that they would receive considerably less than the
full amount of the SUGS funding for these partnerships in the scheme's
devolvement to local services. The future of these pre-existing arrangements was therefore uncertain.

Substance misuse work itself had not been affected by cash limiting in
17 services. However, respondents attributed this good fortune to different causes: to the priority accorded to substance misuse; to effective
access to the community care budget; or to reliance upon statutory
substance misuse teams. Six respondents attributed the absence of
impact to the fact that the probation service did not pay for the services
from which they benefitted locally: primary services were statutorily
funded in the area; relationships were collaboratively, rather than finan-
cially based; or a partnership's funding derived solely from the SUGS
scheme at that time.

While substance misuse was often a priority area for the development
of services, conflicts were nevertheless arising *between* priorities for
expenditure in the light of financial constraints. Six respondents
reported that their service's substance misuse work had suffered, or
was likely to suffer as a result of cash limits. In five of these cases, the

project which was cut or threatened was an in-house specialisation: secondments to substance misuse agencies were particularly affected, but in one case a hostel's future was in doubt. In the sixth case, a big budget cut, combined with a reduction of funds devolved from the SUGS scheme, threatened the survival of a partnership.

The collaborative context

Another transition at this time was the re-organisation of community care funding and service delivery. This was an anxious time for substance misuse agencies, fearing de-prioritisation of their services by authorities operating under financial constraint. Relationships between probation services and substance misuse agencies were clearly modulated by the approach of local authorities to service provision in the aftermath of community care transitions. The crucial role of local social services departments was demonstrated in appreciative reports from some areas that departments had protected substance misuse funding, alongside complaints from others of low priority accorded to such provision.

Perceived accountability of social services departments for the quality of inter-agency collaboration and co-operation was key to the degree of satisfaction in the new arrangements. Fourteen respondents reported that inter-agency collaboration on substance misuse issues had improved since the introduction of community care. Proactive intervention by social services departments to co-ordinate substance misuse services had an important bearing on this outcome, alongside agreement of protocols and development of multi-agency fora for policy discussion. Elsewhere, social services departments were primary targets for blame when inter-agency collaboration was poor. Three probation services had been omitted from consultation on community care arrangements, amid confusion between health authorities and social services departments. One consequence of such organisational disarray could be deteriorating communication between probation services and the substance misuse agencies themselves. Several respondents remarked that it was impossible to navigate a coherent pathway through multiple agencies to treatment: "Clients have to jump through about five hoops, and that is entirely to do with the arrangements made by the social services departments with the various agencies involved."

The gateway to services, under the new arrangements, was the community care assessment process, administered by local authorities. Practical arrangements for assessments varied. In some areas the task was assumed by social services departments; where statutory substance misuse teams existed they often took responsibility; contracting to approved agencies was an alternative approach; elsewhere provision was mixed. Thus, in some areas, voluntary substance misuse agencies had benefited from approval as assessors. Another possibility, however, lay in the approval of probation services as assessment agencies. Eight respondents reported that probation officers were accepted as community care assessors in substance misuse cases. There were mixed views about this arrangement. Some saw this as an inappropriate role for probation officers; one service refused to accept it. Elsewhere, approval had been sought, albeit for limited use.

There were several complaints about delays in obtaining assessments. Apart from the slow response to requests, the new system introduced an extra tier of bureaucracy for approving treatment services. This prevented direct referral to drug rehabilitation centres, requiring probation officers instead to work through the assessment agency. Delays were keenly felt by probation officers, who often worked to time constraints imposed by the criminal justice process, which were not salient pressures for local authorities.

The impact on voluntary substance misuse organisations was also apparently mixed. Seven respondents offered examples of local voluntary agencies suffering reductions in funding and resources. Elsewhere, it appeared that the impact was worse in the anticipation than the actuality. Three respondents reported increased interest in probation partnership funding among local agencies anxious about their financial futures.

Perceptions of the probation service's role in supporting substance misuse services strongly influenced approaches to funded partnerships. Several respondents asserted that the probation service should not fund the responsibilities of the health and social services. Indeed, for these respondents, an important part of the probation service's role was to hold other agencies accountable for their obligations to provide services to the local community. As one respondent explained: "Most services are [there to] provide services to members of the community, and offenders are members of the community. So we don't intend to pay for them, particularly because [offenders] have [the same] right to them as someone who doesn't happen to have committed a crime". The role of partnership, therefore, was to fill distinctive gaps in services for offenders, not merely to sustain agencies' presence in the community.

What we *could* fund was any *additional* service that was required because that person also happened to be an offender. What's happened is, because we've got funding powers at a time when everybody else seems to be pulling back from funding, we're seen as a funding substitute. We can't do that.

To be effective, this strategy required careful analysis of the relative merits of different funding opportunities.

Local drug services have a reasonable amount of funding and we have been trying to dip into their existing resources... With the alcohol services, we have taken a slightly different position, because their funding has been far less than the drug funding. They are very much on a shoe string, and they have not been able to respond within their own service to requests... So we have put some partnership money into that.

Selection

Probation Circular 17/1993, which set out the requirement for submission of partnership plans, implied strong preference for competitive tendering as the method for selection of partners:

Details of local partnership arrangements and the application procedure for grants should be widely available. Plans should outline the selection procedure, and if competitive tendering arrangements are inappropriate, provide details of other measures to invite bids, and to ensure that projects are competitive and take proper account of equal opportunities. (Home Office 1993c)

Within partnership plans, it was frequently unclear whether the proposed method of selection was deemed to be competitive tendering or not. Only one plan contained a detailed procedure for project specifications and tenders; the telephone respondent for this service confirmed its commitment to competitive tendering. Another plan contained a cautious commitment to selective use of competitive tendering: "A future development will be to promote competitive tendering where this is appropriate and to design relevant specifications, to ensure as wide an opportunity as possible to prospective partners". A third acknowledged: "There may be a tendering process if several organizations are interested in providing the service".

Five plans argued against competitive tendering. One offered no less than six reasons for rejecting competitive tendering: a wide network of relevant potential partners already existed; the local voluntary sector would not co-operate; the cost would be prohibitive; there were relatively few potential partners for any one type of project; the "contract culture" reduced flexibility and creativity; if forced to work to tendering processes and tight specifications, voluntary agencies would require 100 per cent funding for each project, where presently part funding was possible. It concluded: "We therefore consider that competitive tendering is neither cost effective or in the spirit of partnership outlined in 'Partnerships in Dealing with Offenders in the Community' ".

Another service declared: "we are seeking to establish partners – not rivals or agents"; and "competitive tendering is neither practical nor desirable". One limited its publicity for partnership funds, "partly through not wanting to raise false expectations of how much was available and what it might be available for. Compared to Local Authorities and Health Authorities, the Probation Service is, and will continue to be, a very small player in the field of grant aiding".

The potential for prohibiting participation by small agencies deterred probation services from competitive tendering. Several plans contained commitments to empowering small and local agencies. For example, one service declared its aim: "To encourage the empowerment of all those community organisations, whatever their size, who can make an effective contribution to the achievement of [probation service] objectives".

Such commitment was hard to reconcile with competitive tendering. One probation service challenged Home Office guidance on this point. Certainly, Probation Circular 17/1993 encouraged probation services to consider that a "disproportionate investment of time and commitment to new or small initiatives in order to foster new partnerships may well produce more successful and useful partnerships in the long term". It also suggested that the "use of 'seedcorn' or developmental funding should be considered where existing services require development; where a specific service does not exist; or where additional costs, such as training, are justified". The service complained: "On the one hand you wish us to select and set criteria for that selection on the basis of an identified need and on the other to empower/assist local voluntary agencies to provide services which they may not be in a position at this point in time to do."

How, then, was selection of partners occurring in practice? Telephone interviews revealed five methods of selecting partners: historical relationships; networking; the "managed market"; competitive tendering; and SUGS. It is fair to acknowledge that in the relatively small world of local welfare systems, there was in practice a degree of overlap between these methods. Nevertheless, the conceptual distinctions which they imply were important to the respondents, as will be seen.

1. Historical relationships

Little more than tacit acknowledgement of this approach appeared in partnership plans. However, 21 respondents reported that their substance misuse partnerships developed from historical links with local agencies. Established relationships provided the springboard to partnership with a familiar agency.

> These agencies we've always worked with, and we've grown up, and they've grown up with us.

> We picked up a partnership with [the substance misuse agency] for reasons that are almost lost in time, that have to do, I think, with us always having had a member of our staff on their management committee. So we had always had some links with them. You end up making judgements about the organisation, and can you work with it. So we did.

2. Networking

As noted earlier, the existence of a strong local welfare network was advanced as an argument against the introduction of competitive tendering. Fourteen respondents reported that their partnerships developed from introductions via local contacts, third parties or mutual membership of working groups. Notwithstanding that the prospective partner's existence may have been previously known to the probation service, the significant trigger for negotiating financial partnership took the form of such an introduction through the welfare network.

> Our service belongs to a drugs data base group, which is attended by all agencies interested in the reduction of offending with drugs [or] reducing people's dependency. So all of the drugs agencies in the county attend that.

> Word of mouth. Grapevine. The voluntary sector has a wonderful grapevine...We also have an information database which we are putting together across the county. So we are sharing that information and building it up.

> Building upon a variety of community initiatives...The probation service was involved in the local crime prevention panel. From that arose discussions about managing drug misusers...For a variety of reasons, we have ways or means to use one another's resources.

3. The "managed market"

This expression was coined by one respondent, although others contrived alternatives. Essentially, although, to the naive observer, the selection process would appear indistinguishable from the methods described by another group of respondents as competitive tendering, these interviewees called it by another name. This device seemed to derive from discomfort with the notion of competitive tendering, and a consequent search for a terminology with fewer connotations of an aggressive market orientation. Five respondents reported using this method from the beginning of the partnership initiative, and a further five claimed that it would be the preferred method in future.

> We would take to the various forums our need to develop something. Then within that ring-fenced group say "What proposals, bids, suggestions are there from people who would like to take this forward with us?" It's a "managed market".

> We will advertise for partnerships against a project specification. Agencies will be invited to bid to take on that work... We don't like to call it competitive tendering, but "open pre-applications".

> We've decided to go down the service specification road, but not necessarily to say it's [competitive tendering]. I suppose it *is* competitive tendering, but it is not only on price.

> What we would say is that the approach we took was a form of competitive tendering, but at the gentle end, in that we did send a proposal out to all the agencies which we identified in the field.

4. Competitive tendering

Four respondents reported that their services had used, or intended to use competitive tendering to recruit partners. In contrast to the sensitivities of the previous group, to these respondents competitive tendering represented a strategic, well-informed approach to partnership development, as opposed to the "spontaneous combustion" (as one graphically put it) of earlier initiatives.

> In terms of our adopting a more strategic approach to it, that's how I think we would do it. We would have a clear statement of need... That would then be put out to competitive tender.

> The service's view is that it is appropriate in this day and age. The service is recognising that it's got to get a lot more commercial and business like about these things.

We are very clear about the services we want to deliver. If there were other agencies who felt they could deliver that, then clearly we would take that into account when we make the decision about funding.

Thirteen respondents who reported that their service, hitherto, relied upon historical relationships or networking for partner selection, thought that competitive tendering was a possible or likely future approach, although the degree of enthusiasm varied. Several were simply resigned to mounting pressure from the Home Office:

It is going to be a big issue ... It's going to be one headache, especially in an area like ours, if they enforce it.

I think that we'll need to go down that road. This is the way of the world in public services.

Viewed positively, competitive tendering was "fair", in that it opened equal opportunities to all organisations, reducing reliance on tradition. One respondent reported receiving complaints from voluntary agencies of preferential selectivity in support of agencies for SUGS funding.

Competitive tendering is a fair system. We shouldn't just keep to what we know. New organisations growing up may be better partners.

We have, over the last eighteen months or so, received a number of vitriolic complaints from individual agencies, who have accused us of being unfair in terms of supporting particular agencies for SUGS funding. That has left us uncomfortable ... So we have been strongly committed now to ensure that we advertise openly and straightforwardly to everybody and that there is a selection process which is set out very clearly to ensure that everybody has an equal open opportunity to bid for the work.

Competitive tendering might also encourage new involvement in provision for offenders:

It might encourage a group to diversify, or a new group to start up.

Those services which have evolved more theoretically, in our minds, rather than having discussions with a particular provider – It's only right that if we are to use public money we do go down this road.

One respondent reported that advertising had extended the probation service's knowledge of available agencies. Similarly, another saw an advantage of competitive tendering in creating choice. Finally, one respondent saw it as simply realistic in the "very competitive environment" which the field of public services had become.

Negative views on competitive tendering were more common, the most frequent objection being that choice between prospective partners did not exist. Nineteen respondents reported only one or very few substance misuse agencies operating in their area. Probation services in three such areas received only one or two responses after encouraging agencies to submit proposals for a substance misuse partnership.

> You can only competitively tender when there are organisations out there that actually want to tender... There's still only one organisation [around here] that is prepared to work with drug misusers.

> There isn't anybody who could compete with the team that is already here for the volume of work that they do. There's just no two ways about it.

> I have to say that we only received one formal proposal, which involved a partnership between two agencies who decided [to do it] together!

> Our efforts to have an open and fair tendering process only revealed two organisations that were prepared to put something on paper for us to consider.

Competitive tendering was commonly expected to create an obstacle to effective partnership, perceived as a quality of working relationships achieved through mutual negotiation and compromise over time. Respondents reflected on the potential damage to be inflicted upon established goodwill relationships with local agencies through a launch into the market place for the services which they had been providing. The point was also made that services for complex problems took time to develop and adapt appropriately.

> We would know to our cost the consequences of going down the competitive tendering route, when we've already got something that is working and valued, and a lot of investment has been placed in it.

> Our existing partner is well known to the probation service, is well known to courts, is well known to magistrates. There is a cost to

saying, "I'm sorry, you're not the cheapest, therefore you don't get it." Because all the ground work which has taken place over ten years will have to be done again by the new organisation.

My personal view is that you are either in partnership, or you are into competitive tendering. You can't do both. So our view of partnership would be that it's about sharing the risks and the gains.

Concerns were also expressed about maintainance of good quality services within a system of competitive tendering.

There is a real danger if you go into competitive tendering that it's all about doing it for the least cost. Therefore quality goes down the plug hole.

We would prefer to know more about the organisation and what quality of service they provide. Not just the cost basis, no.

Some respondents considered that competitive tendering imposed a bureaucratic burden on the probation service and small agencies which was unjustified in terms of the actual investment in provision:

If I was confident that I had an administrative machine behind me that could check out how they keep their accounts, how they staff themselves, what policies they have and all that, yes. Ideally, it would be great, wouldn't it? . . . But it's not like that.

It just takes up an inordinate amount of time, for the actual benefit that accrues to anybody.

Four respondents could see no advantage, even hypothetically, in engaging in competitive tendering. Four said that their service had as yet formed no view on it.

5. SUGS

One respondent ascribed the source of the probation service's partnerships directly to the SUGS funding opportunity:

Because most of the funding has come directly from the Home Office, what happened was that the agency itself approached the Home Office with support from the local probation service. So, basically, all this has been instigated from the agency . . . It's never been strategic

...So some things which have been Home Office funded have been very useful and others have been a waste of time.

6. Others

Three respondents said that selection of voluntary partners was hardly an issue, since, in their areas, there was no choice available between the existing agencies for local services. Two gave no response. One knew of no local device for recruitment of partners at all. Four probation services did not participate in the telephone survey.

Advantages and disadvantages of partnership

The telephone survey explored predictions of the advantages and disadvantages of partnership, both for probation services and for voluntary substance misuse agencies. Responses are summarised in Tables 2.1 to 2.4.

Table 2.1   Advantages of partnership for the probation service, as perceived by telephone survey respondents

Expertise		
	offered by voluntary organisations	28
	enhancement of probation officers' practice	15
Total		43
Service delivery		
	inter-agency co-ordination	9
	additional resource	7
	develop services in community	6
	clarify roles and responsibilities	4
	work with offenders in community	2
Total		28
Non-statutory status		
	quality of relationships	6
	flexibility/creativity	4
	Show strengths	1
Total		11
Professional and organisational effectiveness		
	different perspectives	5
	maintain priority of substance misuse	2
	facilitate strategic approach	2
Total		9

Advantages for the probation service

The most popular advantage of partnerships with substance misuse agencies to accrue to the probation service was the injection of specialist expertise. This was hardly surprising. But a strong theme concerned strengthening the skills and confidence of probation officers themselves. This desired outcome did not accord with any obvious intent that probation officers should be relieved of their case involvement, but reflected the pre-occupation with practice enhancement expressed in the partnership plans. Indeed, not one respondent mentioned facilitating a move towards case management, or in any other sense divesting probation officers of their traditional tasks, as a predicted advantage of partnership.

> Sometimes that access to expert advice enables officers to realise that they can in fact do a lot for themselves. There is no mystique about it.

> There's support for the work that we're doing ourselves, that they provide us with training, they provide us with support and encouragement, and also a safety net.

A cluster of advantages concerned the range and quality of service delivery. Partnership offered improvement in inter-agency co-ordination; clarification of roles, responsibilities and procedures; and an additional resource. It contributed to overall development of services in the community and could increase potential for working with offenders in that context.

The non-statutory status of partner organisations could confer particular advantages: in the quality of relationships with clients, including the type of information which could be divulged; in the flexibility and creativity characterising voluntary organisations; and by enabling voluntary organisations to show their strengths in the statutory context.

A small group of comments predicted that partnership would sustain the professional and organisational effectiveness of the probation service: through the challenge of differing perspectives; by maintaining the priority of substance misuse problems; and by facilitating a more strategic approach to substance misuse.

> It's jolly good to have our sometimes stuck-in-the-mud attitudes challenged.

> A very difficult area of work has now been given priority.

> That helped us to start to look at a new substance misuse policy for the whole service.

Disadvantages for the probation service

Leaving aside issues in coercion and confidentiality, which will be examined separately, the probation service's difficulties in the partnership enterprise were most commonly expressed in terms of its resistance to change, at both organisational and individual levels. Respondents deplored the attitudes of their colleagues in this respect, criticising their reluctance to share clients or their stereotyped rejection of voluntary agencies.

> The problems are first of all within themselves. They have a great difficulty in sharing clients with other probation officers! So sharing them with other *agencies* can be for some a major problem.

> They feel they are frequently working with volunteers, who are not experts or who aren't qualified.

The perceived threat to their jobs also influenced probation officers' responses.

Table 2.2 Problems of partnership for the probation service, as perceived by telephone survey respondents

Resistance		
	probation officer attitudes	12
	threat to jobs	9
	loss of status	2
	change of role	2
Total		25
Inter-professional relationships		
	different perspectives	6
	establish trust	6
	external constraints	3
	informal relationships	2
Total		17
Service delivery		
	ensure delivery	10
	clarify roles and responsibilities	4
	poor liaison	1
	inconsistency	1
Total		16
Increased workload		5

> There's an undercurrent of anxiety that this is the beginning of a major replacement of probation staff through the establishment of partnerships across the board.

> There's been a suspicion and anxiety among staff generally about the erosion of their tasks and also the erosion of service.

Another factor in resistance was the loss of expert status implied by introducing independent resources.

> It's sharing their own lack of expertise. They feel vulnerable because when with someone who specialises in drug or alcohol misuse then they have to admit that they don't know everything. That can be quite difficult for some because they have been seen as the experts in everything. Suddenly there is a whole range of people around who know much more about particular areas of work. Probation officers feel quite vulnerable about that.

Finally, pressure to change role from caseworker to case manager was resented: "Anybody involved with community care will know what difficulties that poses for people who came into the job to be social workers."

A cluster of responses concerned the quality of inter-professional relationships. Differences in perspectives, although potentially creative, also posed difficulties: "Whether the philosophy is the same, whether the values are complimentary, the structure of the organisation." Establishing trust, in conditions of mutual suspicion, was problematic: "How do you develop that trust? You can't just *tell* people to trust one another. They have to *learn* it and *experience* it." External constraints could compound these problems: for example, the impact upon the probation service of working to the requirements of the Criminal Justice Act 1991 and National Standards; or the institutional complexities of working in prisons. Previously informal relationships might suffer.

Issues in service quality and delivery were also troubling. It would be difficult to ensure that the service was delivered as intended.

> We have got to invest to ensure ... that all aspects are covered and the legal statutory aspects of the requirements are fully met. What ... may seem adequate to a [voluntary organisation] worker ... has got to correspond with the number of days or hours required in the order.

Getting access to the service for individuals who might otherwise be seen as a fairly low priority.

Ineffective clarification of roles, responsibilities and procedures, or poor liaison would result in inefficiency. Inconsistency between similar agencies as to what service they were prepared to provide could lead to confusion.

Both our service and the voluntary agencies need to be much clearer in their new contracts about agreements on exchange of information, complaints, boundaries, and accepting that we both can work together rather than be seen as two separate agencies.

It's extremely difficult to work out who is going to supervise who. Who is going to be accountable to who ... Later on you find that you are back-tracking to try and find who agreed what, when. Then there's financial clarity about who pays for what.

Five remarks comprised a category of their own, albeit one implied by all of the foregoing:

It is *very time consuming activity*, setting it all up, monitoring and ensuring that you are getting the service that you are actually asking for.

Advantages for voluntary organisations

The most commonly predicted advantage for voluntary agencies concerned the additional financial income. Secondarily in this theme of organisational advance was the support of a statutory organisation, in the quest for alternative funding, assisting the voluntary organisation to function, and raising its profile in the community.

The probation service as a statutory organisation will underwrite and provide references and support for some of these voluntary organisations.

Using our police liaison meeting to talk about substance misuse issues has helped [them]. They have started a [police referral system].

The professional effectiveness of voluntary organisations could improve. Substance misuse agencies might reach new clients through the probation service: "The clients that they may have had difficulty getting access to may well be the people that we've got on probation."

Table 2.3   Advantages of partnership for voluntary organisations, as perceived by telephone survey respondents

Professional effectiveness		
	reach clients	12
	develop expertise	9
	different perspectives	6
	status	5
	overlapping clients	4
Total		36
Organisational advance		
	income	26
	statutory support	9
Total		35
Inter-agency relationships		
	networking	10
	better understanding of probation service	7
	clarify roles and relationships	2
	trust	1
Total		20

Alternatively, in so far as their client group overlapped that of the probation service, partnership could increase agencies' response efficiency. There was potential for developing expertise in criminal justice issues through association with the probation service. It would also be helpful for voluntary organisations to take on different perspectives: "It has made them look externally rather than internally at what they are doing. It's been quite challenging for them to look at their own practice." Agency status could improve: "They are figures around at court...They are being seen and being valued."

Improvements in inter-agency relationships brought advantages. Partnership offered a gateway to the network of agencies in the criminal justice system and statutory sector: "It does bring them... right into the heart of the criminal justice system." It also usefully increased understanding of the probation service itself: "The kinds of problems presented by offenders and how we supervise and manage them in the community". Partnership would serve general benefits of clarifying roles and responsibilities and of fostering trust.

Disadvantages for voluntary organisations

Fewer disadvantages of partnership for voluntary organisations than for the probation service were predicted. One cluster of responses concerned the quality of inter-professional relationships, most particularly problems of autonomy.

> They have had to struggle with whether they are being compromised by our cash into betraying their own ethos and ethics.

> Probably being anxious about the possibility of bigger organisations pushing them around.

> Difficulties in terms of power... We make great statements about equality, but there is an underlying fear that because we have got cash, that makes it a power based relationship and that they will lose their autonomy and value base, which is very central to what they are doing.

Differences in perspective were now described in terms of "culture clash".

> They would be frustrated by our bureaucracy. Perhaps we appear to be over sensitive about how we deal with the police, how we deal with the courts.

> They haven't understood the constraints of the probation service, in relation to legal matters, in relation to people using illegal drugs, conditions of treatment and the legal aspects of people on conditions.

Table 2.4 Problems of partnership for voluntary organisations, as perceived by telephone survey respondents

Inter-professional relationships		
	loss of autonomy	12
	different perspectives	9
	difficult probation officers	6
	access to probation officers	2
	trust	2
Total		31
Services		
	resources	9
	insecurity	4
	difficult clients	4
	street credibility	2
Total		19

Our turn-around times to do with courts, PSRs and wanting things done and information about breach are usually fairly immediate. Voluntaries sometimes are not geared up to that turn around.

I could think that from the point of view of somebody from outside the service, the probation service is really odd and peculiar and they find it difficult to get on with.

Despite their earlier self-effacement, only six respondents referred at this point to the awkwardness of probation officers as colleagues.

There are all sorts of problems that come from the misuse of [the partnership project]. [For example] probation officers ringing up and saying "Joe Bloggs is in court in twenty-four hours. I am sending him round to you for an assessment."

Probation officers are not the easiest bunch of people to relate to. They can be difficult in their expectations . . . because probation officers, despite being so-called caring people, can be arrogant and bombastic, in my view.

Lack of trust between agencies, and difficulties for partners in gaining access to probation officers were also problematic.

Respondents also predicted problems in service delivery, in terms both of organisational structure and ethos. Insecurity of funding was a debilitating feature of voluntary agencies' experience. Resource constraints would prevent full coverage of service.

We are probably wanting to get access to facilities at a time of crisis. At a time when they can't manage within their own resources . . . the agency might have difficulty in being able to mobilise and respond to those needs in the same time scale.

[The substance misuse agency] workers say "This is wasting our time and our energy when we are already pressed. We could be providing a service for more appropriate voluntary referrals."

The guidance for the contracts is [too] complicated and has an unrealistic expectation of what voluntary agencies operating a very small office can come up with.

The client group offered by the probation service was unattractive: "The probation service spends most of its time working with unmotivated people, but of course voluntaries have this history of working with people who knock on the door and come looking for them." "Street credibility" was potentially compromised by liaison with a statutory service: "If you are seen to be aligned too closely with the criminal justice system, particularly for drug users, then that's a problem in itself."

Substance misuse policy

Thirty-five substance misuse policy documents, from 30 probation services, were received. Five services had separate policies for drugs and alcohol; one of these also had a general statement on substance misuse which explained the distinction between the two issues.

Apart from the aforementioned general statement, 17 probation services had substance misuse policies covering both alcohol and drugs, 10 services had drugs policies and eight services had alcohol policies. All 27 substance misuse and drugs policies supported harm minimisation. Apart from one early drugs policy prepared in 1990, these documents dated from 1991 onwards. The majority were prepared in 1992 or 1993, clearly prompted by the report of the Advisory Council on the Misuse of Drugs (1991) which strongly promoted harm reduction strategies within the probation service. Many drew closely, even verbatim, on the advice contained in that report, particularly with regard to disclosure of sensitive information.

Approaches advocated in the eight alcohol policies were not subsumed under a particular title such as harm reduction. However, broad based strategies pursued control over drinking behaviour as the general aim. The notion of control included, but was not limited to abstinence. Notably, three alcohol policies were prepared between 1985 and 1989, thus pre-dating the probation service's interest in harm minimisation. The remainder were dated between 1990 and 1993, apparently complementing the development of harm reduction policies for drugs. The main difference between alcohol policies and drug or substance misuse policies seemed to be the concerns of the latter with confidentiality and health, particularly in relation to HIV and AIDS.

Implementing a harm reduction policy was not straightforward. For example, it made little difference to the selection of substance misuse agencies with which to foster local relationships. In fortunate cases, this reflected a shared philosophy. Several telephone respondents reported that most agencies in their areas also pursued harm minimisation; a few acknowledged that their service's adoption of harm reduction lagged behind other organisations. A popular, pragmatic view was that a spectrum of services was needed, in order to cater for individual need and preference. Abstinence proponents, therefore, had their place in a broad range of treatment opportunities.

> I don't think we see one answer to the whole of human kind's problems. What we need is a differential approach, which actually requires extremely good assessment skills in order to make those sorts of decisions properly.

> To deal with a complex problem like substance misuse, you need a broad and varied strategy. You don't put all of your eggs in any one basket.

However, defining a harm reduction strategy was in itself problematic. There was no guarantee that agencies claiming such a policy pursued the same goals and methods in practice. For example, one respondent had attempted to canvass views of drug workers and probation officers locally, concluding sadly: "I don't think drug agencies want to mention abstinence because they consider it too unrealistic. Probation officers want to be realistic in acknowledging that harm reduction is necessary, but they would like to have abstinence as a goal!" Another admitted: "Sometimes the drugs projects feel fairly alarming to probation officers in terms of the line they pursue." It was all the more confusing when local substance misuse agencies disagreed among themselves.

> We're in the middle of a fraught situation here... Within [the area] there is a campaigning group, based on the only residential centre [here]. They have formed themselves into a pressure group, where they believe that chemical dependency is the norm, and abstinence is the only solution. They are very intolerant of the street agencies ... Every meeting we have, they have a protest... We have to be very careful... because of course in some cases they are the appropriate vehicle for treatment in our area.

Other problems emanated from within the probation service itself, often rooted in its place within the criminal justice system. A particular concern was a perceived trend towards punitiveness in criminal justice policy, with consequent lack of sympathy for harm minimisation. There was also tension between knowledge of illegal activity and effective engagement in harm minimisation interventions. Moreover, substance misusers were not generally popular clients and probation officers were sometimes resistant to the implications of a harm mini-misation approach.

In the face of such conflicts, it often seemed wisest to allow practice to develop case by case, with individualised agreements worked out between probation officers, offenders and treatment providers. Agency specific policies, backed where possible by multi-agency liaison and protocols, could provide a supportive framework for what essentially must be an individual enterprise at case level. In view of this emergent pragmatism, closer examination was made of existing substance misuse projects, and of issues in coercion and confidentiality.

Projects in substance misuse

As Home Office guidance suggested, substance misuse was a popular target for partnership development. However, because of its long recog-nised relationship to offending, several probation services already had well established in-house projects. For example: five partnership plans described secondment arrangements; two identified strong joint-working alliances; one dedicated a probation officer post to develop-mental work with substance misusing offenders; and one reported a substantial increase in provision following multi-agency collaboration with health and social services departments. The telephone survey revealed more in-house projects, including a probation team specialis-ing in alcohol interventions and a probation hostel dedicated to sub-stance misusing offenders.

Several probation services enjoyed strong links with statutory sub-stance misuse services. Apart from their attractiveness as hosts for se-condments, partnership plans revealed that statutory services were involved in a number of joint projects and in one area were contracted to deliver groupwork programmes. Several telephone survey respond-ents complained that these relationships could not be recognised within the targetted partnership expenditure. This was particularly galling in areas where no satisfactory alternative agency existed in the voluntary sector. Additionally, a range of projects for substance misusing offenders developed through the SUGS scheme. As will be shown later, the future of all these varieties of substance misuse projects became actually or potentially threatened by the combined impact of reduced funding of probation services and lack of recognition for projects located in the statutory sector.

Proposed, or newly developed local partnerships for substance misuse projects were described in several documents, ranging from a contribu-tion to increased staffing of agencies, through contracted groupwork programmes or individual assessment and counselling services, to a day centre in one case and a specialised service for women in another. The scope of partnership projects was explored more fully in the next phase of the study, but the diversity exposed by this initial exploration is worthy of note.

Coercion in treatment

Home Office guidance in Probation Circular 17/1993 reveals enthusiasm for developing partnerships in the context of supervision programmes, both to increase access to specialist resources and to facilitate probation officers' transition to case management. The document also advises that "[s]ensitive issues requiring clarification of role and responsibilities should be positively addressed", citing breach procedures as one such issue.

Partnership plans, however, were reticent on the topic of coercion and enforcement. In fact, there was no discussion of the issue in any of the documents received. Perusal of the projects described revealed a few examples of schemes explicitly targetting offenders subject to special requirements in probation orders; for example, drug and alcohol education programmes. It cannot necessarily be concluded that the use of special requirements was not envisaged, but only that there was no commitment apparent in the partnership plans to invoke coercion on a general scale to gain offenders' co-operation in the enterprise. Moreover, several partnerships described in the plans did not lend themselves readily to the use of coercion; Citizens Advice Bureau surgeries and furniture distribution are among examples already mentioned.

Nevertheless, 13 telephone respondents predicted coercion and enforcement as potential problems for the partnership endeavour. The issue was sometimes presented in terms of a culture clash.

> There are often issues about the philosophical ethos underpinning the organisation. Clearly the probation service is a statutory organisation and inevitably we're dealing with a degree of compulsion, whereas a lot of voluntary organisations want to hold on to those concepts of voluntarism. That can produce headaches.

Some respondents described the dilemma for voluntary agencies sympathetically:

> The voluntary sector has had a mixed response to our initiative. It depends how they see working in the criminal justice system. Some

are sceptical of that, feeling it affects their street agency status. They have not always welcomed it. They are sceptical about dealing with people on a statutory basis. They fear that would put off their out-reach work, particularly with drug abusers. Some voluntary sector provision on alcohol is very much a counselling basis, a self-referral basis, which doesn't necessarily fit with the statutory basis of our work. So they haven't necessarily welcomed getting more central to the criminal justice system.

Others, however, took a more robust view of voluntary sector sensitivities:

> The only thing that would affect us funding a partner organisation . . . is if they were refusing to accept people on conditions of orders. Realistically, we couldn't afford to fund them, because that's what the courts want to do.

> Sanctions is the be all and end all of it really. They are still reluctant to take that on board. I can understand that. But they are going to have to.

A few respondents reported that the issue was not insurmountable in practice, as it appeared to be in principle:

> The voluntary sector didn't find it that difficult really, so long as we separated who did the enforcements. We are the enforcers and they provide the expertise.

Confidentiality

Twenty-eight telephone respondents predicted that confidentiality would be a problem between partners. Strict principles of confidentiality pertaining in the voluntary sector, perceived as crucial for effective interventions with substance misusers, presented difficulties for probation officers seeking to verify that their clients were in treatment. One respondent regarded the strength of professional allegiance to this principle sceptically:

> The agreements seem to be based on trust between individual people, which can't be right, when it's a case of agencies working together in the context of the criminal justice system. So it needs to be moved to an inter-agency agreement.

Others also saw differences between agencies in their approaches:

> With the alcohol agencies, if you had somebody on an order with a condition [of treatment], the alcohol people never had a problem with it. They simply say "Well, he didn't attend." End of story. With the drugs people, they had awful difficulty with it. It got in the way of appropriate levels of care and treatment.

Some respondents pointed out that probation officers also had to make careful choices about disclosure of sensitive information, such as the nature of criminal convictions. There was some feeling expressed that the issue was accorded disproportionate importance for dubious reasons:

> What I've experienced is preciousness around issues like confidentiality and unnecessary barriers being created around that...That's something the probation service traditionally have experienced difficulties with, particularly with drug agencies, who like to think that they're all very alternative and "right on", and that we are agents of social control. They get a bit silly about it sometimes. You would even have situations where someone on probation will tell you that they are using heroin and they are in contact with the street agency, but will not tell the street agency that you know, because *they* have told them not to tell their probation officer!

Conclusion

When the strong reflection, with little departure or innovation, of Home Office guidance in the partnership plans, was raised with probation service managers, responses suggested that the documents might usefully be regarded as strategic devices for satisfying a statutory requirement without voluntarily surrendering autonomy. This presents itself as a reasonable explanation, and suggests a motive to which many might be sympathetic. Nevertheless, the point remains that these documents were offered in response to a request for *policies*. If they did *not* constitute policy, because they were operational statements and/or strategic devices, the question may legitimately be asked: where did partnership policy lie? Uncertainty on this point later emerged as more than an academic nicety, when exploring the problems associated with partnership development in Phase Two interviewing. Many of the problems of the partnership enterprise arose precisely because the policy intentions of senior managers were not accessible to field probation officers.

As heralded in the previous chapter, the elusive definition of partnership, strangely compounded by the Home Office itself in its guidance, continued to require attention throughout the research. However, a further, and possibly related issue was the reticence of the plans on the topic of coercion and enforcement. It may be that this was simply not regarded as pertinent material for inclusion in the partnership plans. Nevertheless, identification by telephone respondents of coercion and confidentiality as the most problematic predicted areas of partnership relationships, suggests that the Home Office rightly advised early clarification of the matter. An alternative explanation for the silence, therefore, might be tentatively advanced.

Avoidance of the issue of coercion both increased the range of potentially useful partnerships, to include activities which would not constitute elements of supervision programmes, and smoothed over a topic which potential partners might consider irrelevant or even injurious to their own enterprise. By also exploiting ambiguity in the definition of partnership, probation services were able to offer the formidable range of inter-agency activity exemplified in the review of the partnership plans, without relinquishing any of its traditional professional territory. Thus, probation services maximised their opportunities in the partnership enterprise while simultaneously diluting a threat to their professional autonomy.

Similarly, despite ambiguities of definition, and diversity of practical forms, the partnership plans offered a unified vision of the purpose of partnership, captured in the term "enhancement". Enhancement of probation officer activity was also perceived by telephone survey respondents as one of the most important potential advantages of partnership. Again, this emerged as a crucial aspect of the partnership enterprise during Phase Two interviewing.

The pursuit of enhancement has implications, not only for the types of service which might be acquired through partnership, but also for the quality of the relationships to be developed between the probation service and voluntary agencies. Strong allegiance was declared in partnership plans, and endorsed by many telephone survey respondents, to qualities of sharing, support and empowerment as vital ingredients in successful partnership relationships. Unease with the terminology of competitive tendering and contracting, and the search for more comfortable alternatives, was partly driven by its associations with an aggressive market place. Such discomfort echoes the earlier experiences of local authorities in the drive towards mixed provision of social care (Flynn and Hurley 1993; Wistow, Knapp, Hardy and Allen 1994).

The vision of partnership as enhancement was also linked to perceptions of the probation service's role in supporting substance misuse services. The telephone survey revealed a range of experiences of the impact of community care arrangements on substance misuse services, featuring local differences in ease of access by probation officers. The problem facing probation services was to provide for enhancement of field officers' activity without underwriting or replacing the responsibilities of health authorities and social services departments to provide treatment for substance misusers. Thus, local authorities emerged as important, albeit indirect, moderators of relationships between probation services and substance misuse agencies, with potential significance both for the attractiveness of financial partnership and for the practical forms which it might take. Resolution of this problem, however, depended on local constraints and opportunities. As will be seen, differences in the availability, nature and quality of local agencies for substance misuse treatment provided an important backcloth to the approaches adopted by probation services. Yet, in working out its approach to these issues, the probation service was confronted with the challenge of defining its role within communities.

Thus, although the preliminary soundings taken during the telephone survey were a tentative exploration of issues in substance misuse work emerging in the context of community care, cash limiting and partnership initiatives, they provided some helpful clues to subsequent phases of the study. Indeed, many of the issues which telephone respondents identified bore an impact upon the projects which were visited in Phase Two, and some emerged importantly in Phase Three. Inheritance of devolved SUGS partnerships, conflict of interests in service development and sacrifice of in-house specialisation, became particularly salient and sensitive issues for several projects.

3
The Organisation of Partnership

This chapter explores partnership development in practice: selection of partners; a profile of partner agencies; and partnership structures, including the nature of services, targetting and coercion.

Selection

Among the 25 projects, there was not one example of a partnership developed through competitive tendering, or the so-called "managed market". Fourteen partnerships grew out of historical relationships: nine of these were funded by the SUGS scheme; two were non-financial. Six originated in networking; two of these were funded by SUGS; one was non-financial. Four partnerships apparently owed their existence entirely to the SUGS scheme. Clear information was not forthcoming as to the origins of one financial partnership, although a pre-existing non-financial project was known to the study.

Historical relationships

Historical relationships leading to partnership took several forms, which were not mutually exclusive. In two cases, involvement of probation officers in founding the substance misuse agency itself spawned long standing relationships.

> [The agency] was virtually set up by a probation officer... [who] put a huge amount of time in. It really was a lot of investment and time. It was...kick started from probation. So right back there's been involvement. (probation officer)

Probation staff sat on the management committees of eight substance misuse agencies.

The problem I'm having is to work out the difference between a partnership as it's recently been described and something that's been happening for years...I am on the council of management at [the substance misuse agency]. (senior probation officer)

We had worked together for a long period of time and in fact two of my colleagues sit on their management as well. So there is an ongoing relationship. (probation officer)

At six partnerships, previous joint project work was conducted on a collaborative non-financial basis. In some instances partnership funding consolidated such ventures.

It began as a voluntary arrangement with [the substance misuse agency]...That voluntary contact was then built upon when the Home Office were persuaded...to provide a three year funding ...That formalised the two years of work which had led up to that. (senior probation officer)

We had the van and a half-time worker...We were tinkering around trying to make a mobile [project] work, make it acceptable, accessible...One of the things we tried was making links with the probation service...It was highly likely that a proportion of offenders might well be people who were involved with drugs and might not be in contact with other services. It was negotiated...[with] the senior here, who was keen that we should do that...Then we hit funding problems...we had to abandon the session...That period coincided with the launching of partnerships. (substance misuse manager)

Elswhere, funding was directed to new projects.

This particular partnership isn't the first enterprise. There's been a long tradition of working together, in particular with the alcohol education groups...We've been running those for seven or eight years in close co-operation. (senior probation officer)

Finally, historical relationships evolved from looser contacts at ground level, through onward referral of clients, and relationships between individual practitioners.

Personally, because I came here as a new officer, I wanted to establish my own liaisons, co-operations with other agencies. I went out of my way to contact them, do an afternoon's induction with them. So they knew who I was and were probably at ease as to what my philosophy was about working with people with substance abuse. (probation officer)

It's always existed informally. There's always been an understanding that there is a bonding between offending and substance misuse and traditionally we've always had links with the probation service. (substance misuse manager)

The impact of formal financial partnership upon these historical relationships was a sensitive issue. Firstly, staff at practice level sometimes felt that their earlier informal efforts were disregarded and devalued by management intervention to create the partnership enterprise.

I was involved eighteen months ago in meeting with [the substance misuse agency] with a view to setting up a partnership ... We had regular meetings and we felt that we had more of a mandate to move the process on than we actually did at the time ... We took that forward a lot, and when we got to the point of printing referral forms, we came to realise that it wasn't as simple as that. The finances hadn't even been negotiated ... We then withdrew and nothing happened until [the funded worker's] arrival here. (probation officer)

Conversely, management inspired ventures could overlook problematic realities of relationships between a selected partner and local probation officers. One substance misuse manager described a most unfortunate experience:

There seemed to be a coincidental collision of two ideas ... I wrote to the [team] seniors ... about a year ago ... My concern was that probation officers seemed to have a different understanding [of our] role as a specialist agency. Consequently, their expectations were perhaps unreal or inaccurate ... Specialist agencies should increasingly be seen as agencies of last resort, and if probation officers did not feel competent, then that was a training issue ... Well, at that moment, unknown to me ... the Home Office was keen to sub-contract some of their work to non-statutory agencies. I got a phone call from the Assistant Chief Probation Officer, saying he would like to talk about a possible development of this particular notion ... I was quite happy to develop it with him, as long as we did not compromise this important principle ... that probation officers should be encouraged to work with drug users...He didn't see there was a contradiction...But later it became clear that some probation officers could not understand. They saw a contradiction, they saw a tension, and they thought..."Let's shove it".

Finally, there was disappointment that popular links with management committees were disrupted by the partnership initiative. This unforeseen product of the partnership enterprise, announced in separate guidance from the Home Office after the establishment of early projects (Home Office 1993d), was poorly received by both probation and substance misuse agency staff, finding themselves forced to surrender a valued commitment.

> I'm part-time...so [evening] meetings were a bit of a pain. But I did get quite involved in [the substance misuse agency] and felt very sorry not to be so involved. So I don't miss the time commitment, but I do miss the actual involvement. (probation officer)

> We have a liaison officer who used to be part of our management committee, but she was told...that she had a conflict of interest because they fund us. She has had to leave. But...communication between me and her was good. (substance misuse manager)

Networking

The minority of partnerships which originated in networking revealed a flair for opportunism among both probation and substance misuse personnel.

> I knew [the substance misuse manager] through inter-agency groups in the city and suggested to her that we could consider it. The [team] were happy to give it a try. Staff at [the substance misuse agency] came along and talked to the team...about what they could offer... and simply went ahead...So it was an informal opportunistic thing. (senior probation officer)

> A care trust had funding to set up a project for young people with alcohol problems...With the best intentions in the world...that project didn't get off the ground and the funding was still there. The director approached probation, who at that time were running their own alcohol education programmes...to see whether, rather than lose this funding, to merge it with the alcohol education programmes. That's how the partnership came about. It was through a

meeting with probation and [the substance misuse agency] and the care trust that they came up with co-ordinating the alcohol education programmes from a central point. (project secretary)

At other times the networking process was purposefully exploited for the occasion.

We commissioned the local council for voluntary services to carry out a feasibility study. They went off and interviewed all the agencies with a drug and alcohol remit...and gave us lots of information about what the voluntary sector could offer us in partnership. I chaired a group within the service in relation to drug and alcohol problems and looked at what we needed to fill the gaps in-house. The outcome of those two things was that we decided to enter into formal partnership with three voluntary sector agencies. (senior probation officer)

Substance misuse workers, in particular, sustained a network of inter-professional relationships enabling them to capitalise on developmental opportunities.

The first we heard about it was Home Office directives...about the money that had to be used...I've always had an interest in working with the law and offenders. So the documents were passed to me by my director, and I got into doing the research...Being the organisation that we are, we're always looking for funding avenues...I was feeding all of the documents I had from [other organisations] to [the senior probation officer]. (substance misuse worker)

SUGS

Four partnerships apparently owed their existence to the central SUGS scheme.

The partnership began when [the substance misuse agency] approached us to see whether [we] would be able to fund this sort of venture. [But] there was some delay. [The substance misuse agency] were however successful in their bid to the Home Office...at which point we had to create a partnership. (probation officer)

The partners

Interviewees at partner agencies were asked to describe briefly their organisation's background, its theoretical approach to substance misuse, and the types of services which it provided. They were also asked about the impact of community care arrangements, changes brought about by partnership with the probation service and their agency's current main concerns. A broad characterisation of partner agencies thus emerged.

Background and current circumstances

Three partners were part of a large national organisation and one, although comprising a single residential facility, provided a national resource. Information on five agencies' origins was not forthcoming. The remainder were strongly rooted in local initiatives: some were helped into existence by health and social services departments; some developed during the 1980s following the release of government pump-priming money for drug initiatives (Dorn 1990); two alcohol agencies also benefited from targetted funding. Some staff attributed their agency's foundation to local groups or individuals, including, for example, parents of drug users and, in four cases, probation officers:

> We were put together in 1989 by senior officers in probation, health, education and police. They decided that [the area] had to have a voluntary organisation dealing with drug and alcohol issues.

> It was started up by some mothers who had children with drug misuse problems. It started at somebody's house . . . Then the demand got more and more. Then more people got involved and then they actually got some funding from [the hospital and the] local authority and started up a project.

> It started off as a phone line, started off by certain interested probation officers, social workers and concerned parents. It has gradually grown from a phone line to a street agency.

One agency ceased to function during Phase Two of the study. Others had grown, some quite substantially, since their foundation. Five were increasing in size at the time of interview, and at least one had firm plans for additional project staff:

> Recently, it has expanded and there has been one new post this year, and myself . . . But the big expansion has been in having been successful in bids to take over the drug and alcohol units which are moving from [hospital psychiatric units]. The hospital is closing next May, so [we] are taking over the running of those services with a twenty bed unit.

We are going through a lot of changes at the moment. We're due to merge with [another agency].

Six agencies benefited from approval as assessors for community care and another received additional funding after its introduction. Two agencies discovered imaginative ways to use community care funds:

We put in for four or five bikes for people who were doing new things and the bikes would enable them to achieve that. For instance...a graduate of [a residential programme]...was a baker and needed a bike...so we got him that and money for his whites.

Substance misuse staff complained frequently, however, about the bureaucracy created by community care arrangements:

We have a lot more demands on us in terms of collecting data, systems, assessment forms and so on, which are in constant conflict with the approach to counselling where we are trying to make it as uninvasive and unobtrusive as possible and to preserve as much confidentiality as possible.

It is a nightmare. If somebody comes from out of the borough we have to get hold of the fund-holders of the borough, tell them the situation, then the client has to go over to that borough to be re-assessed. Usually, they then have to wait for it to go to a funding panel, who then get back to us. We then have to get in touch with the client to say you can come on the programme. Of course you lose so many along the way.

The slow pace of processing could have disastrous consequences.

We did have a residential unit...which following the introduction of community care ceased to get referrals. The referrals we did get were so slow to be processed that the people that were referred had relapsed before being admitted. So we closed the unit.

At eight agencies there was concern about the continuation of funding. Allied to this, major changes in the structure and organisation of local government, health authorities and social services departments would affect agencies' funding arrangements. There was also dissatisfaction as to the types of available funding:

Being expected to be able to get spot funding... The problem with that is that there has to be a core organisation to respond to it. We won't be able to generate income from that kind of market... Yes, if that was in addition to core funding, that would be generating extra income, but if it was seen as a substitute, that's what worries me.

We're very stretched at the moment. One of the problems with fixed term contracts is that when someone leaves a post six months or a year before the end, or the renewal, of funding, you can't find anyone to replace on a six month contract. They just won't take it. So there's a delay in replacing staff.

There is now a statutory team in this health district which is in direct competition with us... So what concerns me is the future funding of an agency which offers a service which is distinctly different from their [statutory] service. The most distinctive feature is that we are not bureaucratic and we are user friendly.

However, agencies were not deterred from forward planning and developmental ambitions. When asked about their immediate concerns, ten agencies mentioned a target group identified as especially vulnerable, or a special project for which funding was sought:

I will be looking for some funding to start up a benzodiazapine clinic. I am hoping that there will be enough funding to set up two clinics.

Trying to respond to crack use. [And] the fact that drug agencies have not been accessible for non-white people.

Our main priority this year was securing funding for a relatives counsellor.

At two agencies a main concern was dealing with the *consequences* of expansion: "The big concern is getting a new responsibility for staff, responsibility for beds, and becoming a much bigger employer".

In this mixed yet active environment, partnership with the probation service was not a survival issue for these agencies, although funding would be sorely missed in some cases:

It pays for a part-time counsellor. It covers eighteen hours and we pay the rest, so that we can have him for four days, but we would effectively lose the position of a part-time counsellor, which would be devastating as we have only got two on the staff!

However, elsewhere it was pointed out that the probation budget was separately maintained and thus did not affect the wider organisation. Substance misuse staff described the implications of losing the partnership in qualitative terms: as a loss for the client group; as a waste of the effort of forging a working relationship; or, conversely, as a link which was sufficiently strong to withstand the withdrawal of funding:

> Not much of a loss. Could be a gain in some respects...The strong links that were there before between probation and the drugs project will have been strengthened tenfold.

> To [the substance misuse agency] none at all, because the money is allocated to the probation service and that's where it stays. The loss to networking, the loss to partnership working and the loss to clients would be great.

> Important for the clients. Yes. [The substance misuse agency] and the probation service can go off and do other things, get funding for other things. It's problematic, but not that problematic. At some level we will always survive. [But] they are an extremely vulnerable client group here, who need help, and there are probation officers who need help and training in drugs work.

How, then, were agencies changed by the partnership experience? At five agencies, involvement in coerced client contact heralded a change in outlook. However, each of these respondents observed that the agency itself did not substantively change, but rather the perspective of substance misuse workers:

> I have moved from being against being involved in conditions of orders. I have changed my mind about that. At the end of the day, if it avoids someone going down, which is very important to me, I've changed. I resent people who occupy some moral high ground.

> I got some rooms at the health centre because I thought that would be away from probation and we wouldn't be seen as an extension of probation. I thought that would be really important, for me to highlight the difference between us...When I talked to the people... they were indifferent. In fact some of them said they preferred to be counselled in the probation office because it was more convenient for them.

At two agencies, partnership involved substance misuse workers in different practice approaches: an abstinence agency participating in a multi-agency partnership for assessment and onward referral to a range of resources; and a counselling agency at which the traditional style contrasted with probation staff's preference for task oriented work:

> There is a need for harm minimisation, there is a need for abstinence, there is a need for all the different philosophies...that is very important to me. But it's different in as much as before I was just working with abstinence, sometimes we don't look at harm reduction, alcohol education, other areas as well. But [here] I'm assessing and seeing which would be best for the client.

> For probation it was very much drink exercises, how much are you drinking, individual drink exercises...So it was all about trying to find out about the drinking, whereas we tend to ask the question why.

At another agency, there was a positive change in staff attitudes towards their mobile outreach project, which was rescued from closure by partnership funding:

> It's altered [staff] attitude towards the van, because before it was seen as [a chore]. Because before the partnership there weren't many people coming on to the van. It wasn't being used to a great extent ... But having come to [the probation site] we've been really busy some sessions. The people who have been staffing the van with me have been pleased. They're willing to come back and staff it again...They are more willing to accept the van as a good piece of work.

One agency's policy of absolute confidentiality was changed in order to permit reporting of attendance at the programme. At three agencies there was an impact on administration:

> Originally, I was a bit careless about recording who came [to the group] and who didn't. It didn't seem that important. Now we've got monitoring forms to check on who is coming. May be important some time, to demonstrate to our purchasers and to probation that we are getting so many people.

> My boss would say the complexity of the financial arrangements is a nightmare. Let's take expenses. Two and a half days a week I'm doing

expenses for [the substance misuse agency] when I drive. Two and a half days a week I'm doing it for the probation service . . . Some of the money for my employment is coming from [the health authority], some is coming from probation. It's all worked out on a different basis.

In general, therefore, the impact of partnership was small, and particularly so in comparison with other agency changes and concerns. As one substance misuse manager explained: "It is very much perceived as a stand-alone project. So it hasn't changed us that much."

Services for substance misusers

Eight partner agencies specialised in alcohol problems. One offered a mixed drug and alcohol service, although the majority of its clients in practice presented drinking problems. One offered a service to alcohol and non-intravenous drug users. The remainder focused predominantly on illicit drugs.

Six agencies described only one type of service. Two of these were residential facilities, although in both cases the partnership project was a separate community-based programme. Four agencies, all of which specialised in alcohol problems, described their service only as counselling. The remainder mentioned a range of services available to clients.

Fifteen agencies, including the four just mentioned, provided a counselling service; this included information and advice giving, as well as short and longer term personal support. Eight agencies offered either a drop-in service or a day centre programme. Although in principle these services are distinguished by their degree of formality and structure, in practice the distinction could be blurred. Thus, while one agency exclusively offered a structured day programme of groupwork modules, some provided a walk-in facility for immediate advice, needle exchange facilities or general befriending, while others offered a mixture of these styles. Seven agencies provided a needle exchange service. Seven also operated an outreach, or detached service which ranged from individual workers making street level contact to, in one case, a van travelling to various sites in the county.

A variety of services were mentioned less frequently. Five agencies offered groupwork: one of these, as mentioned, worked exclusively in this style. Relapse prevention was a popular candidate for selective groupwork. Four agencies provided a residential facility; in two cases this was part of a range of provision. Four mentioned school-based projects for raising awareness, education and publicising support services. Three agencies provided a service to prisoners. Three provided "alternative" therapies, including acupuncture, aromatherapy and relaxation training. Two agencies included methadone prescription among their direct services.

Eight agencies identified the use of volunteers as part of their services, although this may understate the level of volunteer counselling overall.

Theoretical approach

Thirteen agencies described their approach to substance misuse problems in terms of harm reduction. With one exception, these were primarily drug agencies.

> [We] see ourselves having a role at two broad levels. One is...to promote a help-seeking environment...The other part is that, having hopefully created an environment where people can seek help or advice, then we're able to have some impact on reducing the harm that might be related to their chosen drug use.

> Health promotion, harm reduction and harm minimisation and risk reduction. Drawing in the whole field of advice and education and information around safer injecting practices, safer drug use, HIV, AIDS, and sometimes sexual and drug-related diseases.

An important aspect of this approach was a non-judgemental, pragmatic approach to continuing or resumed drug use.

> It's like a child learning to ride a bicycle. We would not dream of taking the bicycle away from a child after the child falls off three or four times. We know about the cumulative process...Likewise, people coming off opiates need that flexibility and need that permission to fail.

> We were the safety net. We dealt with the people [who often] had no fixed abode and were constantly in grief with the law and they needed friends. We're not passing judgement on them for what they're doing. It's their choice. It's about looking at what they're doing, reducing the risks to them personally. That might be just saying, "Well, let's look at your injecting sites and find somewhere that's better for you to inject."

Three agencies pursued abstinence: a residential facility; a community-based programme adapted from the popular "twelve steps" model; and a day treatment facility for alcohol abusers.

It's an abstinence based programme. We don't do here any alcohol education, we don't do controlled drinking, we're not interested in counting units because the people that come here are really beyond that. They are in trouble with drink, and the only way they can get out of that trouble is to stop. Entirely.

This approach did not entail outright rejection of clients who did not sustain abstinence. Some tolerance was extended. Repeatedly relapsing clients would be invited to withdraw to reconsider their options.

It's very difficult to have one particular rule that everyone has to stick to, because they are all different. Somebody might have a couple of lapses, yet want to stop. Some people don't want to stop drinking yet. So usually, after about three lapses, we say "Right. Go away for three months, do your drinking, think about it and then come back." But we always let them know that they can always come back. When they're ready to stop, then they can come back.

They are coming of their own accord and they realise that alcohol and/or drugs is a problem to them ... If they were to relapse then they would either shape up or ship out. Which means that if it happens again, then they would have a six week discharge. It's for the client's good, we feel. Then they would have the six week discharge, to attend [for example] AA meetings, phoning in every Friday, keeping in touch with us. Then coming back after six weeks and looking at it again.

Five agencies described their approach as client centred. Client centredness was considered by some to be integral to a harm reduction strategy:

[Our] general thesis is that abstinence is not a requirement. It's really up to the client to decide what the client wants. It's up to the client. It's client centred.

The approach of three alcohol agencies was described in terms of responsible, or sensible drinking, focusing on the quality of individual choices:

We regard drinking as being the responsibility of people. It is a legal choice to drink or not to drink, to abuse drink ... So we are not taking away choice, but we are giving choice and responsibility back to people. But with the responsibility for drinking goes the responsibility for any consequences there might be...So we will confront people with the consequences of their drinking.

Three agencies, one of which specialised in alcohol problems, were described as eclectic. One drug worker allied eclecticism to the agency's primary aim of harm minimisation:

> It doesn't have an underlying therapeutic philosophy. But it's refreshingly generic in its social work style, [which] makes it good fun to work with as well.

Four alcohol agencies described their theoretical orientation in unique terms: functional; behavioural; cognitive behavioural; and holistic.

> The model is a functional model...We're looking for reasons why people drink, what the function of the alcohol use is, what it's masking...It's controlled drinking or abstinence. Helping people to choose which is best.

> [We] believe that alcohol is a behavioural problem. That people can learn to adapt their behaviour in response to their alcohol use and that whether the goal is abstinence or moderating or reducing their drinking, is entirely in the client's hands.

> We use a holistic approach with clients. We use whatever suits the client. We make sure that we look at the clients individually.

Underlying the differences in terminology, unifying themes of tolerance and flexibility emerged in all these descriptions of agency theoretical approach. Even within the narrower constraints of an abstinence approach, partner agencies were forgiving of their clients' fallibility. All attempted to work creatively to facilitate opportunities for individual change. Thus, notwithstanding the different terminologies invoked to describe their agencies' overall theoretical orientations, many interviewees referred to a particular conceptual model of fluctuating motivation in the process of recovery from addiction (Prochaska and Diclemente 1986).

Structuring partnership

Partnership services

The most popular approach to financial partnership was to appoint an additional full or part-time substance misuse worker to the substance misuse agency. This was the case in 16 partnerships. In only one instance was the post absorbed into the substance misuse agency. Indeed, the appointed worker at this partnership was not offered for interview, since the funding source had no implications for the role played within the organisation; instead, probation clients were given access to the agency's day programme for recovering alcoholics.

In the other 15 partnerships, the new appointment provided an identifiable extra resource for the probation service, usually by dedicating part or all of the funded worker's time to provision for its clients. There were two variations on this theme, both of which involved outreach services. At one partnership, which subsequently participated as Project C in Phase Three, the funding established a new community outreach service at the substance misuse agency. At another, a mobile service was rescued from abandonment by the provision of an outreach worker, enabling the project to resume operation, including sessions at probation office sites.

Partnership funded substance misuse workers usually provided assessments (13 partnerships) and/or direct individual work with clients of an educational, advice or counselling nature (15 partnerships). Consultation on the handling of cases was provided to probation officers at nine partnerships; in one case this was the funded worker's primary role. Other, less frequent activities involved working with prisoners (5 partnerships), training (5 partnerships) and groupwork (4 partnerships). At two partnerships the worker provided research and development: for example, in one case the drugs worker facilitated development and piloting of a harm reduction policy within the probation service. As noted, at two partnerships the primary role of funded workers was outreach, including needle exchange. Finally, at two partnerships the substance misuse workers were devoting their time almost exclusively, at the time of interview, to public relations with probation teams, in the absence of opportunities for direct service provision.

Four financial partnerships adopted a different approach. At each of these, the probation service provided core funding to partner agencies in return for specific services. This concerned, in every case, a groupwork service, either in the context of the organisation's existing provision, or as structured programmes for offenders.

The three non-financial partnerships offered direct individual work with offenders (one), a needle exchange facility (one), and groupwork with prisoners (one).

In addition to the aforementioned two cases, in which no direct provision at all was identified, there were four instances of discrepancy in the descriptions of the partnership service offered by probation and substance misuse staff. At one non-financial partnership, the senior probation officer explained that a misunderstanding led to disappointment:

> The [substance misuse agency] is primarily a needle exchange project ... So they were certainly offering that service. We knew about that. But my understanding was that they were also providing counselling. I think in retrospect, the amount to which they did that was quite limited, and it wasn't clearly promoted for that.

At a financial partnership, the liaison probation officer to the substance misuse agency, when asked to describe the service, declared: "No, because we don't really *know* what it is except that someone has been employed to work with probationers or offenders on their drug problems". The senior probation officer, however, explained: "What was initially envisaged ... was to tie up some of the community care assessments ... Also to try and get more structured counselling". The substance misuse manager saw the partnership rather differently, if equally clearly: "Us being consultants and only responding in very specific cases ... which need more [specialised] advice". The substance misuse worker, however, did not perceive any such clarity: "Originally it was a loose job description in that I was to take referrals from probation for their clients who had expressed a desire to do something about their drug use ... [T]hat was about (all). And to provide consultancy to probation officers who wanted a little more information".

In one case, the very free-ranging comments of the probation interviewee did not offer a clear description of the expected service. In another, the probation officer merely said: "You really need to have good reasons for not referring if there is drug use". These were subsequently classified according to the substance misuse worker's account of the service.

There were serious difficulties at the two partnerships where no service at all could be defined by the funded workers. The nominated probation officer at one partnership declined to be interviewed, while the substance misuse worker disclosed a series of difficulties in agreeing upon the service to be provided: "The kind of service I was to provide was not specified. Probation teams were not forthcoming with ideas about the kind of service they wanted, because there was some suspicion around and a notion of not knowing where the partnership was leading".

A similar account emerged at the other partnership. During an interview concerning a long standing non-financial groupwork arrangement, it emerged that a substance misuse worker had recently been appointed to the partner agency through partnership funding. The probation officer revealing this information could say only: "I don't know exactly about his appointment, but he works for [the substance misuse agency] and his role is to work very closely with probation". When traced for interview, the funded substance misuse worker explained: "The idea was to build on the existing success of [the groupwork] to enable it to grow, and to [develop another group]...There were originally targets about setting up groups which have all fallen by the wayside". This worker was forced to devote his time to attempting to identify a service which probation officers would use.

In most cases, the partnership service matched part or all of the services provided by the substance misuse agency. Clear departures from existing services were infrequent. At one partnership, a residential centre for long term drug dependent people was offering a community based counselling service for young initiates. Similarly, at a substance misuse agency for which the primary service was a rural residential facility, a consultancy service for probation officers was provided from its city-based headquarters. An agency providing individual counselling services joined in non-financial partnership to provide groupwork in a local prison. A multi-agency project involving a probation service and two substance misuse agencies, one offering harm minimisation and the other abstinence services, was established to provide a common assessment procedure for all probation clients in the area.

Target groups

Most partnerships attempted to provide an open, flexible service. Defining narrower target groups within the population of substance misusing offenders could be problematic. As one substance misuse worker explained: "The target group were individuals who were in custody or on probation with identified alcohol problems, or people who were at risk because of their alcohol use in some way. Which really covered all individuals who were under [that] probation service's supervision!"

One way to focus the partnership investment was to target particular points of contact in the criminal justice system. Thus, one partnership concentrated on the pre-sentence report stage: "This acts as an automatic referral scheme. Every pre-sentence report...will be screened for drug and alcohol misuse. Those who show themselves to have a drug or alcohol related problem linked to offending get referred to the project worker automatically" (senior probation officer). Another partnership was designed for prisoners, while a third was primarily intended for offenders sentenced to one of the community disposals.

Offence seriousness provided an alternative focus. Two programmes were targetted on high tariff offenders as alternatives to custody. In a third case, the substance misuse worker set out with this intention, but encountered difficulties in practice. Seriousness of offending was linked, in some definitions, to the seriousness of substance misuse.

> The people who are eligible to come on this course are not occasional, recreational drug users. They are not soft drug users. They are serious drug users with a documented history of serious drug use, and that is likely to be heroin or crack or multi-substance use. A serious criminal record as well . . . It's serious on both sides. (substance misuse manager)

> The ones that we are trying to target are the more serious offenders, in the sense that they have got the more serious drinking or drug problems. (senior probation officer)

One substance misuse manager wanted to clarify the definition of seriousness in terms of drug use, fearing that probation officers were somewhat indiscriminate in their referrals: "Ideally, I would like people who have more intractable problems, who need clear, focused counselling over a period of time". At one partnership, seriousness became a bone of contention affecting probation officers' response to the project.

> They came along presenting . . . a counselling service for offenders who were in the early stages of their drug taking career. That flopped . . . [It] aroused a fair amount of scepticism amongst probation officers, because they felt that they were targetting the work inappropriately. It was inappropriate . . . to be targetting young low tariff offenders as part of a probation project. The service has for many years been seeking to target heavy end, serious offenders . . . [Also] most of the people [here] are [older] people with long established drug habits. (senior probation officer)

Two structured groupwork programmes were offered exclusively to males. One of these provided exclusively for Asian men, the programme being delivered in native language. This was the only example of a programme targetted on a particular ethnic group.

Coercion and enforcement

Given the alleged sensitivity of the issue of coercive treatment requirements, many interviewees displayed surprising uncertainty about their
use in partnership programmes. At four partnerships all interviewees
agreed that offenders were only referred to the programme as a specific
requirement of a probation order. At six, all interviewees agreed that
only voluntary attendance was acceptable. At another two, the question
of coercion was inapplicable because of the nature of the service:
research and development in one case; consultancy in the other. At
seven partnerships the use of specific requirements was apparently
optional, but there was no clear indication as to the balance in practice
between compulsory and voluntary referrals. At four partnerships, interviewees' responses were collectively so unclear that no firm identification of the use of coercion was possible. At two others, responses of
probation and substance misuse staff conflicted. Thus, at a total of 13
partnerships, the use of coercion could not be defined.

Interviewees were asked if they could recount what happened on the
last occasion that an offender was dealt with for not co-operating with
the partnership programme. Only six interviewees – two probation
officers and four substance misuse workers – could recall an occasion
of breach of a probation order, and one substance misuse worker remembered a failure to return to prison after temporary leave to attend a
groupwork programme. In three of the breach cases, poor co-operation
with the partnership programme reflected wider difficulties in compliance with supervision.

Two probation interviewees could remember occasions upon which a
probationer's non-compliance with a groupwork programme was managed informally without recourse to breach proceedings. One substance
misuse manager recalled only: "To my knowledge there has only been
one and that was a confusion".

At the six partnerships where all interviewees agreed that only voluntary attendance was acceptable, it was also agreed that the question was
not applicable. There were two interviews in which probation officers
offered recollections of incidents which did not actually occur within
the partnership arrangement, and indeed pre-dated its existence by one
and two years!

Thus, despite the sensitivity of the topic of coercion and enforcement
in principle, it appeared to play a small part in the practical experience
of partnership. One possible explanation of this was the youth of the
partnership enterprise at the time of the study, providing little time for

enforcement experiences to accumulate. Alternatively, these blurred accounts of compulsory requirements and enforcement activity might reflect the combined antipathy to coercion of both probation and substance misuse staff. Seen in this light, the apparent vagueness of many responses may reflect active management of cases to reduce the potentially punitive impact of coercion and enforcement. Indeed, probation officers' accounts of their management of National Standards for supervision, and their interpretations of drugs policy and practice, supported such a perspective.

National Standards

Probation interviewees were asked how they managed their accountability to National Standards for supervision when working with substance misusers. Responses echoed the inventive approaches to accountability commonly found in studies of welfare bureaucracies (e.g. Lipsky 1980; Rumgay and Brewster 1996). Probation staff agreed that unstructured supervision was neither professionally responsible nor helpful to offenders:

> Drug users are supposed to be chaotic, aren't they? Never able to keep appointments. I think it's [rubbish], myself. They can get their act together to find their drugs and buy them on a regular basis . . . It just feeds into a stereotype of drug users that . . . they can't be held responsible for their actions. They can't help burgling somebody's house because they've got a £100 a day heroin habit . . . Probation officers and other workers help to prolong stereotypes of drug users in the courts and criminal justice system which are not helpful or beneficial in the long term.

Equally, rigidity paralysed professional activity:

> [I expect] we're going to be able to breach people for swearing at their probation officer soon! All I can say is that the courts will be full, all the time. It's so unrealistic. If you breached everybody who breaches National Standards you would never be out of the courts. So they're unworkable. If anybody wants to sack me for not breaching somebody, well, *they* can have a go. Let [the Home Secretary] come and try my caseload!

Probation officers argued that true professional accountability lay, not in mechanistic rule enforcement, but in appropriately balancing regulation and sympathy:

There have to be limitations. You can't just let it go and say that someone is very erratic therefore he shouldn't have to comply with National Standards. It's trying to be as flexible as you can in recognition that particular people have particular problems. But at the end of the day, we do have public accountability and we have to provide the service we say we're providing.

You've got to start from where people are. As long as they're [making some progress] and considering change, you have to accept that for some people it's a slower process than for others. That's what I'm paid to do. I'm paid to carry that kind of judgement. The day that I'm not allowed to do it is the day I'll stop being a probation officer.

Probation officers revealed a flair for creative problem solving which maximised their discretion. One strategy was to study the National Standards, uncovering areas of discretion. This was often presented as positive practice: "National Standards are there as a tool to help us to work with clients, not as a strict rule." National Standards were thus transformed from a mechanism of control into a professional ally.

I know it says weekly contact for the first three months, but there is a rider that says the very minimum standard is six appointments within the first three months. Clearly, that isn't a lot. So if you think you're going to have problems with people not reporting, then it's safer to have them on the lowest setting.

She's exempt. You can get exemptions from National Standards and she is exempt. She is chaotic and suicidal . . . I'm not in it for chasing people up and offering them appointments and them not turning up.

I certainly have no problems in saying that, instead of seeing the probation officer, then it is one of the weekly planned meetings of your probation order that you go [to the substance misuse agency].

Another approach was to ensure that supervision requirements were not constructed in restrictive terms: "We've tried to resist conditions that people will attend [specific activities on specific dates]. These things can be worded in a fairly general way". Officers also adapted supervision practice in order to maximise clients' chances of compliance:

Probation officers, like they have done in the past, have just used their ingenuity. [If] they feel that, however chaotic, there is some basis of a working relationship with a person who is trying to make positive changes, they will work as hard as they can to try to help them to keep from breaking the conditions. They would accept visits at other times than agreed appointments, or follow up missed appointments by home visits.

> If someone is a heavy drinker, you book them in for 9.30a.m., not for 3p.m.

Officers honoured the requirement to determine acceptability of excuses for missing appointments assiduously, to ensure a valid outcome:

> The general finding is that, when you impose National Standards, failures to attend simply get re-classified as reasonable absences. So we keep to the rules, but our clients' behaviour doesn't change much.

> It's simple, really. We have the rules that we must follow and we are allowed to use some initiative. So, if someone claims to miss their appointment because they are ill from drug withdrawal, that is acceptable as far as I'm concerned. [In fact], that's good, that they have thought "Oh, I must tell my probation officer I cannot go in because I am ill".

Finally, officers appealed to the spirit of the probation order:

> If you can argue that someone is co-operating with the spirit of supervision then there is no need to breach. All you have to do is discuss it with a senior manager and get consent [on that], and you can make allowances for chaotic lifestyles.

> The court made this order specifically to assist this person with a drug problem. Therefore we're entitled to be more flexible than we would be normally.

The brilliance of this tactic was to recruit the courts as allies in extending tolerance beyond the discretion available in National Standards. With foresight, sentencers' complicity could be harnessed at the point of disposal:

> I try to allow for much greater flexibility... I put it in the report... [that] it will be necessary to adopt a more flexible approach. I use that in my records as a reason [not to breach].

Indeed, sentencers' reluctance to punish breach was a good reason to invoke it sparingly:

> Ironically, the service is often criticised for being too lenient, but, when you bring somebody back to court for breach, the magistrates are generally reluctant to do anything...They very often don't impose any penalty at all. If they do, it's derisory. So unless courts are prepared to take some significant action, then we're spending a lot of time taking breach proceedings that have very little impact.

Thus, probation officers managed their obligations to National Standards in their daily practice through strategies which maximised opportunities for individualisation (also Maguire, Peroud and Raynor 1996). In doing this, moreover, they perceived themselves to be *fulfilling* their professional responsibilities, rather than evading them.

Drugs policy

Probation service interviewees were asked how their agency's policy on substance misuse helped them in their practice. Their responses might disappoint many authors of the policy documents.

Four interviewees responded that their service did not have a substance misuse policy. While believing in principle that a policy should be developed, they were not greatly troubled in practice by its absence. Two officers thought that "unwritten" policies of harm reduction were implicitly "understood" within their services. Another cheerfully explained:

> I've got no hang-up about it. It is less harmful to smoke occasional pot than to drink seven pints of lager and smash everybody up on a Saturday night...Obviously I have to [remind them that] it's against the law...But I told [one client] "I prefer it when you're doing that to when you're drinking because when you're drinking you're an absolute asshole, quite frankly."

Eight officers confessed to uncertainty as to the existence or contents of a policy. They fashioned practice after personal perspectives, again assuming consensus within their services:

> Well, I hope it's harm minimisation...It's probably implicit in everything we do. That's the ethos of probation, enabling people, offering them choices and then it's down to them.

Five interviewees alleged that the policy did not help them in their practice:

> Well, of course, you're referring to the harm reduction policy. In theory it helps the service in that it enables offenders to talk to their officers about drug misuse, which theoretically they weren't able to do before. In practice it has no impact at all, because people were doing that anyway. [Those who] weren't doing it before are still not doing it. Offenders make their own judgements about whether or not they can trust their probation officer. Just telling somebody there's a policy about harm reduction isn't going to [change] offenders who don't trust their probation officers.

> It's very sketchy . . . The policy doesn't help me. It's more a case of me helping the policy. This sounds big headed, but there is nothing this service could have taught me about drugs and alcohol. Nothing at all. *I told them.*

Two people thought that the policy added to confusion: "But anything is better than nothing". Two simply said that they did not know: "I'm going to have to say 'Pass' there. That is something else that [our partner] would deal with".

More positively, three interviewees described policy as supportive, in officially endorsing harm minimisation: "[It] would help me if I could be clear with clients about what will happen to the information they give me . . . Clear policy guidelines about that are going to be very helpful to me". Three senior probation officers regarded policy as an important aid to partnership: "The harm reduction policy that we have . . . clearly helps, because . . . there's a shared perspective with [our partner] and other agencies with whom we work. So that's enabling." Another thought that partnership embodied policy intentions: "In the hurly-burly of everyday probation work, a lot of this policy is automatically absorbed by the scheme that we have here." One probation officer observed that the purpose of partnership was to develop a policy.

Common themes in these responses were the symbolic importance of a policy endorsing harm minimisation, belief in consensus within the probation service and development of individual practice styles assumed to accord with that consensus. Policy thus had little direct relevance to daily tasks, but a symbolic function of supporting a principle which probation officers believed enabled them to adopt flexible, creative and individualised styles of intervention.

Urine testing

Probation and substance misuse staff were asked how appropriate it would be to use urine testing in offender supervision. By drawing attention to a technology available to many substance misuse organisations, this example confronted the point that enforcement of agency expectations was not exclusively a probation service concern. This, then, was an opportunity to reflect on the potential co-option of technologies of substance misuse treatment as coercive instruments of offender control.

Responses from probation and substance misuse staff were remarkably similar. They frequently questioned the purpose of urine testing, professing inability to perceive its relevance to offender supervision.

> I don't think it's relevant to the probation order in itself. I understand why *some* agencies use it, but I couldn't foresee why *we* would need to use it or why we *should* use it. (senior probation officer)

> What would you use it for?...I can't imagine what you would do it for...Why would probation ask us to do it? All they want to do at the end of the day, as far as I know, is to write in their report that a person is addressing their problem. They have to believe that's true. They can't just write it. (substance misuse worker)

Probation staff repeatedly described their task in terms which illuminated their inability to perceive any usefulness of this technology for their agency:

> I can't see that simply knowing more facts makes much difference. It's more to do with how someone's life is going, how they are adapting, maturing. That's more important.

> I can see the point if someone is living in a drug free environment. I don't have any problem with that. But there's no way *I* could do it. What *I* would hope to achieve is that there is a relationship between myself and the drug abuser where they can just say "Yes, I used." If there isn't that relationship, then the reason why there isn't needs to be addressed.

> People change largely because they want to change, not because they fear that on Monday morning the project leader's going to ask them to pee into a bottle or blow into a bag.

Agency culture was at stake here:

It would have to be part of a much firmer shift to the right in the way the criminal justice system works with offenders...If you go down that route then you're a policing organisation, not a social work based organisation.

[I'm] against it. My personal view is that the probation service has got sucked too much into the punitive aspects of the criminal justice system. That leads us down the road of being prison, rather than probation officers.

There is not a drug project [here] that really has any need for that sort of provision. It spoils the quality of contact with clients, it makes the workers lazy and it introduces a very different culture. It introduces helplessness and the purpose of treatment is empowerment.

Drug testing, in the opinion of probation officers, concerned substance misuse treatment in ways which had little relevance for their own work in offender supervision. Substance misuse staff similarly perceived an agency specific purpose of drug testing:

There has to be a purpose. If somebody is on the methadone programme, the idea is for them to come off the other opiates...If you test them for the methadone and there is nothing there then obviously they are selling it. So there is a justification for testing. We had a request from social services the other day to test somebody. I sent them away. It would be inappropriate for us to police people.

If they were to have a urine test it would be just the same as anyone else having a urine test. Just because these people have got probation orders, that doesn't mean they have got to be checked. They would be given the same treatment as anyone else.

They also believed that there were preferable alternatives to technology:

Unless there's anything really positive to be gained from it, my personal feeling is that it's a waste. If somebody tells me that they are using something, then I've been around long enough to be able to ask a few more questions or look for tell tale signs, and I'll know whether they have or not.

They can't keep it hidden for long. Fortunately, we're old hands at this. We can usually see if somebody's had a drink...The drinkers that come here are in deep trouble with drink and it is an extremely difficult thing to have to hide.

In fact, 11 partner agencies did not test for drugs or alcohol; at several others it was seldom, or selectively used. At counselling agencies, in particular, no value was attached to information gained through technology: "The only information useful to us is what the client tells us. Ideally we'd like the truth . . . [But] we would never, ever use any form of meter to check it. Never." Testing was considered largely irrelevant to harm reduction:

> We weren't prescribing for the people who came in. As long as they didn't hurt us, we didn't mind . . . It's about people's rights. How can they be valued if they're being [checked]? And it's about responsibility. I know that's difficult to say about people who misuse drugs, but they have to take some responsibility for their own destiny.

For substance misuse workers, as for probation officers, relationship was the crucial tool:

> It has a place in a clinical setting. It has no place in a therapeutic relationship, or a relationship which ought to about trust. If you're clear about what your expectations are and negotiate clearly with the clients, then there is no reason why they shouldn't be able to tell you if they're not able to do what they committed themselves to doing. You don't have to ask them to wee into a bottle to find that out.

> I wouldn't dream of it. It's most undignified. You're supposed to build up trust with the clients. What trust are you showing them by making them do that? It's humiliating.

> Our nursing treatment service breathalyses people, if they're giving them medication during a home detox and they're concerned about using alcohol at the same time. But in the relationship that *I* have with clients, any kind of verification of what they tell me would absolutely destroy the counselling relationship. We wouldn't entertain it.

The only substance misuse worker with experience of urine testing as part of probation supervision told a salutary tale:

> I do at the moment have one client, where I'm supposed to be taking weekly urine samples and feeding back to the probation officer. But

it's a complicated case. The guy is diabetic. He's been having a lot of trouble with his insulin lately, so he has been comatose twice in the last fortnight. So I don't know what happens there...We wouldn't touch it without [the client's] written consent...Our philosophy is that hopefully it will help the client.

Thus, probation and substance misuse staff agreed that urine testing had little value in offender supervision. Its merit lay only in certain types of substance misuse treatment. They also agreed that the primary intervention tool was the relationship between worker and client.

Confidentiality

Confidentiality was the problem most frequently predicted by telephone survey respondents. Yet, while interviewees in Phase Two could talk at length on the principles at stake, pragmatism and commonsense resolved most dilemmas easily in practice.

At two partnerships where community outreach services were provided through the partnership, all parties accepted total confidentiality as a fundamental principle of successful harm reduction. Probation officers, therefore, were not informed of their clients' contact with the outreach service, except at the expressed wish of the individuals themselves. Only voluntary attendance was acceptable at these projects; thus there was no conflict for probation officers in terms of accountability for their clients' compliance.

At a partnership where the service was circumscribed in terms of joint assessment and consultancy, questions of confidentiality did not arise, since the substance misuse worker did not interview clients alone. At several partnerships, periodic joint interviews ensured clients' participation in sharing information.

Partners quite commonly agreed that probation officers would receive confirmation of their clients' attendance at the programme. Disclosure of the content of contact was discretionary, the general rule of thumb being the "need to know", for example, concerns for personal safety. However, information was rarely passed without the knowledge and consent of clients; offenders were generally more surprising in their acquiescence than their resistance to disclosure. Moreover, probation officers were not unduly inquisitive about the content of their clients' discussions with substance misuse workers. They required information, not for its own sake, but for its utility value.

Thus, the sensitivity of the issue of confidentiality in principle was dissipated through a variety of pragmatic, commonsense approaches to information exchange on the basis of necessity and utility. Indeed, probation officers' vigorous pursuit of individualised practice, to which the ideology of harm minimisation and even the rigours of National Standards were harnessed, and their lack of interest in information acquired for its own sake rather than purposefully, arguably rendered confidentiality principles virtually redundant in the problem solving routines of offender supervision.

Conclusion

Contrary to the impression created by the partnership plans, probation services relied heavily on historical relationships, supported by opportunistic exploitation of local networks, for their partnership development. A theme emerging from several interviews was the haste of partnership negotiations, driven by Home Office requirements. In such circumstances, probation services' dependence on familiar, accessible relationships was predictable. Nevertheless, whether by accident or design, probation services had chosen their partners well, although this conclusion rests on grounds not anticipated in Home Office directions.

The disappearance of coercion and confidentiality as contentious issues in the practical realities of the partnership enterprise is remarkable. Acknowledgement by some substance misuse interviewees of a change of attitude on the issue of coercion, reflected the broader point that it played a relatively small part in the partnership experience. Some partnerships were constructed in such a way that neither compulsion nor confidentiality were relevant issues in the use made by probation service clients of the substance misuse service. Elsewhere, it seemed that a commonsense, pragmatic approach reduced the potential impact of contentious matters of principle in daily practice.

British probation officers' resistance to co-option as law enforcement agents is legendary (Clear and Rumgay 1992; Raynor 1985; Vanstone 1993). In the area of substance misuse probation services forged alliances with partners whose ideologies and technologies virtually ensured their inability to assist in any attempts to force offender supervision down the path of surveillance and enforcement. The ideology of harm minimisation was an ideal vehicle for development of services for offenders characterised by patience, tolerance and persistence in the face of personal fallibility. The primary technology of substance misuse work in partner agencies was relationship. Partner agencies not only opposed involvement in drug testing for enforcement purposes: many lacked the resources to do it; others used it sparingly for specific treatment purposes. Whatever else their differences, probation officers and substance misuse workers shared a distaste for intrusive or coercive practice, working creatively to reduce punitive impact of programmes. There was never a true clash of cultures on this issue.

As for the partners themselves, their mixed experience of broader changes in the delivery of welfare testified to forward planning, expansion and new initiatives. In this context, partnership with the probation service was for many an optional, rather than a necessary venture; its value was perceived more frequently in terms of good practice than financial advancement. The self-containment of many partnership arrangements, the fact that for many partner agencies this was one initiative among several arising during a period of flux, and the limited prospects for probation service funding contributed to this perspective. There was little evidence, then, that substance misuse staff feared a substantial loss of professional or organisational autonomy as a price of entry into partnership.

Thus, in the organisation of partnership the potential flashpoints of ideological differences were dissipated through selection of partners with complementary approaches to substance misuse and its treatment, lack of reliance on partnership for the survival of substance misuse agencies, and commonsense, pragmatic approaches to coercion and confidentiality in daily activity.

4
Partnership and Conflict

Qualitative dimensions of the partnership experience were crucial to projects' success. These included perceptions of the significance of the enterprise and the quality of relationships between probation staff and substance misuse workers.

Successful and problematic partnerships

Projects were assessed for their degree of success or difficulty at the time of contact. While this might appear a harsh judgement, given the youth of some of the projects, the data yielded no basis for making confident predictions about future improvement or deterioration. Moreover, projects which were successful at the time of interview had been so since their inception, for reasons which will be examined. An initial categorisation was made on the basis of the relative weight of favourable or unfavourable comments concerning inter-agency communication, relationships between agency personnel, the level of referrals to the project and the quality of the intervention. Projects were then further examined for features which might account for their relative success or degree of difficulty.

Of the 25 projects visited, 13 were categorised as successful, and 11 were particularly problematic. In respect of one, identified during interviews regarding another arrangement, there was insufficient data to make a justifiable assessment. Examples of problem-free partnerships were rare. Equally, some projects which experienced acute problems displayed positive qualities. All six partnerships at which there were difficulties in defining the partnership service were problematic. Departure from agency tradition in the partnership service, however, was not uniformly linked to lack of success. Nor, notably, was the fact of funding: of the three non-financial partnerships, two were problematic.

Scrutiny of the 24 assessable partnerships revealed two features which reliably distinguished successful from problematic projects: championship; and enhancement.

Championship

At 10 of the 13 successful partnerships, an individual within the probation service clearly took a pro-active role in developing the project, promoting it among colleagues, liaising with the substance misuse agency and assisting its workers to establish their presence and acquire knowledge to raise their effectiveness.

> The way it has been publicised up to now is by me attending seniors' meetings, and seniors going back to their teams to talk about it...[The substance misuse workers] have had an induction programme which has involved them coming to teams, getting themselves known within teams. They've had a formal session from me about pre-sentence reports and the Criminal Justice Act, to get them into the new thinking in probation...I've spent time with [them] going through the plan they prepared, to look at how that should be framed and structured. (senior probation officer)

These project champions, spurred by personal interest or professional duty, invested considerable time and energy in the role. Two senior probation officers remarked:

> I would estimate that this project takes up half my time. Now, I haven't got half a job normally. I manage a very busy team...This role has taken up a lot more time, effort and energy than I would have anticipated when I took on this responsibility. I keep saying that it will get less as it goes on...But of course, it won't. Because the strategy has got to continue.

> The amount of work involved in maintaining good partnerships is often enormous. That goes for not only hours involved in committee meetings and liaison, negotiation, monitoring, research and preparation. The number of issues to be dealt with are never ending. Voluntary agencies go through difficult times. Problems can be hard to work with.

All project champions realised that their role was not temporary: "You constantly have to work at things. You can't just set something up and leave it and let things evolve."

Effective championship by senior management was appreciated by one substance misuse worker:

> The person with overall responsibility for partnerships wrote a circular to every single senior probation officer, saying what I have to offer. I was invited to a meeting of all the seniors, and I addressed them on what I could offer, my experience, my philosophy... Then the onus was on each senior probation officer to invite me to their team meeting, so that I would talk to the probation officers. The reason they did it that way was that they wanted it to be fully backed. People knew that this was serious business, not an *ad hoc* arrangement, that this is something to be taken seriously.

This was the only probation service experiencing both a successful and a problematic partnership, with an important difference between them in their management. At the problematic partnership, senior management relied on historical links at ground level, which were actually somewhat tenuous and did not produce a project champion. Strong co-ordination of the successful project, on the other hand, acknowledged a new relationship with a voluntary partner.

Elsewhere, champions were self-appointed at ground level, often believing that their efforts were not fully supported by senior management. One probation officer felt that considerable preparatory work by practitioners was disregarded: "We thought we had more of a remit than we actually did. It was dispiriting. A lot of effort went in and then nothing seemed to get off the ground." Another complained: "Some workload relief for me to concentrate on enhancing the project and developing it from our side. That would improve it." Project champions testified to uncomfortable conflicts:

> I do have a heavy workload anyway... I would not see the partnership as being the primary focus of my work. Maybe that's what is needed. The partnership needs more than I'm able to give it because of all the other tasks that I have to do that would take priority.

> [The most difficult thing] at this particular moment is to make time to offer [the substance misuse worker] enough support and supervision. That isn't meant to mean that I don't want to do that. But it is difficult because I've got a whole team of [probation officers] to supervise and all sorts of other things to deal with.

The three successful partnerships where championship was not identified displayed special features. Firstly, at two projects, the probation service interviewee was a potential candidate for the role in terms of interest and support; perhaps modesty should not be ruled out. Secondly, at one of these projects, the probation officer interviewee, who was Asian, participated in running a native language groupwork programme for Asian men. At the other, the substance misuse worker was an experienced former probation officer, and consequently confident in dealings with the service. At the third project, the partnership funded an administrator within the voluntary agency to co-ordinate a groupwork programme jointly led by probation officers and substance misuse workers. This project was unique in encouraging interview with administrative staff, whose role was crucial: "I've been told I'm the centre. The centre pin, of the centre cog, of the whole works" (project secretary).

At problematic partnerships, project champions were not identifiable, nor were there special compensating conditions. Instead, all the pitfalls anticipated by project champions emerged. Firstly, a nominated liaison officer did not guarantee success. Four projects nominated liaison probation officers, but only two were successful. At the others, enthusiasm for the project's health, spontaneously expressed by champions, was lacking. As noted, one liaison officer could not describe the partnership service. Another liaison officer's remit had changed, leading to partial withdrawal and uncertainty about the role. Here, when asked about communication between the partners, the substance misuse worker appeared unaware of the liaison officer's existence: "That's basically what *my* job is. *I* am the liaison between probation and [the substance misuse agency]".

Secondly, hopes that the project required only "start-up" investment ended in disappointment. Some staff, with hindsight, were rueful. Senior probation officers remarked:

> I don't think I did anything other than set it up, which was a few telephone calls, team meetings, contact with the workers when they were here...At that point I really saw it as being down to them to continue the project.

> I guess that more time and attention from myself and local managers of the service should have been involved in this...It's meant to be a partnership, which implies that we have got to do something as well. We've got to engage fully.

Thirdly, some interviewees keenly felt the absence of championship.

> I would have a liaison person who would interact between the two agencies. I would promote it better. I would make sure that it was a well used resource. It feels sporadic to me. (probation officer)

> Nobody has taken a great deal of interest in what I do one way or the other. Nobody has said "How many bodies have you seen?" or "Have you been helpful?" There's not been a great deal of management of the partnership as far as I can see... It has to be more directed than that. (substance misuse worker)

Finally, self-appointment of champions potentially confined a project's success to the local sphere of that individual's activity. This contributed to partial successes, with substance misuse workers reporting good use of their services by some probation teams and neglect by others.

> What was significant about the way the substance misuse partnership was received was the approach of the senior probation officer here. She had previously worked with [the substance misuse worker] and she had a lot of respect for and confidence in him. This affected his reception... People were originally cynical. But the senior probation officer introduced him and had confidence in him. People took her confidence as an authoritative statement. (probation officer)

This surmise was corroborated by the substance misuse worker's report that he was ignored by another team: "One probation office, after two clients, has decided not to use me. I don't know whether it was a conscious decision or just the way it is." Moreover, at the same partnership:

> [Another substance misuse worker] found it more difficult because her area was more reticent. [One] in his area had a good relationship with a senior probation officer who had a lot of dealings with our organisation and knew us very well... But [the other] had to build a lot of bridges. (substance misuse manager)

Senior management's reliance on the emergence of self-appointed local champions, or the substance misuse workers themselves, contributed to unhappy experiences. Substance misuse workers recalled:

I don't think anyone asked the probation officers...a) whether they wanted it, b) whether they thought it was a good idea, or c) whether they thought there were alternatives. So it came...from top down, and it was then decided it would be difficult to impose, so go softly, softly.

Not enough groundwork was done. When I went to the team meeting no one really knew about partnerships and where they were going to lead...There was hostility...So instead of a structure to introduce the partnership to probation as a whole, I had to win over individual officers. The Assistant Chief Probation Officer did say at the beginning "What if you don't get any clients?" But I was naive. I didn't realise that this meant that probation might not refer. So probation *did know* that there might be resistance.

Enhancement

At successful partnerships, probation staff strongly appreciated enhancement of their work, perceiving no threat to their traditional casework role from partner agency workers:

I've no problem with it. Absolutely no problem. Because, the way I look at it, services are there to help the client as much as possible, and I can accept that there may be issues that they want to discuss with [the substance misuse worker] but they don't want to discuss with me...Now some people feel that as some sort of personal slight, or reflection on their capabilities...But that isn't a problem for me.

Probation officers are not drug specialists. Having the partnership enables their awareness and their ability to work with drug offenders to be hugely increased...So the probation officers are learning, the clients are getting their service...and we are offering them the hope of being able to do something about their drug problem.

Some probation officers observed that effective use of the partnership demanded their own skills:

It's been a learning experience for me...As a probation officer referring clients I thought all I had to do was say "Joe Bloggs has an addiction. Let's refer him to [the substance misuse agency]". It doesn't work like that. It has to be more in depth.

How was enhancement experienced? "Focus" was a popular description.

It was sometimes hard to see where the boundary lines were ... So the very narrow focus of [the partnership] brief is helpful, because we know clearly what [the substance misuse worker] is there for. She's there for assessments, and you can use that resource very well. (probation officer)

I like the fact that this service is now much more focused in its approach to substance misuse. That we can now offer a definite service to substance misusing clients ... so that's a great improvement. (senior probation officer)

It can give more time and more focus for something quite specific that probation officers might not have had time to address, and that might be a big element of offending behaviour. (substance misuse worker)

Probation staff reported boosts to awareness or confidence:

[I]t *is* possible to work with drug using offenders. One *can* do something for these people. Before we started working in partnership with drug agencies, probation officers thought "We can't do anything with these people, they are beyond our ability to help." It has given us the hope that we can do something constructive with this group of people.

An additional resource was available: "Simply having one more string to one's bow is an extremely worthwhile achievement" (probation officer). Opportunities for joint work were enjoyed: "The advantage of doing joint assessments, getting a more complete picture, where perhaps I bring to it more knowledge of the person and [the substance misuse worker] can have the specialist knowledge" (probation officer).

At problematic partnerships, anxiety about encroachment upon professional territory predominated. The assurances in partnership plans about the purpose of partnership were either not communicated to field staff or not trusted. Probation interviewees complained:

The biggest problem that probation officers fear is loss of jobs. It hasn't happened yet, but given what's happening in other public sectors, predictably that's the direction. The fear is that the more bits of our work that go out to specialist agencies, the less work there is for probation officers to do.

It would be difficult to expect probation officers to accept the notion of partnerships and funding for partnerships very readily, because the reality is that it costs jobs... There is no increase in budget to allow for this.

Partners, in fact, displayed every desire to contribute a distinctive service. This was explicit in the work undertaken at successful partnerships. Substance misuse workers explained:

I'm sure there are some probation officers here that are quite knowledgeable about drug use. They have been working with clients, some of them for years. So I do see it as a two way thing: I'm here on a consultancy basis, but at the same time I don't want to undermine probation officers if they already have that knowledge. I'm here if they want to use that resource.

It seemed to me that the probation service in this area does very well in working with people with alcohol and drug problems. Some of the things that other partnerships are doing, like running alcohol education groups, aren't necessary here, because they are already run within the probation service. So it's genuinely using what an agency like [ours] has that is different... rather than in any way moving over into the probation service work.

I am the resource for the probation officers. That is very clear. I am not the resource for their clients... I do everything through the probation officer... They are the ones who are in control. They have to be, because I couldn't just delve in and out and only home in on the drug problem.

At problematic partnerships, however, it sometimes appeared that no amount of reassurance was accepted. Consequently, substance misuse workers reported difficulties accessing clients and identifying work which was acceptable to probation officers:

When I have asked the teams what they wanted, they have not been able to identify very much at all. I have offered a great deal, lots of different things, and they have said no to most of them. So it has been very hard working with those teams... There are political issues about the impact on their own jobs, of the seeping privatisation of the service.

I wanted to have a Drinkwatch group as aftercare for those who have been through the alcohol education programme, to continue the support for changing drinking habits... [It] has been difficult to get going as... there has been some fear on the part of probation that the alcohol education programme will be contracted out in partnership. So there was initially resistance to doing anything linked to that programme. So I then asked if I could come and sit in on the last few sessions but probation officers said that this would disturb the harmony of the group.

This issue aroused anxiety about the wisdom of entering into partnership in at least one agency.

We had this awful feeling that this was a cost cutting exercise. We were in a double bind... because we knew that the Home Office was going to cut [the probation service's] budget, which actually meant, in pretty terms, "downsizing". In real terms, people lose their jobs. So... obviously that would influence the way we would be welcomed into the probation service... But then again we also knew that probation officers themselves, although they are very skilled, were not really dealing with the alcohol issues that clients were bringing. So we identified client need, but we also knew that it would be a very contentious programme. (substance misuse manager)

Occasionally, failure to identify enhancement had different sources. Naturally, where the partnership service could not be defined, it was hard to perceive enhancement potential. At a project targetted on young offenders with minor drug problems, probation officers disputed its relevance to their needs for high tariff programmes for serious misusers. Where a partner agency offered a self-contained day programme, probation officers lacked information on their clients' progress. Finally, entry into partnership with an agency at which the manager had previously advised probation officers to do more with drug users themselves, was greeted with amazement and anger.

Up until the partnership time, we had been told by [the substance misuse agency] "What we do isn't any different from what probation officers do. We have the same skills." That led us to ask what the hell is the point in us having any contact with [the substance misuse agency]? We don't actually believe it. We don't think that we can hold the amount of knowledge about drug use, types of drugs, effects on behaviour... and so on. (senior probation officer)

Inter-professional relationships

Comments on the quality of inter-professional relationships illuminated the problems of partnership. These are summarised in Table 4.1.

General issues

Although not directly asked about the quality of *intra*-agency communication between senior management and field teams in the probation service, 21 interviewees remarked on this when reflecting on the partnership experience. At successful partnerships most remarks showed appreciation of consultation and information exchange between senior management and field probation staff.

> In our service, [the Assistant Chief Probation Officer] asks staff what their views are on areas that we should be considering for partnership. (senior probation officer)

> I went round the teams yesterday delivering the forms...There's team meetings next week to explain exactly, and they'll probably fire a lot of questions at us...We'll be giving them information, explaining to them more fully, so they're more aware of exactly what it is. (probation assistant)

At two successful partnerships, probation officers were less complimentary about management handling of projects, but independently committed themselves to the enterprise. One senior probation officer thought the key to a non-financial partnership's success was "minimal intervention from management"!

Complaints about poor communication at problematic projects usually alleged that senior managers failed both to consult before entering into partnership and to explain its purpose to field staff. Probation staff explained:

> This particular partnership was sold to us as a two-day training course. Practically every probation officer put themselves down for it. It became apparent when we were on the course that it was a much bigger commitment than that...It was a major piece of work over six months. A number of people would have been keen to do that...but only four out of 14 have stayed with it. That was purely because of the misunderstanding. People were dissatisfied about what was happening, and couldn't commit themselves so much.

Table 4.1 Inter-professional relationships at successful and problematic partnerships

| Interviewees | Probation | | Substance misuse | | |
Partnership	Successful	Problematic	Successful	Problematic	Total
General					
Probation internal communication					
– good	4	–	2	–	6
– poor	2	7	–	6	15
Roles and relationships an issue	7	2	8	7	24
Good working relationships	4	6	8	2	20
PR by substance misuse worker	3	–	5	7	15
Mutual assistance	2	2	2	–	6
About probation officers					
Suspicious	–	3	–	4	7
Sabotage	–	1	1	4	6
Unresponsive	–	–	–	4	4
Unprofessional	–	–	–	3	3
Unsupportive	–	–	–	3	3
Defensive	–	–	–	2	2
Intimidating	–	1	–	–	1
Cynical	–	1	–	–	1
Total negative comments	–	6	1	20	27
Receptive	2	–	3	1	6
Supportive	1	–	5	–	6
Good qualities	–	–	2	3	5
Total positive comments	3	–	10	4	17
About substance misuse workers					
Superfluous	–	3	2	2	7
Personal qualities problematic	–	4	–	2	6
Refused	–	1	1	3	5
Unresponsive	1	3	–	–	4
Unprofessional	–	2	–	1	3
Suspicious	–	2	–	–	2
Defensive	1	–	–	–	1
Total negative comments	2	15	3	8	28
Enhancement	20	12	5	11	48
Personal qualities good	5	2	–	–	7
Accessible	4	–	1	1	6
Stimulating	3	–	–	–	3
Respect	1	–	–	–	1
Supportive	–	1	–	–	1
Total positive comments	33	15	6	12	66

It was negotiated and set up at headquarters level for both organisations. It should have been set up by myself and other people at senior grade in consultation with staff, to get the detail of the partnership together, to set target dates to achieve the objectives of the partnership. It was set up and ignored. The level of communication from our headquarters to staff, including myself, was very poor.

While two substance misuse workers appreciated management influences on their reception at local teams, others described serious deficiencies. Two managers recalled:

I could tell they were a bit pissed off, to be perfectly honest with you, that they were not consulted, that this arrangement was between me and the Assistant Chief Probation Officer, rather than them... Of course, the less you consult, when you're trying to put it into practice you're going to have a lot more work, because people are going to try to sabotage it.

Well... [the headquarters staff] believed in all sincerity that they communicated incredibly well with senior probation officers and probation officers. But the resounding response from the ground was no, they hadn't... The response shook them. They hadn't expected the anger and aggression from probation officers in some offices, which was quite shocking. We had assumed in our innocence and ignorance that the probation service had prepared their probation officers for this, when in fact they had not.

There was general agreement that roles and responsibilities of the different agencies were important. At successful partnerships, clarity was achieved.

We held several meetings and there was a lot of discussion between the two organisations when the programme was designed. Then, of course, the leaders held meetings before each group, to decide exactly what needs to be done when the session runs. (probation officer)

As long as you work out where the responsibilities lie. That's the real lesson of this. People need to understand the limits of their powers and their responsibilities. (substance misuse manager)

At problematic partnerships, interviewees repeatedly complained about blurred role definitions and boundaries. Firstly, there could be role confusion between probation officers and substance misuse workers.

> Weeks and months were spent when neither side knew what the other person's job was...Some probation officers see their job as counselling, and that's very much the way they work. So to have another person coming along who does counselling also, was something that needed quite a bit of talking about. Because quite clearly the counsellors feel they do superior counselling and what we do is less than superior. (senior probation officer)

> There has never been a service level agreement...We need to review that. I meet with [my managers and the Assistant Chief Probation Officer] on a bi-monthly basis to see how things are going on. To clarify direction. I suppose that's the only form of supervision and feedback. (substance misuse worker)

The difference between partnership work and general use of the agency was contentious. Substance misuse workers reported:

> All of a sudden somebody would show up on the doorstep and say "I have to be here"...A lot of times [the probation officers] will tell people they have to attend [the substance misuse agency]. And people don't *want* to attend.

> It was difficult to see the difference between [a client] attending voluntarily through probation or any other way...It was just like employing another worker rather than somebody as specific as a probation partnership worker.

At one partnership, the funded worker's accountability was disputed.

> Soon after she had been appointed, there seemed to be some confusion about the role. [The substance misuse worker] was clearly saying "I'm paid for by the Home Office. What has it got to do with probation?'...So there was some confusion about accountability. Clearly a line of accountability is to their own managers in their agency, and there is the accountability to provide a service to us. Otherwise the partnership money would go to somebody else. That didn't seem to be very well understood. (senior probation officer)

Ambiguities in relationships with partners were exacerbated by links with other similar agencies.

As we'd been negotiating this partnership...we were developing our links with the [statutory] addictions team. There was a lack of clarity about who occupied what role and function between the addictions team and [the partner agency]. Should we refer drugs cases to the addictions team, who are interested in taking drug cases, who are prepared to come down here and meet clients, to work with officers and their clients, to do a lot of negotiation for us on a voluntary basis? And it's free! (senior probation officer)

[One probation team] have had long contacts with [another substance misuse agency] and really weren't sure why I was here or what their involvement was. It took a long time for seniors to respond to all that, so the communications are foggy some of the time. (substance misuse worker)

Complexities also arose between partner agencies and other types of organisation linked to the probation service.

We were going to be the next [court based outreach team]. But we have immense problems with the court, because they have got NACRO there, offering an advice shop. There's also a mental health diversion worker who was going to have access to the cells. The clerk to the justices thought we might be able to link in with that. But they didn't get back to us. (substance misuse manager)

With the assessment form, my policy in the past has always been to say to the probation officers [that they can use it as they see fit]. But apparently some other agency kicked up a bit and said if they submitted an assessment report it was used in its entirety or it wasn't to be used. So the probation service said to [my manager] "What's your view?" Slightly reluctantly, she said that we had better follow suit. (substance misuse worker)

This last decision made matters worse: "Probation officers were not happy about a memo from higher up in [the substance misuse agency] which communicated an arbitrary decision without reference to probation officers' needs" (probation officer).

While these issues could arise at successful partnerships, their resolution posed no great difficulties, nor did they subsequently rankle. For example, at a partnership where a harm reduction and an abstinence agency were jointly engaged in assessments and onward referrals for the probation service, a potential conflict of ideologies was placed in simple perspective.

We have agreed to disagree. At the end of the day, we're looking at the client. We are assessing agents. We shouldn't be blinkered by the background that we come from... We should be able to step back from our backgrounds and make our recommendations for the best outcome for the client. (substance misuse worker)

At successful partnerships, substance misuse workers observed the importance of publicising their services and developing relationships with probation officers:

I'm going to be involved in the team meeting at [one] office next week, I'm involved in the team meeting at [another office] in the following week, where it's going to be sold to the probation officers and talked from the very beginning right the way through – the process, the structure and anything else.

I used the initial time getting as much resource information as I could... making sure that I had that up to date and ready. So I was prepared. From the word go I had my information ready.

At problematic partnerships, however, public relations activity was usually associated with antagonistic relationships and difficulties in generating referrals. Probation officers appeared oblivious of these efforts, if their lack of mention is a guide. Two substance misuse managers recalled:

I've had some feedback from probation officers that [the substance misuse worker] is not really marketing herself, or being firm and clear enough about what she offers.

Being the first organisation we got the brunt. We decided that rather than attempting to do any work at all, we would just focus on PR, on going and meeting probation officers, discussing with them what their needs were. Also looking at what we had to offer and how that could complement skills that they had to offer. But I do believe that a lot of probation officers felt that we were taking the cream work.

Probation and substance misuse staff appreciated good working relationships and mutual support. This included probation officers at some partnerships which had experienced considerable difficulties, linked perhaps to an ability to distinguish between organisational deficiencies or principled resistance and the individual helpfulness of substance misuse workers. Only two substance misuse workers at problematic partnerships, however, spoke of good working relationships.

> It's been a good humoured working arrangement with genuine efforts on both sides to make progress... It just could have been set up more clearly than it was. But I would blame internal probation matters for that. (probation officer)

> I like meeting with probation officers because on the other hand, you know, with some probation officers there's really a very good relationship. (substance misuse manager)

Probation officers at two other problematic partnerships also commented on the relationship's mutual benefit, although here their perceptions were not reciprocated:

> I still think there's a need for it, these partnerships... I think we can learn, like they can learn from me. Because I get phone calls from [the substance misuse agency] about the legal sides... So we can help them more.

At successful partnerships interviewees presented mutual benefit as a return on investment.

> A meaningful partnership has a benefit on both organisations. Throughout both organisations there is a better understanding of the rather foreign culture of the other field. Something new is produced from it, which is usually better service for clients... The achievement so far has been to allow some of that to happen. (probation officer)

> I've worked very hard to build up a relationship with an officer that will refer to us, and then be able to pick the phone up and say... "I've encouraged the client to talk to you about an issue. Will you be aware of that?" That's nice to know that. That is local help. (substance misuse manager)

Comments on probation officers

Five substance misuse workers praised the personal or professional qualities of probation officers:

> I like working with probation officers. They are funny and entertaining and good to work with as they are irreverent, which is refreshing.

I very much like my contacts with the probation officers who have asked to use me. I've met some delightful people with enormous concern for a very difficult client group in the face of huge difficult-ies...I admire that. I'm not sure that I would be that sort of person, to work with a deeply frustrating group.

I saw two incredibly impressive interviews...I was impressed by how forcefully, calmly, objectively, she laid out exactly what her obliga-tions were...So they were dealing with it in a very focused and clear and honest way...I also have noticed that a lot of probation officers work until eight o'clock at night.

Surpisingly, three of these accolades came from substance misuse workers at problematic partnerships, who also recounted exposure to hostility or unprofessional behaviour. The experience of probation of-ficers as strong, contrasting personalities was captured by another sub-stance misuse worker, who began by paying tribute to the originator of a groupwork programme and concluded rather differently:

Some people enjoy leading groups and have larger-than-life person-alities. If it hadn't been for [the first probation officer], I don't think we would have got the group going. She had a very big personality ...I couldn't work with her as a team, she was diabolical!...She was still very likeable. All the group loved her, except me, I suppose.

Substance misuse staff appreciated receptivity and supportiveness:

I had a very warm welcome, when I got in there. I wasn't sure whether I would get a good welcome or a bad welcome or an indif-ferent welcome, [but] it's been really good.

I've found the partnership arrangements supportive. It's been nice to have that environment. In other areas of my work I'm quite a lot on my own.

One probation officer troubled to telephone the substance misuse worker at intervals early in the project to offer support. Probation staff occasionally observed that colleagues were receptive to partnership:

People here are very used to, and very good at using what's around. They won't rely just on themselves to give the best information to clients. They will use people in specific fields who will have better knowledge.

Substance misuse workers generally understood that the behaviour which they encountered occurred in a wider context, and indeed was an interactive phenomenon. Two, for example, describing probation officers as defensive, rationalised this behaviour:

> Communication and the relationship has been a problem. Not necessarily to do with [us] and probation officers, but to do with the wider perspective on the defensiveness, on what this means to probation officers themselves.

> There are also occasions when I think I have mishandled things. I was out with [a] team and talked to them about what I could offer. I was trying to promote the motivational interviewing course, but did it in a way that made them defensive and feel that I wasn't valuing their skills. I came away thinking "Well, they don't need me", because they were all getting defensive. It has taken a while for some of that irritation to work through.

Unresponsiveness in probation officers was all the more disappointing after investing considerable effort in public relations.

> One team being actively hostile, one being so stretched and burdened... We sat up there with no referrals for several months and phoned them up on a regular basis, but still no referrals. So that was a disaster. (substance misuse worker)

Suspicion was acknowledged by some probation officers: "Some seemed wary of change... It seems at the moment that... probation officers are starting to rival farmers in their propensity to complain."

Three substance misuse staff gave distressing accounts of unprofessional conduct by probation officers:

> [I am] negotiating the necessity for having formal procedures in place, whereby if a probation officer has a complaint or concern about the work, they have a procedure that they can go through to get heard. This came about because... [the substance misuse workers] are meeting an awful lot of probation officers, each of whom has their own way of working... In one probation centre [a worker] was verbally attacked and abused by a probation officer. As far as I was concerned that wasn't appropriate.

> Certain idealistic views came to the fore, very strong, I couldn't believe I was hearing it. [For] instance, [a prisoner said] his mother

was killed in an accident. He was very bitter about this. He did not go to the funeral, it was denied him. He said it was just like when his father committed suicide. Then [the probation officer] said "Well, where were you [when your parents needed you]?"...The guy really was upset, just having to listen to someone say "It was your own fault."

I find that what is acceptable in the probation service I would not be comfortable with...It wouldn't sit comfortably with my professional ethics. Displays of erotic material behind somebody's desk, for example, which, if I were a manager, I would not allow. I wouldn't feel that it gave an impression of the service that I wanted to promote.

Some substance misuse workers felt unsupported in their efforts to develop the partnership, occasionally implicating their own colleagues:

Because the project relies so much on one person...it sometimes feels like it is me against the whole service...So, yes, it has been hurtful...Development work is quite a lonely thing.

The probation service...offered me absolutely no guidance about the population they work with...bearing in mind [I] did not set out to work with people in prisons. So that hasn't been easy for me.

Some accounts suggested sabotage. One method was for probation officers to favour collaboration with another agency. At the only successful partnership where this was attempted, it was swiftly countered.

One team was reluctant to invite me...They tried to say "We want to invite the local drugs service as well." But I said "No. I am not their resource. I am your resource. It would be good if we could have a discussion first"...They did go through a very strict protocol. That has been very good for me as well, that we have bided by that...They had to have ownership. (substance misuse worker)

At problematic partnerships, sabotage became a chronic issue.

That has been the story of very much that we have set up. It has fallen down on the probation side...[For example], it was discovered that I was doing a prison release course with the prison officers. The probation officers felt it duplicated work they were doing and undermined the close liaison they were trying to build with the prison officers

...So it got harpooned, so it didn't happen. (substance misuse worker)

Substance misuse workers in these situations were frustrated and disappointed: "It has felt as if there has been a burden placed on me to do something magical, which I can't do". A senior probation officer recognised the challenge: "That's quite intimidating for a worker from any other agency to come in and talk to a team the size and strength of this team, with some powerful opinions." A probation officer also acknowledged a formidable attitude problem: "There was a feeling that this was the first move away from a professional probation service...So probation officers had cynical feelings about partnership."

Comments on substance misuse workers

Probation officers were more complimentary about substance misuse workers, although again there was a preponderance of complaints at problematic partnerships, some of which were acknowledged by agency staff.

There were complaints from only one successful partnership, where some defensiveness and unresponsiveness in the partner agency was perceived: "Undoubtedly they do offer very high quality services...but we find, as a commissioning agent, making any criticisms or giving any ideas, we are faced very often with either a wall of silence or an aggressive and defensive posture."

Criticisms by probation staff of professional standards were not lurid:

There was a certain lack of professionalism within the [substance misuse agency]. For example, they said they would provide promotional material before the project started, and they didn't. So when they came here, nobody knew that they were coming.

I have a feeling of amateurishness about working with [the substance misuse agency]. I guess that underpins everything I've been saying. We regard ourselves as fairly professional. I think they are struggling to be so.

One substance misuse manager acknowledged poor professional conduct: "A probation officer who had a particular interest in substance misuse did phone our office, and got a raw deal from one of the staff. She actually complained to the trustees. So that might have put them off."

Overlapping skills prompted some interviewees to question the superfluity of the partnership.

We are able to run alcohol groups in the prison ourselves very adequately. It's nice to have someone from the outside who, theoretically, is a specialist in this field, but not absolutely essential... In the future we might go it alone, because in truth we can manage without an outside agency. (probation officer)

A chunk of the probation service training seems to be about the very things that we are doing. Motivational interviewing. So if the probation officer can do it, why have the partnership? I don't know. (substance misuse worker)

At successful partnerships, such doubts were rapidly dispelled.

There were one or two that were reluctant because they felt that they had all the expertise and that their local drugs service was fine for them. They didn't see that I would be any use, but they were obliged to invite me. As it turned out, without exception, all the teams have used me. They could see that I did offer something different. (substance misuse worker)

Two probation interviewees reported that substance misuse workers were suspicious of probation officers:

It was stated to me that there are some probation officers who they will discuss clients with. There are some they will not... We're not policemen. They know that. But we are in a position of authority.

It took [the substance misuse agency] some time to realise what probation officers do and to have some faith in that.

There were a few examples of substance misuse workers refusing to meet a request. At a successful partnership, this was merely because of "the Home Office wanting us to sign a ridiculous contract... But that's sorted now" (substance misuse manager). Elsewhere, refusals were symptomatic of deeper problems in inter-professional relationships. One substance misuse worker refused to work with a probation officer whose approach to clients was considered unprofessional. Others thought that they were asked to undertake inappropriate tasks:

One probation officer asked me to counsel in prison and I couldn't. We didn't feel that was appropriate – the venue, the fact that he had no access to booze. How can you work on controlled drinking with somebody who is banged up?

It was decided that a client should go to a particular inpatient treatment centre. Would I be available to drive him down there? Probation officers are very busy people. They know I'm retired and working
only part-time. I didn't think it was a particularly good idea, but I
took that one to [the substance misuse manager]...She didn't think
it was a good idea. It's a probation service job, they've got probation
volunteers...It's not appropriate for [the substance misuse agency].

The personal qualities of substance misuse workers, as perceived by
probation officers, were important influences. As one probation officer
at a problematic partnership explained: "I have good liaison with [the
substance misuse worker], who is a lovely man. The partnership's success [here] is a lot to do with [his] personality and that he fits in well
with the team." Elsewhere, perceptions were less favourable:

To put it bluntly, probation officers didn't like him as a project
worker.

The [substance misuse worker] is reluctant to meet clients, is slow to
engage, isn't accessible, won't respond quickly...I'm disappointed in
[her] as a worker.

Two substance misuse managers also acknowledged unhelpful person-
alities: "The person who was running it was not very well motivated.
She probably didn't help. She has had problems and finds outreach
difficult." One substance misuse worker, however, was deeply offended
by prejudicial attitudes:

Probation officers have access to me. They are making decisions on a
personal level about what I might or might not be able to do. Or how
I might or might not be able to relate to their clients...I take strong
exception to criticisms of my middle classness, as being inappropriate
to work with offenders...Knowing what I know about counselling
skills, however I speak or however I dress, or whatever my background is – which, as it happens, is not middle class – doesn't affect
the way I can form relationships with clients.

Probation staff at successful partnerships praised the substance misuse
workers: "We happen to have got someone who is ideal for the post, in
terms of her get-up-and-go, and ideas, and clarity of thought. So it's a
pleasure supervising [her]". The substance misuse worker's accessibility
was also appreciated: "One of the things that has been really good is that

most times that I try to get hold of [the substance misuse worker], she is available. If not, she will get back to me quickly". Other favourable comments concerned the substance misuse worker's supportiveness, stimulating ideas and deservingness of respect.

At problematic partnerships, boundaries between organisational and personal inadequacies became blurred. As a senior probation officer remarked: "Staff will personalise. They're buggers for it!...That isn't the issue. The issue really is about the poor quality setting up of this."

Table 4.1 also includes references to the enhancement of probation officers' practice in terms, as described earlier, of focus, increased confidence or awareness, an additional resource, or joint working. Although such enhancements were appreciated by probation staff at problematic partnerships, those at successful projects recognised them more frequently. Greater recognition of enhancements by substance misuse workers at problematic than successful partnerships might tentatively be explained by their struggles to create roles acceptable to probation officers, thus raising their awareness of this issue.

Table 4.1 shows a clear trend for favourable remarks about interprofessional relationships to emanate from successful partnerships. Unfavourable remarks predominated among problematic partnerships. Successful partnerships are marked by the *absence* of complaints about both probation officers and substance misuse workers. Compliments were more liberally bestowed upon substance misuse workers, even though probation officers could be highly esteemed. Probation officers appreciated good relationships with partners, even when this was an isolated success within a generally problematic partnership.

Thus, when inter-professional difficulties arose at successful partnerships, they were isolated issues, swiftly resolved, and did not rankle. At problematic partnerships, multiple difficulties were experienced, which were pervasive, poorly resolved and persistent.

The benefits of partnership

Comments on benefits and problems of partnership were categorised and classified according to their sources in probation officers or substance misuse workers, and successful or problematic partnerships. Benefits concerned six topics: advantages for the probation service; advantages for substance misuse agencies; criminal justice advantages; improvements in service delivery; partnership learning; and personal gains. The results of this analysis are shown in Tables 4.2 to 4.7, with a rank-ordered summary in Table 4.8.

Advantages for the probation service

Introduction of culture change was the most popular advantage for the probation service, recognised at both successful and problematic partnerships, although the benefits were rather more obvious at the former. Some remarks referred to the need for change within the probation service itself. Senior probation officers remarked:

> The one thing that we've been trying to learn for a long time in the service is that we can't provide everything. By bringing in other agencies that sends a message to probation officers that they can work with other people.

> This project has enabled this service to have an overall drug and alcohol strategy. So no longer is it the case that it depends on which probation officer you go to as to what model of intervention you will be referred to, or whether drugs and alcohol is recognised at all. Now, equal opportunities should apply so that whoever you are, whoever your probation officers is, you will have the opportunity for assessment and intervention.

Benefits of culture change within partner agencies accrued most tangibly to the probation service in terms of increased willingness to engage with criminal justice issues and offenders. Thus, substance misuse staff acknowledged moderation of their resistance to coercion and good practice examples:

Table 4.2   Advantages of partnership for the probation service, as perceived by probation and substance misuse staff at successful and problematic partnerships

Interviewees	Probation		Substance misuse		
Partnership	Successful	Problematic	Successful	Problematic	Total
Culture change	4	2	4	2	12
Relieve pressure	3	4	–	–	7
New people involved	–	2	–	–	2
Good for image	2	–	–	–	2
Improved links with partner	–	1	–	–	1
Involve staff in policy	–	1	–	–	1
Total	9	10	4	2	25
Percentage of total comments	36	40	16	8	100

I'm very impressed. I have talked to the manager about changing the ethos in [the substance misuse agency], because we are under so much pressure all the time. How we can slow that down...Maybe it would be possible to deliver a better quality service. [What] I like about the probation service, is that it's slower, so there's more quality.

Relief of pressure was the most obvious organisational advantage at problematic partnerships. Probation staff observed:

The partnership has freed up probation officers to get on with other work, as long term substance misuse counselling is very demanding and not very effective in terms of outcomes.

That particular client group can cause enormous pressure...It's very beneficial to people that they have got and will increasingly have a close link with someone who can take a lot of that pressure off.

Introduction of new people to the organisation was welcomed: "It got people into the probation service who were not probation officers, who were able to offer a service" (senior probation officer). Partnership was good for the probation service's image: "It's helped to improve the image of the probation service, even if only in such a small way, as an agency that does care about drug users and is willing to help and listen" (senior probation officer). One senior probation officer thought that partnership had improved communication, a sentiment sadly not reciprocated at the partner agency. One probation officer approved of using a partner as consultant on harm reduction policy: "It's not often that we get involved in trying to write policy. That has been very welcome, that the main grade has been consulted about what the real problems are."

Advantages for substance misuse agencies

Most popularly, partnership with the probation service was seen to expand the substance misuse agency, in terms of staffing or horizons: "We have been short staffed recently and having an extra person here has been wonderful. We have been really grateful for that" (substance misuse manager).

Partnership's contribution to developing a new service was a source of pride: "It's provided a service for the clients of this office that isn't provided anywhere else in the country" (probation officer). Elsewhere, starting the programme was itself an achievement: "It's a massive achievement to set up this programme that only eighteen months ago

Table 4.3   Advantages of partnership for substance misuse agencies, as perceived by probation and substance misuse staff at successful and problematic partnerships

Interviewees	Probation		Substance misuse		
Partnership	Successful	Problematic	Successful	Problematic	Total
Expansion	3	1	3	2	9
Develop new service	3	1	2	1	7
Starting the programme	4	–	1	1	6
Getting the money	1	1	–	1	3
Probation service support	1	–	–	2	3
Influence other organisation	1	–	2	–	3
Improved links with partner	–	–	3	–	3
Professional recognition	–	–	–	2	2
Good for image	–	–	–	1	1
Total	13	3	11	10	37
Percentage of total comments	35	8	30	27	100

was still an idea, and now it's a functioning project" (substance misuse manager). More modestly, getting the money was welcomed.

Partnership provided access to probation service support for new initiatives: "We worked closely with probation at [the prison]. [Some] probation officers came down and unofficially spoke at our AGM, saying what a good service we provided . . . they put in a funding application to give us some money" (substance misuse manager). Partnership activity actually or potentially influenced other organisations: "We're going to be feeding in to the magistrates' training, changing their attitudes . . . stop them stigmatising our client group" (substance misuse worker). Improved links, and the professional recognition which the partnership symbolised were enjoyed: "Voluntary organisations are often looked upon as being very amateurish, which we are not, we are a professional service, all our counsellors are fully qualified. We're not a tinpot service, and it's like we're being validated" (substance misuse worker). One substance misuse worker thought that partnership was "good advertising for us, it's good public relations."

Criminal justice advantages

The single criminal justice advantage, identified by a few, was provision of a sentencing option for courts: "The most important thing is that we're now working quite realistically with people who may otherwise have gone down" (substance misuse manager).

Table 4.4 Criminal justice advantages of partnership, as perceived by probation and substance misuse staff at successful and problematic partnerships

Interviewees	Probation		Substance misuse		
Partnership	Successful	Problematic	Successful	Problematic	Total
Sentencing option	1	2	3	1	7
Percentage of total comments	14	29	43	14	100

Improvements in service delivery

This category attracted most comments, although with interesting discrepancies in perceptions. At successful partnerships, probation staff identified many improvements in the service to their clientele, while substance misuse staff were less enthusiastic, making few more comments than personnel of either agency at problematic partnerships. The most commonly cited benefits were reaching the client group, accessibility and a generally better service.

> A significant proportion of the people who have made contact with the van when it's been at probation offices have not previously had contact with the drugs service, so that would probably be our biggest achievement. (substance misuse manager)

> When [clients] come to see their probation officer there is the direct possibility of immediate referral to a drugs worker. That makes it easier for the clients... to keep appointments and work on the problem. The ease of access is very important. (senior probation officer)

> You can give a better service to a group of offenders that we know we have needed to develop a better service for. We can have an improved service. That's the main thing. (senior probation officer)

Probation officers applauded the additional expertise: "If someone had asked in which area we would like specialist help and relief, alcohol would have stood out, so the probation managers were in touch with our needs on that point!" They appreciated partner workers' good relationships with their clients: "I find them very client focused, very non-judgemental and very practical... The right balance between sympathy for people and getting on with the job".

Curiously, few advantages were observed in harm reduction and non-statutory relationships with clients. However, substance misuse workers

Table 4.5   Advantages of partnership for service delivery, as perceived by probation and substance misuse staff at successful and problematic partnerships

Interviewees	Probation		Substance misuse		
Partnership	Successful	Problematic	Successful	Problematic	Total
Reach client group	7	1	6	6	20
Accessibility	8	7	1	4	20
Better service	10	3	3	3	19
Expertise	2	5	1	1	9
Help clients	–	–	4	3	7
Good with clients	2	3	–	–	5
Exceed probation officer's expectations	3	–	1	1	5
Harm reduction	2	2	1	–	5
Effective	2	–	2	–	4
Concrete resource	2	–	1	1	4
Realise need	1	–	2	–	3
Empower clients	–	–	2	–	2
Innovation	2	–	–	–	2
Non-statutory relationship	–	1	1	–	2
Uptake by probation officers	–	–	1	–	1
Total	41	22	26	19	108
Percentage of total comments	38	20	24	18	100

were pleased to be helping clients: "Giving a chance to people who really did feel that they were on the scrap heap". Clients benefited more from the service than some probation officers expected: "The counselling clients who I am seeing are doing far beyond what the probation officers ever thought they would. They were hopeless cases as far as they were concerned" (substance misuse worker). Similarly, effectiveness was recognised at successful partnerships: "Out of five [group members], four totally abstained for the eight weeks" (substance misuse worker). Partnership increased recognition of the extent of need: "There are some very real needs. You're looking at damaged goods" (substance misuse manager). Two substance misuse workers enjoyed empowering clients through inclusion and choice in service planning; one perceived uptake by probation officers as tribute to the programme's worth.

Developing concrete resources, such as reports, posters or materials, was rewarding: "A lot of material has been translated into other languages" (probation officer). Two probation interviewees were proud of their project's innovative nature.

Partnership learning

Appreciation of the process of partnership development was strengthened. Substance misuse staff, in particular, recognised the benefits of networking: "The biggest lesson is about liaison and networking. It's so important". Similarly, different partners could work together: "They are also going to visit each other's project, because they are totally different, and it's important that they can cross-refer" (senior probation officer). Bringing clarity to the enterprise through formalisation was approved: "Because there is a better understanding of expectations...a clear understanding of what we need to know" (senior probation officer). The probation service's investment in dedicating time to the project was also important.

Less enthusiastic remarks revealed willingness to learn from mistakes. The experience could illustrate pitfalls awaiting the unwary, as a substance misuse manager philosophically explained:

> Nothing is ever a negative experience, it's always a positive. We learned as an organisation that we needed to put the service agreements in so that we knew what their expectations were and vice versa. So we grew from that.

A few were pleased to be involved in a new kind of enterprise:

> It's an example of a partnership between a statutory and a non-statutory agency. The government are trying to encourage community partnerships and community safety. (substance misuse manager)

Table 4.6 Advantages in learning about partnership, as perceived by probation and substance misuse staff at successful and problematic partnerships

Interviewees	Probation		Substance misuse		
Partnership	Successful	Problematic	Successful	Problematic	Total
Networking	–	1	3	2	6
Formal clarity	1	2	2	1	6
Investment in success	2	1	2	–	5
Different partners co-operate	2	–	1	–	3
Illustrated pitfalls	1	1	–	1	3
Provide an example	1	–	1	1	3
Tested demand	–	1	–	–	1
Total	7	6	9	5	27
Percentage of total comments	26	22	33	19	100

It was an effort to develop inter-agency working, but it tested out whether or not there was a demand. So it told us something about whether our probation clients wanted that kind of service, and probation officers. (senior probation officer)

Personal Gains

The most common personal gain was the variety which the work offered. This was particularly true for substance misuse workers at successful partnerships:

It's fairly different. I have a different style for the group. It's very different from one-to-one work. I'm pleased to do something different once a week.

I do like the nature of the post even though it has been difficult. That I'm not at one place, that it is a liaison post, that hopefully there is room for development within the post and that I can bring some of my own creativity to it.

It's really interesting. You can't stereotype these [clients]...There's a variety of people.

Table 4.7   Personal gains of working in partnership, as perceived by probation and substance misuse staff at successful and problematic partnerships

Interviewees	Probation		Substance misuse		
Partnership	Successful	Problematic	Successful	Problematic	Total
Variety	1	–	7	3	11
Challenge	2	–	3	2	7
New institutional insights	2	–	1	3	6
New perspectives	4	–	–	1	5
Personal satisfaction	2	–	1	1	4
Excitement	2	–	1	1	4
Intellectual stimulation	3	–	1	–	4
Like clients	–	–	2	2	4
Method	1	–	–	1	2
New skills	–	–	1	1	2
Identified with project	1	–	–	–	1
Working for the agency	–	–	1	–	1
Personal support	–	–	–	1	1
Total	18	–	18	16	52
Percentage of total comments	35	–	35	31	100

Several comments identified a psychological boost: challenge; excitement; personal satisfaction; intellectual stimulation; and simply being identified with the project.

> I have liked the challenge of working with a totally different group – offenders – having the privilege of viewing the difficulties in their lives and doing what I can to support them... I find that rewarding. (substance misuse worker)

> This sort of programme for ethnic minorities, if they really mean to provide them equality of opportunity to meet the needs, must be sensitive to their needs. I've derived a personal satisfaction from involving myself in this partnership, which has fulfilled those requirements. (probation officer)

> Getting this thing from [the idea], to seeing it in place has been very challenging and very rewarding. At every stage there have been challenges along the way... Good fun though! (senior probation officer)

> Criminal justice does interest me. I enjoy, find it a challenge doing drugs work. There is a percentage of people who have problem drug use and have contact with the criminal justice system as a consequence of that. So the work that I do I think is important. I enjoy that work. (substance misuse worker)

Interviewees enjoyed opportunities to gain new insights into the operation of a different organisation, and exposure to new perspectives.

> I understand now that there is a big care element in [probation officers'] work. I didn't realise that before, but there is a huge care element in their role. A social element. I thought it was purely law enforcement. (substance misuse manager)

> It has been a huge insight to go into a prison. It is not what I would choose to spend my working life doing. But it's not everybody who has that opportunity to do that. (substance misuse worker)

> I like being able to work with the voluntary sector, because that is totally different from working within the [probation] service... It really does broaden your horizons and broaden your perspective. (senior probation officer)

Table 4.8   Benefits of partnership summarised in rank order

Interviewees	Probation		Substance misuse			% of total comments
Partnership	Successful	Problematic	Successful	Problematic	Total	
Service delivery	41	22	26	19	108	42
Personal gains	18	–	18	16	52	20
Advantages to substance misuse agencies	13	3	11	10	37	14
Learning about partnership	7	6	9	5	27	11
Advantages to probation service	9	10	4	2	25	10
Criminal justice	1	2	3	1	7	3
Total	89	43	71	53	256	100
Percentage of total comments	35	17	28	21	101	

Some substance misuse workers discovered a liking for the client group, one liked working for the agency, and one derived personal support through the partnership. One substance misuse worker – and one probation officer – liked the method of intervention: "I like using solution focused brief therapy. It works well with this client group and it works well for me as a person."

Sadly, not one personal gain was mentioned by probation officers at problematic partnerships, while even at highly problematic projects, substance misuse workers offered some positive comments on their experience. Indeed, as Table 4.8 shows, probation officers at problematic projects saw many fewer benefits than staff of either agency at successful partnerships, and also fewer than their substance misuse counterparts. Given the strong disappointment of substance misuse staff at problematic partnerships, their ability to discern professional benefits, and even personal gains, was surprising. The enthusiasm of probation staff at successful partnerships for their benefits, perhaps testified to their own investment in the enterprise.

The problems of partnership

Problems associated with partnership clustered into five topics: the probation service; substance misuse agencies; organising partnership; service delivery; and the personal costs of working in partnership.

These topics are summarised in Tables 4.9 to 4.13, with a rank-ordered summary at Table 4.14.

Problems for the probation service

The most commonly mentioned difficulty for the probation service was the threat to the quality and quantity of professional appointments. This was particularly evident at problematic partnerships.

> Probation officers are pretty cheesed off that partnerships were inflicted on the service and that partnerships directly threaten probation resources. We have had a 4.5 per cent cut in our budget this year, and 5 per cent more of our budget has to go on partnerships. So there is less money for the probation service through partnerships, not more. (probation officer)

> It is a deprivation. A lot of probation officers came into the service to work with people and that's been taken away. So that's a valid reason for being cheesed off. (substance misuse manager)

Partnership exposed the probation service's insularity.

> The probation service has been a) insular and b) downright arrogant, at its worst, in believing that we are the only ones who can provide for offenders, that we are the only ones who understand. I would honestly doubt that. Offenders are human beings first of all. (probation officer)

Table 4.9 Problems of partnership for the probation service, as perceived by probation and substance misuse staff at successful and problematic partnerships

Interviewees	Probation		Substance misuse		
Partnership	Successful	Problematic	Successful	Problematic	Total
Threatened	3	7	1	9	20
Insularity	3	1	1	2	7
Internal problems	2	–	2	1	5
Service not wanted	–	1	–	2	3
Lack of interest	1	–	–	2	3
Low status of project	–	2	–	1	3
Management diverted	2	–	–	–	2
Total	11	11	4	17	43
Percentage of total comments	26	26	9	40	101

They're quite an insular crew...People are enmeshed in their own work. Often it's so complicated to look around for [alternatives]. Some probation officers just have tunnel vision, don't they? (substance misuse manager)

Three partnerships did not provide a service which probation officers wanted: "For example, [the substance misuse worker] isn't qualified as a community care assessor, which seems an absolute nonsense" (senior probation officer). At problematic partnerships, the project's low status was lamented: "We're a blip in policy...We're a little project in the corner of [the county]...We don't really fit nicely" (substance misuse worker). So also was lack of interest: "I don't think probation pushed it enough, they could have done a lot more" (substance misuse manager). At successful partnerships, there was concern to manage the balance between the project's health and that of the probation service. Internal problems distracted attention from the partnership enterprise: "The restructure is causing such low morale there. I feel the low morale on the telephone. I feel it when I see probation officers" (substance misuse manager). Conversely, investing in partnership diluted management support of probation officers: "Whilst I've been doing this, I haven't been doing other things. This is not a team which can develop without seeing me" (senior probation officer).

Problems for substance misuse agencies

The partner agency was sometimes too small to bear the demand from the probation service without compromising its other commitments, or to offer the range of services expected.

[A] couple of them are part-time and they only have three full time workers. So they had some difficulty in committing a worker to this group. But then they had taken the responsibility. (probation officer)

I was stretched as a manager. They really needed someone [to push them] to get this to work. I just didn't have the time to do that, so it made me very frustrated...I was under pressure all the time to raise money to keep the project going. (substance misuse manager)

Similarly, the partner agency's expansion could pressurise its workers: "We need to [be careful] that we get our share of [the substance misuse worker's] time, and the agency gets its share, and that she is not run ragged in the process...She's got to fit her lunch break in somewhere!" (senior probation officer).

Table 4.10 Problems of partnership for substance misuse agencies, as perceived by probation and substance misuse staff at successful and problematic partnerships

Interviewees	Probation		Substance misuse		
Partnership	Successful	Problematic	Successful	Problematic	Total
Too small	7	5	7	3	22
Inconsistency of probation officers	–	–	6	7	13
Difficult probation officers	1	–	1	6	8
Difficult substance misuse staff	2	–	–	1	3
Expansion	1	1	–	–	2
Exclusiveness	–	–	1	–	1
Insularity	–	–	1	–	1
Total	11	6	16	17	50
Percentage of total comments	22	12	32	34	100

A problem observed by substance misuse staff at both successful and problematic partnerships, but escaping the notice of probation staff, was the variability of individual and team practice within the service:

> The biggest difficulty has been making sure that the probation officers take account of the presence of the partnership. For example ... at one of our sessions there wasn't much uptake, because a lot of the officers were out, so there weren't many clients coming in. We started to query whether we should come, but then one officer started to run a women's group on that day, so we stuck with it. Then that officer moved on and the women's group either was moved to another day or died. Things like that have quite an impact on the success of the partnership. This team will be making decisions about how they plan and organise their work. The difficulty is making sure that they take into account the impact on the partnership.

> I did find that individual probation officers have a great deal of flexibility in the way that they work with their clients ... They have a wide spectrum of skills. You have to fit in with each individual.

Patience had been sorely tried by the difficult behaviour of individual probation officers at problematic partnerships.

> When the liaison officer told me that the probation officers were [complaining], I said "Look, can you tell those wimps to get off

their backsides and start using this project. They either use it or they don't, but if they don't use it then it goes. It is as simple as that"... I lost my temper. (substance misuse manager)

Difficult behaviour by individual substance misuse staff was reported at two successful partnerships, but was a problem more for the agency than for the probation service: "Having a difficult Chief Probation Officer would not impinge directly on the work of the partnership in my organisation. Having a difficult director of a small voluntary organisation has a massive effect even though the staff lower down the chain try to ameliorate it" (probation officer).

One substance misuse manager acknowledged insularity in some voluntary agencies. Another was concerned about the potential exclusivity of a service dedicated specifically to probation clients.

The organisation of partnership

This topic attracted the greatest number of comments overall, from staff of both organisations and at both successful and problematic partnerships. Culture clash was noted equally by substance misuse staff at successful and problematic partnerships, but was less apparent to probation staff at successful projects.

> For me, if they're going to do a programme, they should be *doing* the programme. It starts at 9 o'clock on a Monday and finishes at 5 o'clock on a Friday. It should be a routine. But they have so many different slots. Clients tend to pick and choose the bits that they like... There is an expectation that clients should do two weeks solid, but there has been flexibility. Once you start off on that foot, things can only get worse. (probation officer)

> All the probation officers have been very nice, charming people, lovely, nothing the matter with them at all. But they have not had the same kind of training, so they have a different outlook. They give people advice, which I hate. It's not empowering, it doesn't help. (substance misuse worker)

Effective partnership took time to develop, a point noted less often by probation staff at problematic partnerships.

> At first we thought "We'll employ two workers and it will all be wonderful." The whole thing has taken a lot longer than I would

Table 4.11 Problems in the organisation of partnership, as perceived by probation and substance misuse staff at successful and problematic partnerships

Interviewees	Probation		Substance misuse		
Partnership	Successful	Problematic	Successful	Problematic	Total
Culture clash	3	6	8	8	25
Takes time	6	3	6	7	22
Financial arrangements	3	2	4	2	11
Business naivete	4	5	–	1	10
More work	5	2	–	3	10
Monitoring	1	1	1	4	7
Objectives unclear	2	2	–	2	6
Lack of preparation	2	1	1	2	6
Poor management	–	1	–	3	4
Cost driven	1	1	–	1	3
Formalisation	–	–	1	–	1
Total	27	24	21	33	105
Percentage of total comments	26	23	20	31	100

have expected. From the very start, to getting funding, to recruiting, to contracting, right the way along, it has taken a whole lot longer than any of us could have expected. (senior probation officer)

In a way it's only by going through an evolutionary process that we have managed to achieve the level of clarity that we now have. It would be nice to have the best of both worlds, to have the freedom to allow things to evolve as well as being much more clear from the beginning. (substance misuse manager)

A similar theme was poor preparation for the reality of partnership: "The problems stem from the fact that this was put together in haste ... This wasn't driven by need from the probation service. It was driven by the Home Office ... So it was a knee jerk reaction" (senior probation officer).

Complaints included unclear objectives and poor management.

I don't know that it went wrong exactly, because we didn't have a clear idea of what it was supposed to achieve. So we tried it and it didn't work. (senior probation officer)

There has been a lack of recognition about what partnership involves on both sides. In the probation service, there has been a lack of consultation between management and case officers ... Also [the substance misuse agency] had not thought through the confidentiality issue, they had not thought about what it would mean to work with compulsion. (substance misuse worker)

Several probation interviewees deplored the service's business naiveté, leaving it poorly equipped to meet the partnership challenge: "It's quite a different role to find yourself suddenly negotiating with people about how much of someone's time you're getting and whether you're getting value for money. That's not something that comes up anywhere else in my role as a senior probation officer." The partnership created more work: "[At first it was] no problem for the support staff to take telephone calls and messages for [the substance misuse worker]. When the numbers increased they took more calls and more messages, so the probation support staff got pressured" (senior probation officer). The financial arrangements were sometimes troublesome, in terms of cumbersome administration, the inconvenience of managing separate budgets, or the insecurity of short-term funding. Perhaps partnership development would be driven by cost priorities rather than need: "I believe that partnerships with non-statutory organisations were introduced purely for cost rather than community values. So that is a moral dilemma" (substance misuse manager). The inadequacy or bureaucracy of monitoring was troublesome: "We have had problems in not knowing exactly what to record, how much detail and how to measure effectiveness of the scheme" (senior probation officer). At one well established non-financial partnership, success necessitated formalising an informal process: "It started out to be a very simple system and grew" (substance misuse manager).

Service delivery

Probation staff at successful partnerships found few problems in service delivery, while elsewhere a broader range of concerns were raised. Nevertheless, this topic attracted comparatively few complaints. At successful partnerships, practical problems were noted, usually concerning administrative detail. Three substance misuse workers disliked the amount of travelling required to cover probation service commitments; one probation officer objected to the distance of the project from the probation area.

The difficulty of the client group could result in high drop-out rates, problems for substance misuse workers in relating to clients, and the need to clarify professional boundaries.

Table 4.12 Problems of partnership in service delivery, as perceived by probation and substance misuse staff at successful and problematic partnerships

Interviewees	Probation		Substance misuse		
Partnership	Successful	Problematic	Successful	Problematic	Total
Practical problems	4	–	3	–	7
Drop outs	3	1	1	1	6
Travelling	–	1	1	2	4
Drift to coercion	–	1	1	2	4
Relating to clients	–	2	–	1	3
Boundaries	–	–	2	–	2
Lack of resources	1	–	1	–	2
Service misconceived	–	–	–	1	1
Not integrated	–	1	–	–	1
Sentencers don't change	–	–	1	–	1
Total	8	6	10	7	31
Percentage of total comments	26	19	32	23	100

> One of the problems has been making referrals and people then not turning up. We would expect that . . . but at the end of the day, if you have two hours blocked into your diary and nobody turns up, that is disappointing. (senior probation officer)

> I don't think many people could have done it, frankly. Because I have long experience of working with all sorts of groups, including aggressive teenagers. But some of these intensive probation groups have to be seen to be believed. (substance misuse worker)

> I can tell that they're not disclosing certain things . . . that they are still apprehensive about who I am, what I am, how confidential my work is. (substance misuse worker)

There were concerns about the wider context within which the partnership enterprise occurred, in terms of drift towards coercive treatment, failure to force sentencers to change, and lack of resources for addiction problems.

> I have a feeling that social work is no longer the main focus of the probation service. I'm very sorry about that . . . Probation is becoming much more a corrective agency, and it's so difficult to cope with clients' needs. (probation officer)

We now have the opportunity to come into contact with a lot more offenders who have dependency problems. That's good...But the government rarely imposes change on the judges and magistrates who pass sentence. It is conceivable that drug and alcohol agencies and probation services will devote considerable time to constructing new services...only for sentencers to continue sending this group to prison. (substance misuse manager)

There were two complaints about the partnership service. One substance misuse worker thought that groupwork deterred clients: "It's misconceived. My impression is that drinkers don't like groups...it's too terrifying." A senior probation officer blamed the "lack of integration into the day-to-day work of supervision" for many of a project's difficulties.

Personal costs

Probation staff at problematic partnerships described no personal costs, just as they described no personal gains. For the remainder, some personal costs concerned their role within the partnership endeavour. Role conflict, earlier seen to be an experience of project champions, was also identified by some substance misuse staff. This generally related to the discomfort of alliance with authority, but was different in one case.

I did start keeping notes. I haven't told my director that I'm doing it, which makes it seem rather mean, keeping secrets from my director. We've had different probation officers involved with the group, they change every six months. One or two didn't know much about the kind of group that I was trying to run. I got quite angry about this. I just wanted somewhere that I could write down what happened without worrying about them reading it. (substance misuse worker)

Lack of training for their role was also lamented by substance misuse workers, and one modest probation officer.

I happen to think I wasn't bad, but I could have been lousy...How does the probation service know that I am the right sort of person to run this type of group? It so happens that for part of my career I worked at [an alcohol dependency unit]...but that has not been declared to the probation service because it's not relevant to what I do as a probation officer. (probation officer)

Table 4.13 Personal costs of working in partnership, as perceived by probation and substance misuse staff at successful and problematic partnerships

Interviewees	Probation		Substance misuse		
Partnership	Successful	Problematic	Successful	Problematic	Total
Role conflict	6	–	3	2	11
Lack of training	1	–	2	3	6
Fear to disappoint	2	–	1	–	3
Being excluded	1	–	1	1	3
Complex arrangements	1	–	1	–	2
Witness injustice	–	–	1	–	1
Prisons	–	–	–	1	1
Justifying project	1	–	–	–	1
Lose control	1	–	–	–	1
Being on trial	–	–	–	1	1
Goal posts moved	–	–	1	–	1
Total	13	–	10	8	31
Percentage of total comments	42	–	32	26	100

I would like to learn more. Nobody has offered me any guidance or support or training. So I'm as knowledgeable about the prison system, courts and offenders as I was when I started... Lack of personal development training. I would have welcomed being included by the probation service... they obviously have access to training that I might have benefited from. It might have made the partnership better because I might have understood more what I was doing. (substance misuse worker)

Loyalty to the project aroused anxieties about disappointing others: "The worry, the anxiety about going to talk to other people and raising their hopes and expectations, and bearing the responsibility of that. You want to produce the goods for them, yet some of their expectations are going to be disappointed, because there are only twenty hours. That feels quite a weight" (substance misuse worker). One substance misuse worker disliked "the fact that it has been said that I have to prove myself and I have been on trial. It has been quite uncomfortable." A senior probation officer resented having to justify a successful project. Investment in the project led to frustration when an individual was excluded from decision making: "Nobody tells me anything. I really don't know what's going on between probation and my director. So I'm the guy who is doing it and no one tells me what else is going on. I just *run* the group!" (substance misuse worker). One substance misuse worker

Table 4.14   Problems of partnership summarised in rank order

Interviewees Partnership	Probation		Substance misuse			% of total comments
	Successful	Problematic	Successful	Problematic	Total	
Organisation of partnership	27	24	21	33	105	40
Problems for substance misuse agencies	11	6	16	17	50	19
Problems for probation service	11	11	4	17	43	17
Service delivery	8	6	10	7	31	12
Personal costs	13	–	10	8	26	12
Total	70	47	61	82	255	100
Percentage of total comments	27	18	23	32	100	

complained about his treatment on appointment: "They suddenly said that equal opportunities hadn't been practised, when they had already said it was my job...What annoyed me was the goal posts being changed all the time. Because of our project's need for funding, we had gone along with it every time. But, like the Murphy's, I'm not bitter."

Managing the partnership commitment also involved personal costs. At one partnership, both the senior probation officer and the substance misuse worker were concerned about the arrangement's complexity, involving two voluntary agencies. A senior probation officer remarked: "You feel you've lost some sense of control, because the worker is within an agency which has its own policies, procedures."

Two substance misuse workers disliked exposure to aspects of the criminal justice system. One complained about social injustice: "The partnership exposes me to a substantial amount of outright discrimination, by the systems that offenders struggle to live within. That's what I hate about it." Another disliked contact with custody: "I find it distressing to work in prisons. I find it difficult to walk out knowing that they can not."

Conclusion

As argued earlier, basic strategies for partnership development artfully maximised preservation of the probation service's professional territory, while minimising potential ideological conflict areas. These were not the true problems of partnership. Indeed, it can now be seen that, at ground level, ideological dilemmas of compulsion and confidentiality virtually disappeared from the reckoning of practitioners as to the important issues for their projects. Differences in the qualities of statutory or non-statutory relationships with clients also became unimportant.

Instead, a wealth of data reveals that the fundamental problems of partnership lay in poor management of their introduction, failure to invest energy in the enterprise, and consequent resistance of field staff. Thus, championship and recognition of professional enhancements, which characterised successful partnerships, were absent or ineffective at problematic projects.

The telephone survey revealed awareness within the probation service of the likelihood of resistance to the introduction of partnerships. At that stage, resistance by probation officers was presented largely as an internal problem for the service. Yet we now see that its impact was keenly felt by substance misuse workers. Nevertheless, the failure to deal proactively with resistance led, at problematic partnerships, to resentment, unhappiness and embarrassment, not only for substance misuse staff, but also for those probation officers who testified to the damage inflicted upon standards of professional behaviour and interprofessional relationships. The crucial importance of management roles was therefore examined in Phase Three case studies.

Some seemingly surprising, counter-intuitive findings emerge from this exploration of partnership qualities. Substance misuse staff at problematic partnerships, while identifying the greatest number of difficulties, also discerned nearly as many advantages for their own agencies as those at successful projects. And while probation staff at successful projects recognised many more advantages of partnership than any other group, they also identified a relatively large number of problems. Perhaps most curious of all is the comparative silence of probation staff at problematic projects on the very question of the problems of partnership.

These findings may not be so surprising. The key to their interpretation may lie in the considerable personal investment in the health of their projects offered by all substance misuse staff, and by probation staff at successful partnerships. At problematic partnerships, neither a single personal gain nor one personal cost was mentioned by any probation interviewee. Here, field staff reflected the detachment of their senior managers from the partnership enterprise. Conversely, substance misuse staff at these projects derived personal gains, as well as costs, from their efforts in the face of their difficulties. At successful projects, the earlier prediction of some telephone survey respondents that the partnership endeavour would increase workload rather than reduce it was borne out. There, enthusiastic and committed probation staff perceived many advantages of partnership, appreciated enhancements to their professional practice, enjoyed good inter-professional relationships and derived personal gains. Their investment, however, exposed them to a critical awareness of the pitfalls of partnership and exacted a price in personal costs.

5
In-house Specialisation

In-house specialist projects were analysed according to the same themes as were the partnership projects. Each project was unique and none was problematic.

Defining in-house specialisation

In-house specialisation differed from partnership by the dedication of probation officer time to direct service provision. Defining the boundaries to each specialist project was less simple. The specialist arrangements of two probation services were classified as separate projects, because different specialists undertook distinctive work. In two areas, specialist officers' activities were best understood as team projects. One probation service fulfilled both these categorisations, offering both a team project for alcohol problems and a specialist officer for drug issues; these arrangements were joined administratively in one unit more for thematic consistency than for integration in practice, and therefore were classified as two projects. Thus, nine projects were studied, in seven probation services.

Background to the specialist projects

All projects except one had substantial histories: one residential project traced its origins back twenty years. The youngest project began contemporaneously with the service's partnership development. Project histories revealed debts to the enthusiasm of key individuals alongside capitalisation on local opportunities.

> [The hostel] was started by a recovering alcoholic ... They had connections building up with probation, to the point that, when the

original manager left, the probation service was the major funder and had already appointed an in-house deputy to work alongside the team. By the early 1980s it was fully controlled by the probation service.

It started because of the interest of a senior probation officer in alcohol many years ago... He persuaded management that a specialist team would do the work better. Probably to his surprise, that was agreed! And the unit was set up about 1984.

Specialist services

Each project is briefly described, because summarisation in terms such as secondment, specialist team or hostel would be misleading.

1. A six-bedded house for male and female alcoholics, established jointly by the probation service and a local housing association. The project manager was a probation officer dedicated half time to the project.
2. A half-time secondment to a statutory community substance misuse team with in-patient treatment facilities. The probation officer participated in the full range of work undertaken by the multi-disciplinary team: "[The multi-disciplinary team] shares expertise, but we don't take on the clientele particular to our [seconding] agencies. We take anybody. I work as another drug worker." The remaining time was spent within a probation team, with particular responsibility for the substance misuse groupwork programme.
3. A half-time specialist probation officer, within the same probation service as the previous project, but in an area which lacked a secondment opportunity. The specialist officer liaised with a local voluntary residential rehabilitation centre and co-led a recovery group and a family support group with its outreach worker: "I go to strategy meetings at [the residential project]. I go there twice a week to make myself known to the residents... The object of the recovery group is to be a self-support group, with a programme that is varied according to need."
4. A full-time secondment to a voluntary substance misuse agency. The first seconded officer at this young project was developing a role focused on probation clients, including groupwork programmes: "I should hold a maximum of ten probation orders with drug or alcohol provisions, but it took time to build those

up. So at first I was taking on anybody, any voluntary clients who had no connection at all with probation. Now I have eleven probation clients, but I also have cases that are voluntary."

5. A hostel, fully funded by the probation service, offering bail assessment and a twelve week residential programme to substance misusing offenders, with voluntary after-care support. The staff team comprised a senior probation officer as manager, a probation officer as deputy manager and assistant managers drawn from diverse backgrounds: "I would not say this is a residential treatment facility. I would say it is a criminal justice residential service ...I see it as another unit, in the same way that community service, or the bail hostel, or our day centre are units. We're a unit with a specialist function of providing a residential option for offenders who have acknowledged problems associated with alcohol or drugs."

6. A specialist probation officer liaising with a residential rehabilitation centre which attracted referrals nationally. The specialist officer held all cases of residents subject to probation orders, liaised with "home" probation services, and participated in many activities, including assessment of applicants.

7. A specialist team of three probation officers led by a senior. The three specialists were seconded half-time to statutory substance misuse teams, where they dealt with all forensic referrals. They were otherwise located in field teams, where they contributed the substance misuse elements of the probation service groupwork programme, offered advice and consultation to probation officers and counselled substance misusing clients. Cases remained the overall responsibility of referring officers. This project subsequently participated as Project B of the three case studies.

8. A specialist team of a senior, three full-time probation officers and an assistant, offering an alcohol resource area-wide, with responsibility for the groupwork programmes, assessment and counselling. Cases remained the overall responsibility of referring officers.

9. A specialist probation officer working half-time in the statutory community drug clinic and half-time in the probation service, based in the specialist team just described. The half post at the clinic was funded from health monies originating in initiatives for HIV/AIDS prevention, and thus did not constitute a secondment, allowing participation across the range of work. However: "The main focus of the work is to do assessments for courts...Then I have the resources of the community drug clinic to link into...If

I'm not using the community drug team for health and medical issues, then I operate on a counselling level ... When I've finished I will pass them back to the field officer."

Theoretical approach

Apart from the residential projects, in-house specialisations were most commonly described as pursuing harm minimisation, complementing the ethos of host substance misuse agencies. Specialists explained:

For a lot of people first coming to us, that might be the first time that they have ever thought about their drinking and what harmful effect it might be having on their lives. They don't necessarily come committed to reducing their drinking and a harm reduction approach enables us to do something with them which is of value.

We do aim for abstinence in our work with some people, but we wouldn't foist that on them. So the overall aim is harm reduction. By that, we include the harm caused by offending. In fact, that is the main harm that we would seek to reduce.

At residential projects, a therapeutic abstinence ethos linked with broader notions of harm minimisation:

We're a strictly drink and drug free house ... The vast majority of people who come here don't want to stop using or stop drinking. But we disrupt their using ... Realistically, some of the younger people we get here aren't going to be ready for abstinence. So we try to introduce harm reduction.

Tolerance was extended to individual fallibility:

If we're talking about a person who has had a habit for a number of years, it's not easy to stop ... When an individual lapses we manage that lapse, learn from that lapse. But if an individual lapses again, he or she is asked to leave ... Evidence has shown that people drift in and out of substance use. We have a policy whereby if somebody does return to problematic use, we have them back.

We will try to work with it. We'll put them on a five day programme and we look at the relapse, what led up to it, how it happened, the aftermath. So that they can see the [dynamics] of their misuse.

Target groups

The most closely targetted project was a residential programme for high
tariff offenders: "We're not open to any offenders...Most of them have
over twelve previous convictions and most of them would be facing a
custodial sentence". Moreover: "We're probably now dealing with more
drug users than drinkers, and we've moved to be attractive to people in
their early twenties". The other residential project defined itself differently: "It's not specifically for those within the criminal justice system.
It's a resource within the region for those who wish to stop drinking
alcohol."

For one seconded officer, targetting was irrelevant: "We don't like
referrals from probation. We don't like referrals from *anybody* except
the person. It's about the person wanting help". Another was increasingly focused: "My feeling is that I should be directing it towards
people who are offending or who have offended as a result of drugs
or alcohol". The team of half-time seconded specialists received all
forensic referrals to their host agencies, irrespective of clients' contact
with the probation service. At the specialist team for alcohol problems,
referral opportunities were limited to probation officers. The drugs
specialist here, however, explained: "I'm a probation officer to the
staff [at the clinic], but ...I try to see people who are there for non-
offending reasons...I'd rather have a wider knowledge of the [clien-
tele]."

A specialist liaison officer to a residential centre received all cases of
residents and ex-residents subject to probation orders. The liaison officer
who ran community based groups in collaboration with an outreach
worker, by contrast, loosely defined clients' connection with the probation service:

> People who have been in the house, who are at the second stage
> house or who are in the community can go [to the recovery group].
> People known to the probation service can go. One or two people
> who don't fit those categories have gone too. It's a flexible world,
> dealing with people who take drugs!

The flexible targetting of specialist projects reflected their links with
community based services which themselves offered broad access. As
will be seen, specialisation symbolised much more than a narrowly
defined service for offenders.

Coercion and enforcement

One specialist residential project worked exclusively with offenders sub-ject to special requirements, for assessment while on bail, for residence as a condition of a probation order, or in some cases as part of parole supervision. At the other residential project, and one secondment, coer-cive requirements were rejected.

At one specialist team, special requirements were discouraged, although acceptable. At a specialist team for alcohol problems, however, additional requirements of probation were popular. The senior proba-tion officer here was pragmatic:

> Historically [this probation service] has a high use of conditions in orders for alcohol work...It shouldn't be part of the supervision package of an ordinary probation order, to my mind. You should specify in reports what work you expect to do and the agency should be able to provide that to the court's satisfaction. You shouldn't have to put conditions in. But the courts are used to it now...It would be a big undertaking to re-educate the staff...It's not worth the effort in the current political climate.

By contrast, the drugs specialist in this area discouraged coercion: "The nature of the client group is so chaotic. Their commitment and ability to keep appointments is really difficult. We felt it was unfair to the court to indicate that because of the condition, they were going to attend. That's not really being honest."

Responses from both the specialist probation officer and the sub-stance misuse worker at one project were unclear, due to the variety of community-based activities and ambivalence about coercion at the residential centre. The probation officer commented: "In the past they would have said that attendance as a resident as a special condition was not what they wanted. These days they're easier about it...[But] I can't remember somebody being admitted under such a condition."

When asked to recount the last occasion on which an offender was dealt with for not co-operating with the programme, six probation interviewees recalled an incident. At the residential project which rejected specific requirements a probationer was evicted: "He was asked to leave because of continual evidence of alcohol use...His local probation officer was notified. It was up to the individual and his probation officer to deal with [it]." At the other, targeted project, interviewees recalled residents being sentenced to custody after breach action, although alternatives were sought where possible.

Elsewhere, probation interviewees and all substance misuse staff offered no account, either because voluntary referrals were the norm, or because they discontinued involvement after reporting to supervising officers. One specialist officer confided: "My feeling is that probation officers don't do anything about them."

This outcome partly arose from use of open phrasing in requirements which maximised probation officers' discretion when offenders failed to sustain treatment: "We use the same condition for all of them, to attend [this unit] as directed. That gives us flexibility about whether they come to the group or attend for one-to-one counselling, or both. It gives us a lot of flexibility." Moreover, creative approaches to disciplinary problems were possible:

> The condition on his probation order is very specific. He had to go to a rehabilitation centre for a certain length of time and comply with treatment. But he cut his programme short there. Now he's in contact with me again and seeing me regularly, so in many ways he's complying with National Standards. So I have to breach him . . . I'll be saying to the court that he was two weeks short of completing it but he is now complying with a community based programme.

Thus, the theme common to all projects was maximisation of opportunities to reduce the potential impact of coercion and enforcement. Specialist projects could even be structured to enhance offenders' conformity to National Standards of supervision:

> We have noticed, since we started the rolling programme so people link in with us very quickly, that the breaches have gone right down. We breach far less now, under National Standards, than we used to! That's because people get on with it quickly . . . The way that we operate fits in well with National Standards, because they see their field probation officer and then have seven appointments with us. Which is the requisite number of appointments.

Specialists also perceived urine testing as serving specific treatment functions, of little general relevance to probation activity:

> It's to do with the safety of the hostel. They know we are serious about abstinence, and they do know that they could be urine tested or breath tested. No, it doesn't cause me problems.

> We do [breathalyse] and we've had no conflict or doubts about that . . . We have the rule of being alcohol free in the group and for

most appointments... It's not a major problem for most people to get here alcohol free. If it *was* a major problem they wouldn't be on the group... [Also] there quite often is someone in the group who has decided to stop drinking or who is trying very hard to cut down. Then to sit next to someone who smells of alcohol, that is a very distressing experience.

If they go to the methadone unit, then it's an expectation. It's in the contract. That's part of the programme... If you're trying [to help] people to face up to the reality of what they're doing, then I don't see a way round it.

The specialist role

Interviewees commonly remarked that an important aspect of specialisation was a focus on probation service interests. This priority was adapted to each project's structure. For example, at the targetted residential project: "Our focus has shifted on the alcohol or drug using behaviour. We are making progress if we stop them *offending*."

A seconded officer saw that pressured staff at the host agency could not develop additional programmes exclusively for offenders:

They're short staffed and historically they've concentrated on individual work. I feel that the probation service could benefit from groupwork programmes... That's what *I'm* here to do. If I wasn't here... they would not provide those services, even if probation was asking for them.

At a specialist team, the framework of statutory obligations was important: "We've worked hard to fit in with National Standards *and* to devise work that's of good quality." Interviewees affirmed that the probation service needed in-house expertise for effective assessment and supervision of offenders. Specialisation raised the overall quality of intervention by supporting non-specialists, recognising the frequency of substance misuse problems among offenders:

The provision that is out there, outside the service, is not adequate to cover the extent of problem that we see... There are a lot of people seen by the probation service who have drink problems, who don't go to other alcohol agencies and who wouldn't contemplate going to them, but whose main reason for committing offences is that they misuse alcohol. If they can be helped *not* to misuse it, they will stop or reduce their offending. These people are around in very large numbers.

In-house specialisation was therefore cost effective:

> Other probation services don't do enough...*More* probation resources should be plugged into alcohol and drugs, not [less]. Having a specialist team is one way of doing it, and it works well here.

Specialisation demystified substance misuse, raising confidence overall, by offering training, advice and consultancy:

> I wish that more probation officers would do a lot of this work, that I *know* probation officers can do. *I'm* a probation officer and *I* can do it...We've been trying to do training to help them to feel more comfortable and more aware that they have a lot of expertise. Lack of confidence means that they don't use it.

> I'm very much against people being precious or thinking they're experts...I don't believe in any cult of experts. Probation officers have got the generic skills to work with people with alcohol and drugs problems. They just need persuading...It's some knowledge and training that comes on top. That's all.

Specialists were important intermediaries between probation and substance misuse services, facilitating offenders' access to treatment:

> If [a probation officer] rings up and [asks how to get a client into the programme], I know I can get them in quicker because I'm around. (probation officer)

> The probation officer would be in a better position to motivate clients, to address the horrible issues that they don't want to discuss...[The clients] don't always feel that our facilities would be made accessible to them. The probation officer would facilitate that. (substance misuse manager)

Specialists were committed to this multi-faceted role: "I've felt very pressured, under pressure from the whole job. But because I've liked doing it, I've put myself under pressure." However, loyalties to different agencies could inspire role conflict.

> The clinic in itself is confidential. So I could know somebody is on probation. But if [a probation officer] were to ask me, I would say "I

can't tell you. It's confidential". I've had to explain to teams that I'm bound by the confidentiality of the clinic, which means I'm bringing in conflict to this agency.

Conflicts also arose in apportioning time between multiple activities:

Outside of the hostel I have a liaison and consulting role ... I would like to engage more in the programme, because I'm further removed from it now than I've ever been. It would be helpful for me to get the feel of the odd group session, but that's probably just wishful thinking now!

I have had to do a lot more work in terms of publicity, in terms of PR, getting organisations within the county to consider this as a resource. More time has been spent on PR and funding, issues that I didn't think I would be getting myself into.

Inter-professional relationships

Inter-professional relationships at in-house projects may be considered from two perspectives: internal relationships within the probation service; and inter-agency relationships. Interviewees' comments are summarised in Table 5.1.

Internal relationships

Accessibility was important. The frequent presence of the specialist in field teams created communication opportunities and sustained probation officers' interest:

I'm still very closely linked to probation. I spend probably a day every week on average at the probation offices ... which means that I've developed much better links with the officers ... There is a lot of contact.

When I [took up post] I went round the teams and kept people informed about changes that were happening. I'm open to approach at any time. I know it's easy to say that, but I do get a lot of main grade probation officers coming up and asking questions. They come into my room and get all the leaflets.

No specialist complained about inadequate referrals. Field staff received regular feedback about their clients' progress: "Every contact with the unit, any contact at all, is fed back to the field officer very

Table 5.1 Inter-professional relationships at in-house specialist projects

Interviewees	Probation	Substance misuse	Total
Internal			
Accessible	6	–	6
Management support	5	–	5
Feedback	4	–	4
Good working relationships	3	–	3
Supportive	1	–	1
Roles and responsibilities clear	1	–	1
Total positive comments	20	–	20
Resentment	2	–	2
Insularity	1	–	1
Total negative comments	3	–	3
Inter-agency			
Improved by specialism	5	1	6
Welcome	2	1	3
Good working relationships	1	1	2
Facilitated by specialism	1	1	2
Community partnership	1	1	2
Improving	2	–	2
Gain worker	1	–	1
Stimulating	1	–	1
Relaxed	1	–	1
Stood test of time	–	1	1
Resolve confidentiality problem	–	1	1
Reduces uncertainty	–	1	1
Total positive comments	15	8	23
Status an issue	3	–	
Contribution not recognised	–	1	1
Roles and responsibilities unclear	–	1	1
Total negative comments	3	2	5

quickly and very fully." Also: "There is a clear system in terms of responsibility and roles which has been worked out."

Nor did specialists complain about the level of management support. Several volunteered their appreciation:

> It has to some extent been led by management. One Assistant Chief Probation Officer has taken alcohol and substance misuse problems on board. That has been the case for a number of years.

> The Chief Probation Officer and Assistant Chief Probation Officer are
> both really supportive of the concept of [the project] . . . My Chief has
> been very good and the Assistant Chief has spent a lot of time
> negotiating with the Home Office for it.

Officers appreciated the quality of working relationships between specialists: "There's a lot more sharing in the team about the specific work,
about the client group, than there is in any other team I've worked in."

Only three negative comments about internal relationships were
forthcoming. Two specialists wondered if their apparently well-favoured
role was resented: "When teams are very busy and flooded with reports,
we are a team that's been given the time to do the job properly. It
wouldn't surprise me if people felt that we had an easy time of it and
could feel quite resentful at times. It's never been said on a personal
level." Another ruefully understood the insularity of colleagues from an
external agent's perspective:

> I'm finding in this job just how hard it is to get information across.
> When I started I knew no more than the average probation officer
> about drugs. I did see it as my job to try to get information across
> about local agencies, about the substances we deal with, about the
> problems. I duly drew up a fact sheet about the agencies and sent that
> out, only to get the impression afterwards that most of my colleagues
> hadn't read it!

Inter-agency relationships

Comments about inter-agency relationships, by both specialist and substance misuse staff, were predominantly favourable. In-house specialisation improved relationships between the probation service and external
agencies, not only at secondments, but also at self-contained projects.

> We've managed to make links with agencies which really want to
> have contact with us. It's reciprocal. For instance, the sexual health
> clinic. We will take people who want to go there, but they come in to
> provide educational group sessions. That's interesting. Also it's really
> personal stuff that the staff here skirt around. (senior probation
> officer)

> It's brought two agencies closer together. If there's a client who needs
> support . . . we won't have any hesitation in contacting probation.
> Speaking on the telephone with probation officers now is an

everyday occurrence, whereas before . . . it would be treading on egg-shells. (substance misuse worker)

Probation officers appreciated their welcome at substance misuse agencies, reciprocating where possible:

A substance misuse worker from the clinic is working two days a week at [another town]. We found a space in the probation office for her to work and she does a lot of joint work. I know she's very welcome. They really enjoy her input.

Good working relationships and communication between specialist and substance misuse staff were recognised: "Because of the continued activity between two agencies, if there was any query, that would get resolved fast" (substance misuse worker). Establishing a project was a source of pride: "The whole outlook at the moment in terms of drug services is about having community partnerships. So we've got that link. It's very strong" (substance misuse manager). Host agencies gained a worker, which represented a contribution to inter-agency good will. Specialists enjoyed the stimulation of different perspectives, and the relaxed quality of relationships.

Substance misuse staff saw that the project stood the test of time, resolved problems of confidentiality and reduced uncertainty:

The basic achievement is the time. We're talking about ten years . . . That says everything, really. Both see the need for it to continue.

Because . . . we're definitely not telling tales about the client, we can discuss confidential information. It's not betraying any confidentiality.

It strengthens [the link], rather than wondering if [the probation officer's] going to be there, who's going to come next, or if there *is* going to be someone next.

Only five negative comments about inter-agency relationships were offered. Three specialists were concerned by disparities in agency status:

You have better status in the probation service [than] in the health service. People regard you generally in the community as having more clout if you're a probation officer than if you're a drug worker. God knows why.

> The job description is written very much from a statutory agency point of view... Other secondments here are completely incorporated into the agency, so I don't think it was envisaged that I would still be so much a part of probation.

Substance misuse staff did not mention this, although one manager seemed more concerned for the specialist officer:

> They expect the seconded worker to provide a lot of their needs. Their training needs, for example... She's got a heavy caseload here, she's got a heavy caseload in probation, she's then also supposed to provide education to her colleagues... To help that work, we've offered to utilise some of our other staff to work with probation officers in educating offenders... but they expect that it comes via that one person. I don't think that's always the best way.

Another manager remarked that the role and responsibilities of the newly seconded officer were not yet clear: "The remit of the probation officer within [the substance misuse agency] is a bit obscure. So it needs to be defined, because it was new."

The benefits of in-house specialisation

Benefits of in-house specialisation fell into four categories: advantages for the probation service; criminal justice advantages; advantages in service delivery; and personal gains. These are outlined in Tables 5.2 to 5.5, with a rank-ordered summary at Table 5.6.

Advantages for the probation service

The most frequently cited advantage for the probation service was the spread of knowledge internally. In-house specialisation increased the knowledge base, both of the specialists themselves and within the service generally. Specialists found many opportunities for passing on knowledge, ranging through relatively informal daily contact, consultancy, joint work, and formal training.

> The dependency manual, which is now our bible, was drawn up by our [senior probation officer]. Most of the probation service's policy has stemmed from us. Over the years we have put a large amount into the probation service. We used to run their alcohol education groups. We give inputs into other groups that they run... We get frequent

Table 5.2 Advantages of in-house specialisation for the probation service as perceived by probation and substance misuse staff at in-house specialist projects

Interviewees	Probation	Substance misuse	Total
Expertise			
Spread knowledge	10	1	11
Enhance practice	6	1	7
Training	4	–	4
High quality staff	2	–	2
Relieve pressure	1	–	1
Sub-total	23	2	25
Public profile			
Public relations	6	–	6
Professional philosophy	3	–	3
Social work	2	–	2
Influence other organisation	2	–	2
De-mystify	1	–	1
Respond to local need	1	–	1
Sub-total	15	–	15
Better than partnership	5	–	5
Total	43	2	45

phone calls from probation officers asking for our advice on how they should handle a case. (probation officer)

It gives to the probation service, I hope, a lot of new knowledge, regularly updated, on the drugs scene, taken in across the whole team of probation officers, who deal with a lot offenders who have some form of substance use. (substance misuse manager)

Practice was enhanced through participation in specialisation. All specialists believed their experience raised the quality of mainstream tasks. Rotating specialist appointments returned skilled officers to the field, while others learned.

I'm more aware of what using substances means to people than I used to be. I'm far more likely to be asking them questions which are relevant to that at the start, doing a report. I won't just ask them ''Well, do you use drugs?' I will go on from there. I'll break it down much more. I get far more interesting answers than I did before! (probation officer)

There is a drug using problem around and it's not addressed. But it's improving. The eighteen month rotation should help that. More probation officers will become more aware of when to bring drugs into the conversation. (substance misuse manager)

Specialists' involvement in training reflected both their increased knowledge and participation in multi-disciplinary work, from which many benefits accrued. One explained:

There's the bigger event of training magistrates. But then I would be looking at using a consultant psychiatrist and a clinical psychologist as well ... Magistrates aren't going to turn up for [a probation officer and social worker]. If you've got a consultant psychiatrist and a clinical psychologist they probably will turn up.

The high quality of specialists' work was a universal theme: "The main grade probation officers are all absolutely excellent, and I'm a paid up cynic! I've known a lot of probation officers in my time, but my staff operate at a very high standard."

The probation service's public profile was a crucially important aspect of in-house specialisation. Specialist projects had wider significance, beyond the probation service itself, in terms of public relations and contributing to the health of the community.

[O]ne of the neighbourhood watch members called in to congratulate the team on the way everything has calmed down since our night supervisors have taken a part in the neighbourhood watch scheme ... So it was very positive. I thought she was going to complain, but she just showered me with compliments!

We also run a licensees' information course, which is ... an information course for licensees on how to retail alcohol sensibly ... It's the first course in the country ... [I]t's called server training, which is widespread in America because bar owners have to have insurance to cover them against possible claims by victims of drunk drivers who have left their bar ... My predecessor went to the States to get trained in this. He came back and set it up. The [local] court makes it a condition of new licensees that they have to come on this course ... We run it because it's good crime prevention, it's very popular locally among the alcohol agencies ... You have to put a lot of work into getting good PR mileage out of working with offenders, but everybody loves this.

Influencing professional philosophy and promoting social work values were important:

> The biggest achievement is the shift it's made from being almost fundamental in its abstinence policy to a facility which is very structured, that has targetted an important group of offenders, that has put together a programme which other people come and make use of and it's gathering the expertise really to support people.

> My role in the clinic is trying to put forward social work values and get away from the medical model. At the moment I'm trying to influence prescribing policy. So I'm proactive in the clinic in terms of changing the way it works.

So also was demystifying perceptions of substance misusers, meeting a community need and influencing other organisations: "We had a recent exhibition which was targetted at a significant number of the major employers within the county."

Specialists offered unsolicited comparisons with partnership ventures, perceived as less effective methods of delivering services to offenders:

> Probation is quite specialist and unique. I'm not [being precious], but how could someone from a voluntary agency understand the complexities of monitoring court orders and statutory responsibilities? They don't have those responsibilities. The court isn't going to ask them to work it out. It's going to ask a probation officer.

> There will always have to be a probation service which is capable of working with people on their drinking. I don't see how other agencies cope with it...I don't think they've any comprehension of the numbers of people that the probation service deals with.

Poor local – and in one case national – provision strengthened the specialists' case: "It would be an incredible loss to the whole country. We get referrals from everywhere, it's not just a county resource. You don't need a crystal ball to see what our residents' futures would be without this place."

Criminal justice advantages

One advantage was transmission of expertise in criminal justice.

> We're now much more knowledgeable about the legal system. So when we deal with our clients, if it involves criminal activities and

Table 5.3 Criminal justice advantages of in-house specialisation as perceived by probation and substance misuse staff at in-house specialisms

Interviewees	Probation	Substance misuse	Total
Extend criminal justice expertise	2	2	4
Influence sentencers	3	–	3
Reduce risk of re-offending	2	–	2
Sentencing option	1	–	1
Total	8	2	10

> they're checking the possibilities for sentencing, for example, we're more able to give [accurate] information. (substance misuse manager)

One interviewee mentioned providing a sentencing option, but specialists saw wider potential for influence: "We've had a number of judges from the Crown Court here to explain [why we don't take conditions of residence]. That's been important in getting them to think about their own ideas about alcohol and what goes on here."
Specialists cited reduced risk of offending as an advantage:

> They need all the support they can get. They are at risk of re-offending . . . The fact that they go along and are supported in [the recovery] group makes re-offending less likely and raises the quality of their lives . . . At the family support group, we have the parents of two people who are currently on probation. Now I *know*, without doubt, that it did help them to cope with their problems . . . We have to think more and more in terms of preventing re-offending.

> Once your community credibility [is damaged], it's gone [forever] . . . We have a big responsibility, because the offenders that are referred here have different offences in their backgrounds . . . So we need to be clear that we're not putting anybody at risk, both within the hostel and outside, and that we have a way of minimising these problems.

Service delivery

The benefits of multi-disciplinary working were recognised at all types of project.

> It helps the drug and alcohol service with it's multi-disciplinary team . . . It provides the exchange of skills, the exchange of knowledge

Table 5.4   Advantages in service delivery as perceived by probation and substance misuse staff at in-house specialist projects

Interviewees	Probation	Substance misuse	Total
Multi-disciplinary working	6	2	8
Use skills	5	–	5
Access services	4	–	4
Reach client group	3	1	4
Flexible	3	–	3
Better service	2	–	2
Accessibility	2	–	2
Follow-up provision	2	–	2
Concrete resource	2	–	2
Positive about change	2	–	2
Helping clients	2	–	2
Effective	1	–	1
Innovative	–	1	1
Voluntary	1	–	1
Extend help to families	1	–	1
Total	36	4	40

between different professionals and allows joint working, which is imperative in this type of work. (substance misuse manager)

Probation staff could use their skills, often underestimated in the context of mainstream activity, to full advantage:

Over the years, possibly more by default than anything else, probation officers have learned on their feet. They have got a tremendous amount of knowledge about alcohol and about the criminal justice system. They're weighing these up constantly in their heads in a sophisticated way.

Access to wider services was created: "I've got the resources of the community drug clinic to link into, so I can refer them into the clinic and have them see a psychiatrist, blood tests. I've got so many more resources available to me." Services reached out to new client groups, including, for example, families of substance misusers. Two specialists commented:

[The substance misuse agency] has reached an area of the community which they wouldn't necessarily have reached if the secondment wasn't in place.

> I like the fact that it's within the criminal justice system. It's target-ting offenders who otherwise would never get past the first stage of [other] treatment centres.

Specialists further identified flexibility in broad based and adaptable services: "We're not a closed shop, we are open to change, we don't get bored with what we are doing and we do take on board ideas from outside." Offenders received a better, more accessible service, including opportunities for after-care: "We have maintained a significant number of ex-residents, assisted them to cope with everyday ups and downs when they leave. We have been successful in getting move-on accom-modation."

Developing a concrete resource was a source of pride: "When we first produced this [information brochure], I used to carry it around in my briefcase and take it out and look at it!"

Opportunities for optimism about offenders' potential for change was important:

> When you see people change, that is good. When you see people who are physically damaged move on and develop confidence and skills ... That's a good thing. You see people change, you see people man-aging differently, managing better.

A substance misuse manager saw the project's innovative impact: "It was unusual seven years ago to have a probation officer in the drugs service ... It's a flagship for the probation service..That was a great thing for them to do, and they should be applauded for that."

Personal gains

The particular programme or method of intervention gave specialists satisfaction:

> I like the package, the clear model that I've got. That's been a good feeling, a good achievement.

They applauded the opportunity for professional development.

> As a field work officer you don't necessarily get that many opportun-ities to do different things, to be creative ... Certainly that was one of the main reasons why I went for the post. To have an opportunity to develop things, plus being able to specialise in a particular area. It's brilliant.

Table 5.5   Personal gains from specialisation as perceived by probation staff at in-house specialist projects

Interviewees	Probation
Method	5
Professional development	3
Best of both worlds	3
New institutional insights	3
Challenge	3
Excitement	1
Fascination	1
Gaining credit	1
Personal autonomy	1
Integration into second agency	1
Variety	1
Belief	1
Total	24

Specialists experienced the best of both worlds. A substance misuse manager reflected this point: "We're getting two people in one. We're getting someone who knows the legal system inside out and someone who has been trained in social work, which is invaluable." Similarly, specialists appreciated the insight into another agency.

Excitement, challenge, intellectual stimulation and autonomy were lauded, and also positive feedback for achievements:

> I like being challenged. When I first knew I was going to come here and manage this project, I thought "It is a loser. There is no way that it can move from where it has been in the past to where I feel it ought to be. I'm presiding over it's future closure." But the more I've been here, the more possibilities I see. So I have a sense of vision.

> The credit that I've got from being in this position, because appraisals have said that I've built up relationships. That's been positive feedback for what I've achieved in a short space of time.

Specialists enjoyed the variety afforded by different styles of working and integration into another agency: "The worker is expected to do everything the team does, because it makes a very close team. I like that...I prefer to be a member of the complete team."

Finally: "I have a real *belief* in the value of (this project). For a long time before I was managing it, I could see its potential. I know that there are other people who see it is in a unique position".

Table 5.6 Benefits of in-house specialisation summarised in rank order

Benefits	All Interviewees	% of total comments
Advantages to probation service	45	38
Service delivery	40	34
Personal gains	24	20
Criminal justice	10	8
Total	119	100

As Table 5.6 shows, the advantages to the probation service were the most popular benefits seen to derive from in-house specialisation. This contrasts with the low level of organisational benefits identified at partnerships.

The problems of in-house specialisation

Problems were of four kinds: problems for the probation service; for the organisation of the projects; for service delivery; and the personal costs of specialisation. These are shown in Tables 5.7 to 5.10, with a rank-ordered summary at Table 5.11.

Problems for the probation service

One problem was mentioned several times: loss of individual professional identity. However, certain strategies protected probation service identity within a multi-disciplinary context. For example: full time secondments were reduced to half time, with specialist officers retaining a presence in their agency; frequency of rotating the specialist post was increased; or seconded staff focused on probation referrals.

> I was seconded full time once. It was a much easier job than [this one]... You lose touch with the agency that pays you. You have to work very hard at belonging to [the probation service] if you're at the

Table 5.7 Problems of in-house specialisation for the probation service, as perceived by probation and substance misuse staff at in-house specialist projects

Interviewees	Probation	Substance misuse	Total
Loss of identity	5	–	5
Generalists under stress	1	–	1
Total	6	–	6

[substance misuse agency] all the time…It's much harder work being half and half, but if I'm honest I prefer it, because this way I've got a foot in both camps and I belong to two teams. It's much harder work, but at least I do belong. If I went full time I'd lose my probation bit of me.

One specialist team manager recognised the challenge for management in protecting a valued specialisation while field staff were under pressure of mainstream work.

Organisation

Seconded specialists were burdened by their accountability to two agencies' bureaucracies: "Working for two agencies means almost double the amount of paper work, I've needed to learn a whole new set of procedures that apply to [the substance misuse agency]…so it definitely increases paperwork".

Two specialists struggled with culture clash:

There is a difference of opinion over prescribing practices. I feel very torn about this because I can see both sides of it…Prescribing practice [at the clinic] is for a decreasing programme over eight weeks. Maintenance is rare…The psychiatrist would say "I'm not an agent of social control…I'm here to keep people well. I'm a doctor." But probation officers would say they would like people to stay on a programme longer because it reduces their [illegal] use. As a probation officer I would like them maintained longer. As a drug worker I see the reasoning why they are not.

Table 5.8 Problems in the organisation of in-house specialisation, as perceived by probation and substance misuse staff at in-house specialist projects

Interviewees	Probation	Substance misuse	Total
Two bureaucracies	3	–	3
Culture clash	2	–	2
Staff changes	–	2	2
Reduction of specialism	1	1	2
Objectives unclear	–	1	1
Lack of consultation	–	1	1
Rota constraints	1	–	1
Bureaucracy	1	–	1
Monitoring	1	–	1
Total	9	5	14

Probation is very structured...[But at the clinic], clients are just as manipulative and difficult and abusive and sometimes worse than at probation, because at least here you've got that structure. But in the clinic you've got this unstructured and fairly volatile [atmosphere]. It's quite intimidating...I dislike the chaos in the clinic.

Practical organisation, paperwork and monitoring were frustrating: "I dislike the struggle of getting sensible evaluation that really means something...I'm not a statistician."

Perspectives of substance misuse staff differed. Difficulties associated with probation staff changes could extend beyond specialist posts: "The National Health Service has occasionally had changes in personnel at a senior level. But probation seem to do it more rapidly. If the rotation is going to be 18 months, it would be much easier for me if I had the same senior to work with for that period." Two interviewees at different projects were concerned about reductions in the specialist service. One substance misuse manager was not unsympathetic: "The probation service is obviously going through changes itself and they need to allocate resources where they see fit. The good thing about it is that they still see a need to put a resource into a substance misuse service." This manager thought the secondment's objectives needed re-clarification and was annoyed by management handling of the reduction: "The project is a great idea, but when change had to come, we weren't consulted. It just happened. That left rather a sour taste in my mouth."

Service delivery

Overload was specialists' most frequent complaint:

I don't know exactly how it happened, but suddenly I had a caseload of thirty and just didn't have the time to do the other things I was meant to do. That has been a big problem. Now I have to pull back and say "That's it. I'm not taking any more." I have to transfer certain cases, which is difficult because other [substance misuse] workers are equally snowed under.

Time management caused anxiety:

There are certainly problems in terms of time. No question about that. It's a big commitment [to run two groups each week]. Quite a drain. A pleasant way of working, but a drain.

Table 5.9 Problems of in-house specialisation in service delivery, as perceived by probation and substance misuse staff at in-house specialist projects

Interviewees	Probation	Substance misuse	Total
Overload	5	–	5
Time	4	–	4
Too small	3	–	3
Community care	2	–	2
Space	2	–	2
Practical house keeping	2	–	2
Difficult clients	2	–	2
Losing clients	2	–	2
Funds	1	–	1
Confidentiality	1	–	1
Drift towards coercion	–	1	1
Skills under used	1	–	1
Total	25	1	26

Being part time in both agencies. You've got limited time. I try to manage them as best I can... [but] time is very limited. You do get criticism: "We never see you, you must be skiving." It is quite easy to get lost. You have to convince people that you aren't lost, you are working, but it's a massive area to cover.

Unsurprisingly, therefore, specialists complained that projects were too small to meet demand. Physical space could be inadequate. Problems, particularly for residential projects, arose from community care and funding arrangements. Residential projects also encountered common practical housekeeping problems: "We don't have a housekeeper, we've got a cook who doesn't like cooking and a cleaner who doesn't like cleaning!"

Specialists were sometimes disappointed with the client group's uneven progress: "There are more instances of difficult clients and aggressive clients. I find that hard." Confidentiality could be problematic: "The understanding is that you keep your work [at the clinic] confidential... Sometimes I think officers find that difficult... but they have to take it on board." Another specialist thought that pressures in both agencies prevented full use of specialist skills: "Counselling skills are under-used. They are valued, [but under-used]."

One substance misuse worker raised the issue of "compulsory orders. There is definitely concern within this agency about that. I don't think it's the seconded probation officer's job to smooth them over."

Personal costs

Specialists were anxious about the many calls on their expertise, fearing to disappoint colleagues:

> A lot of my time and attention has been taken up within the hostel. It's harder for me to make the contribution we would like around the county, with the other drug and alcohol programmes for which I should be providing supervision. I feel stretched to do that.

Paradoxically, another source of stress was justifying the project, within the probation service or more widely:

> Where you've got something odd like this, you're forever bending over backwards to justify yourself. Really, generic probation officers in their own little rooms with their own little clients should have to justify what they do. But it's only people like us, who are doing a good job anyway, that have to do it, because we're seen as being unusual.

Uncertainty for the project's future was the only personal cost mentioned by a substance misuse worker. But for specialists:

Table 5.10   Personal costs of in-house specialisation, as perceived by probation and substance misuse staff at in-house specialist projects

Interviewees	Probation	Substance misuse	Total
Meeting expectations	4	–	4
Justifying project	3	–	3
Uncertainty	1	1	2
Isolation	2	–	2
Lose control	1	–	1
Total	11	1	12

Table 5.11   Problems of in-house specialisation summarised in rank order

Problems	All Interviewees	% of total comments
Service delivery	26	45
Organisation of specialisation	14	24
Personal costs	12	21
Problems for probation service	6	10
Total	58	100

That produces anxiety, because we can't turn to the staff and say their future is absolutely secure. I do know that the probation service will do what it can to retain everybody here. But it's about feeling valued, keeping the staff feeling that the work they do is important enough.

Potential isolation was an anxiety: "It's important for me to be part of a probation team. If I was on my own I would be isolated . . . [But still] I could sit at a whole team meeting and not be involved, because the focus is always alcohol." Reduced control over case management aroused some anxiety for a senior probation officer.

In contrast to the experiences at partnerships, Table 5.11 shows that at in-house projects issues in service delivery dominated over other types of problem. These issues predominantly concerned specialists' difficulties in coping with the demands on their time and energies. While organisation was not straightforward, it did not present problems on the scale experienced at partnerships. Problems for the probation service were few, largely connected to the need to protect specialists' professional identities and remedied by a variety of strategies.

Conclusion

Enthusiasm for projects' success infused all interviews. The absence of problems of role and service definition, referral rates and conflict, which beset problematic partnerships, was striking. The success of in-house specialisation, however, might too simply be attributed to confidence in professional security, which was challenged at problematic partnerships. Although this cannot be ignored, successful partnerships demonstrated that it was not insurmountable.

It was at specialisations, rather than at partnerships, that interviewees referred repeatedly to the probation service's public mission. The role of in-house specialisation was perceived more broadly than the delivery of special programmes to offenders. Rather, it encompassed a range of activities seen to enhance the quality of professional standards within the probation service, deepen its contributions to the health of the community, and foster relationships with other agencies and the public. Senior management's active support recognised this contribution.

Appreciating the value attached to this mission helps to explain some other issues. The striking diversity of in-house projects and, even more, the extent of involvement in services for non-offenders is best understood as a reflection of this vision of the specialist role. Improvements in services for offenders were perceived as products of wider investment.

For example, criminal justice benefits were identified as products of the extended sphere of probation service influence.

Such contributions were recognised by substance misuse staff. Benefits accrued to substance misuse agencies through multi-disciplinary working, reaching additional clients, access to criminal justice expertise and social work perspectives, and, indeed, through enhanced knowledge and practice within the probation service itself.

The experience of in-house specialisation also illuminates the absence of ideological conflict at partnerships, whatever their other difficulties. Despite the insistence in policy documents on the difficulties of reconciling harm reduction with the statutory role of the probation service, specialist staff experienced little or no such conflict. Their strategies for responding to their clients' difficulties in sustaining sobriety were similar to those described at voluntary partner agencies. There was little emphasis on coercion at most projects. Enforcement occurred in the context of activity designed to reduce punitive potential. In-house specialist projects thus demonstrated the ease with which the probation service accommodated contemporary ideologies of substance misuse treatment.

This analysis points to a vital role for in-house specialisation within the probation service. It is not, however, intended as an apologia for in-house specialisation as opposed to *successful* partnership. The balance which might appropriately be struck between in-house specialisation and partnership will be explored in the concluding chapter.

6
Treatment Under Coercion

Project A was established to offer an alternative sanction for offenders at risk of imprisonment. It centred on the appointment of a counsellor at a city-based street drugs agency to provide assessment and counselling as a requirement of probation.

Background to the partnership

The partnership at Project A grew from historical relationships between the probation service and a local voluntary organisation. Four probation officers, seeing a gap in local provision, founded the partner agency.

> This came about while we were on a course in the bar at two o'clock in the morning... [S]omebody said to us "If you're so concerned about the drugs problem, then why don't you do something about it?" (senior probation officer)

Funded by the government pump-priming initiative, the agency opened in 1986 with a Co-ordinator and three counsellors, offering a telephone help-line, drop-in advice and counselling. Participation in the first needle exchange schemes stimulated growth of work with injecting street users. Three detached workers were appointed to extend needle exchange opportunities to those unable or unwilling to approach the project. Needle exchange thus established the agency as a service for the "hard to reach". Later, posts were dedicated to working with prisoners and women, including street prostitutes. Community care arrangements provided accreditation for assessments.

At the time of study, the agency employed 15 staff, supported by volunteers. Probation officers continued to serve on the management committee; a senior probation officer, one of the founders, was chair. The Co-ordinator saw an important relationship between policy priorities in the fields of health and crime:

> There's a new kind of agenda...I think we're likely to see health [priorities] subsumed by criminal justice [priorities]. People will become complacent about HIV, which is what has driven drug service provision to date, and will be into community safety and reducing crime.

The partner agency's origins, continuing relationship with the probation service, specialist "niche" as a service for the "hard to reach", ongoing work with prisoners and the Co-ordinator's perspective on the shifting policy emphasis indicate openness to criminal justice interests. However, an initiative with an explicitly coercive structure was not introduced lightly. The agency's relationship to the criminal justice system was discussed periodically after 1989, when the prison specialisation developed. It was recognised that specialist drugs services should be involved in alternatives to custody (Advisory Council on the Misuse of Drugs 1989). In 1990, an application for SUGS funding to develop an alternative to custody for young offenders was unsuccessful.

> The probation partnership work for us meant crossing a line. Before that we'd always worked on a voluntary basis with clients...But we've had a debate within the organisation [for some time] about whether we wanted to cross that line and have a close relationship with the criminal justice system...We decided that, on balance, we wanted to go for it. We needed to try it and see whether our fantasies about the impact it might have on our service were real or not. (Co-ordinator)

The partnership proposal, however, emanated from the probation service's senior management, acknowledging the active relationship with the agency.

> [The Home Office] had already got a lot of schemes up and running, but then...they decided to devolve money to areas. As the centrally funded projects finish up, that would release more funds which would also be devolved to counties. So we got...a windfall, back in the beginning of '93/94. The Chief Probation Officer rang me, knowing my interest in the drugs project, and said would we like a worker

to work with the probation service on diverting drug using offenders from custody... That's how it came about. (senior probation officer)

The project began in January 1994 with the appointment of a full-time drugs counsellor, funded by the probation service.

Aims and principles of partnership

Project A's aims married criminal justice and substance misuse policy priorities. Firstly, it aimed to augment community supervision opportunities through implementing Schedule 1A of the Criminal Justice Act 1991, which provided for substance misuse treatment as a requirement of probation. This was an attempt at "tariff stretching" for offenders facing custody.

> It's specifically targetted at people who would otherwise be going to prison. So we're not talking about theft of a packet of bacon from the local [grocer]. We're talking about mid-to-heavy-end range of offences. People who otherwise might not fall into the community penalty band, but are edging their way towards the inevitable custody. (senior probation officer)

Substance misuse staff were familiar with this professional terminology of the probation service for describing such concerns.

> We receive funding to employ one member of staff who is offering structured counselling and other interventions as a community penalty. We are particularly targetting a population who have a high risk of custody. We've been very clear about that. We don't simply want to move people up the tariff. (Co-ordinator)

Secondly, the programme followed the substance misuse agency's harm minimisation philosophy. This offered the counsellor a distinctive role in offender supervision:

> Although the probation service has a harm reduction policy for drugs, that's not all they are there for. It's *all* I am here for – to reduce harm and improve the quality of life.

Thus, the primary objectives of both partner agencies were twinned, providing focus and rationale to the project. The enterprise, therefore, was clear to both probation officers and substance misuse staff in terms of its tariff status and practice approach.

> I regard it as a good challenge. It's about making relationships with unmotivated clients and confronting that resistance. We're used to that. [The counsellor] is seen as one of the counsellors. He goes to the counselling peer supervision group and he can bring his cases and get support... [H]is stuff isn't different except for the type of people he gets. (substance misuse worker)

> It's about chaotic drug use, how much it is an underlying factor, and how motivated they are, as much as seriousness. It's about suitability and seriousness, and offering a package to keep them out of custody. (probation officer)

The programme's compulsory nature structured the approach to confidentiality. Probation officers were routinely informed of offenders' attendance, thus fulfilling their statutory accountability. Equally, the content of contact remained confidential, thus honouring the partner agency's ethos.

> For the substance misuse project, which has a range of services, many of which are aimed at harm reduction... it's important that offenders, as well as any other client, feel safe to use the full range of services. So that, where somebody may be telling their probation officer that they're not using any more, if they are still using, then [the substance misuse agency] will want them to be using the needle exchange scheme, or whatever primary health care is [needed], for their own safety. So it's very important. (senior probation officer)

> It's not a problem for me because it's an absolute, really. I report on attendance. That's [all], unless [clients] tell me that they want anything else out... It's not an issue at all, just because I have an absolute blanket on it. Nothing goes out of that session. (counsellor)

Project A, then, combined aims of supplementing high-tariff sentencing options and minimising drug-related harm. Principles for translating these aims into practice included compulsory substance misuse treatment, targeting high tariff offenders, and regulating confidentiality.

Management

The Assistant Chief Probation Officer discerned changes in the probation service's approach to partnership:

> Before we had grant aiding powers, we couldn't give money, so we gave people, via secondments. At that stage, the emphasis was on helping worthy community groups which had some common interests with us, but not necessarily an identity of interest. It was very much about our wider community investment... Then we got cash awarding powers. We were probably quite naive in the way we approached this. We went and bought services which we provided before in-house. In parallel with this, we inherited the SUGS schemes, some of which we had little to do with and no great interest in... We were naive in not taking responsibility for ensuring that... the Home Office... represented our interests. Now... we have become businesslike... We now negotiate to tailor what they deliver more closely to what we want.

This Assistant Chief was excited by the prospects opened up by a business-like, commercial approach: "Within a strategic framework, it's opportunistic and entrepreneurial. I know what my partnership strategy is and who my key players are. But at times specific funding opportunities will emerge which we can respond to." For example: he negotiated with a building company for provision of training places for probationers; by locating a community service project making articles for community groups within a carpentry school, he planned that offenders "will get qualifications as a by-product of punishment".

This approach encouraged a robust view of relationships with partner agencies, although the Assistant Chief saw no reason for his perspective to foster insensitivity. For example:

> I suspect there may be issues around confidentiality [for the substance misuse agency]. But if they want to go into the market place, and do see us as partner, they're going to have to be responsive to our needs. Equally, we need to be sensitive to their agency ethos. We may need to write in some form of protocol.

The senior probation officer endorsed this perspective: "I don't think the voluntary sector can afford to say 'That doesn't fit with our ethos'. If you're in the voluntary sector you have to say '*That's* what you want? *We* do that. You want grommets? *We* make grommets.' You can't just sit and say 'We don't do grommets. We only do thingies.' "

The Assistant Chief's partnership strategy aimed to purchase opportunities to enhance the service's interventions with offenders. The opportunities for employment training, described above, exemplify this approach to accessing services distinct from probation officers' mainstream activities. Where partnership potentially replicated work which probation officers were competent to undertake, the Assistant Chief sought complementarity, rather than substitution of effort:

> With our primary direct service delivery partnerships, we [originally] said "You employ staff and offer direct work with offenders." Part of the supervision was bought out. Now, we say "You employ staff and we will work alongside the employee to deliver services together"... In future it will look more like joint working... with both the probation officer and the [agency employee] working in collaboration.

The senior probation officer appreciated this shift: "[The counsellor's] role is changing, partly as a result of evaluating his work and partly as a change in emphasis since [this Assistant Chief] took over the partnership role. He's not about to buy in probation officers' roles... But he sees partnership as much more about partners enabling probation officers."

The vision of partnership thus embraced a business-like, entrepreneurial approach, designed to create access to opportunities for offenders beyond the skills and resources of probation staff.

By virtue of his dual interests, the senior probation officer was a natural champion for the partnership enterprise. Easy communication stemmed from the "inter-agency osmosis" achieved through the mediation of a party who was active in both organisations. Thus, Project A developed in conditions of mutual familiarity of concepts and interests between the partner organisations. As far as the project itself was concerned, the senior probation officer explained:

> I try to keep a little to the sidelines of all this anyway, because I don't want to be involved in operational issues in the [partnership]. It's not my role as the chair. That's [the Co-ordinator's] role... although I am irretrievably identified with the project for obvious reasons.

As the last comment indicates, there were tensions in his role:

> I try to stand one pace removed from [the project], because I see that as being something that [the Assistant Chief] organises direct with

[the Co-ordinator]. I try to maintain my role as being chair of the committee which oversees the work of the whole [substance misuse agency]. But inevitably I do get dragged in . . . I tend to be seen by my colleagues as being responsible for all this, so that when people can't get [the counsellor] on the phone, they come and say, "Hey, I can't get hold of [him]", as if I could do something about it. Or as if somehow it's my fault, or a shortcoming of my management of the project. [But that] may be saying more about me than it does about them.

This tension required an even-handed approach to the interests of both agencies, as was observed during a meeting of the senior probation officer's field team, attended by the counsellor. There were stresses both within the team, which wanted additional assistance with drugs issues, and for the counsellor, in terms of competing demands from other teams. Pressure mounted on the senior probation officer to make representations for additional use of the counsellor's time. Observing that this might be counter-productive, through appearing to exploit his link with the partner agency, the senior probation officer encouraged the team collectively to produce a statement of need for training, using a resource with local knowledge, to be submitted alongside information about the substance misuse agency's competence and costs. This suggestion produced general agreement that training would increase team members' confidence and self-reliance in drug issues.

Service delivery

Three features distinguished service delivery at Project A: the programme structure; coercion in treatment; and the contribution to supervision of offenders.

Programme structure

After receiving a referral, the counsellor offered an assessment interview and thereafter met jointly with the client and the probation officer preparing a pre-sentence report. Given a successful conclusion to these meetings, the probation officer proposed the making of a probation order containing the additional requirement of attendance at the substance misuse agency for drug treatment. When an order was made, the offender was offered weekly appointments, usually for three months, or a total of twelve sessions. The supervising officer was informed of attendance.

Structured programmes require management to prevent drift from their intended outcomes, or confusion between participants. Project A's programme was controlled by several mechanisms. The counsellor explained the project's aims and procedures at preliminary meetings with probation teams and magistrates, thereafter distributing leaflets to probation offices, courts and clients. Referrals were channelled strictly through the probation service. On one occasion, an offender was sent to the project directly by the court. The counsellor negotiated an outcome to this referral which did not jeopardise the offender's position, while clarifying the appropriate procedure and its justification with all agencies. On another occasion, the counsellor was offered a fee by a solicitor for confirmation that he was in contact with an offender of whom he had no knowledge. Procedural correctness, therefore, protected both the overall professional integrity of Project A's relationship to the courts and the individual counsellor.

Probation officers considered the personal suitability of offenders for referral carefully. Most could think of clients they would not refer, including chaotic or unmotivated individuals, entrenched users and people needing alternative services. Accurate targetting of high-tariff offenders was fundamental: all referrals reached a designated threshold on a measurement of offence seriousness. Notably, the offender mentioned above, who was referred directly by the court, fell far short of this threshold.

The meeting between the counsellor, probation officer and client was used to insure against subsequent conflict by establishing that the client understood the commitment to treatment, and clarifying the boundaries to confidentiality. Probation officers generally saw confidentiality as a strength of the project. One even recognised a significant advance: "I'm happy about it being confidential, because I get to know if someone turns up. If it's a voluntary contact, I don't even know the counsellor's name!"

Coercion in treatment

Probation officers appreciated the "tariff stretching" aim of Project A. Most endorsed the use of a compulsory requirement: "It's important for the court. It's important as a sentencing option, so we can keep more people out of prison." Some also perceived a therapeutic advantage in coercion, through strengthening motivation to comply with treatment:

> I've mixed feelings about it...I've seen it working when, had the condition not been there, I'm pessimistic as to whether people would have done so well...If someone elects to do it, that's a powerful sign

of self-help. But the condition can be of benefit if they're not able to organise themselves. So it can be a prop, not a stick.

Because of public protection. We're not just there for [offenders], we have to consider the public. They are pretty anti-social, and drugs are not really an excuse. They have to start taking responsibility.

Coercion was a serious issue requiring individual handling, which perhaps explained the attention to personal suitability for the project.

It could be a disaster if people feel they're pushed into it. You can set them up to fail. They have to be ready, they have to want to do it.

[O]bviously it's something the court feels is important, it's preventing people from being banged up. But by making it compulsory you're almost saying that you can force people. And you can't . . . So part of me thinks it shouldn't be compulsory and then you would know who is motivated and who is not.

The counsellor perceived coercion as a tool for engaging clients in treatment:

Although there are difficulties working with conditions, the fact that this is new means that a lot of people I see would otherwise be serving short sentences and not dealing with their drug use at all. So it adds something to the armoury.

He also saw a positive effect of partnership in introducing new clients to the substance misuse agency. Project A continued the agency's tradition of working with the "hard to reach":

The scheme does definitely bring new people in. Because they're forced to [come]. There are some people who have had contact . . . with the [agency] before they come to see me on the condition, but the majority of my clients are new to [the agency]. In a sense, they have to be. If someone were in full counselling with [another counsellor] here, I would refuse the condition on the grounds that they shouldn't have to come to see me as well . . . [But] that hasn't happened yet.

The counsellor initially assumed that offenders would be threatened into compliance by their brush with custody. Learning that offenders saw things differently, he adopted a more flexible approach:

It's not an alternative to custody. It really isn't. It's a specific scheme that operates for those people who are high enough up the tariff to warrant a custodial sentence. I know that sounds like semantics. But [the idea] an alternative to custody doesn't matter to most of the people that I work with. If they're going to go down...they'll deal with it. So the whole [idea] of me saying there's a threat behind it [is nonsense]. They see it as another thing along the line that they can do...I treat all the people who come to see me as voluntary clients, because they *are*, to the extent that they turn up.

This perspective also evolved from observing probation officers' reluctance to use enforcement as a primary method of problem solving:

The probation officer may be supervising an order when, if he or she had done the pre-sentence report, he or she wouldn't have recommended the condition. So in a sense they have been coerced as well.

Realising that breach proceedings were relatively rare, the counsellor adapted to changes in clients' lives affecting their compliance, negotiating enforcement issues individually with supervising officers:

One client came for two sessions and then got a job. I don't work outside office hours. The probation officer said that was OK, he would continue working with that. The client then came back to see me a few months later because he was feeling vulnerable to relapse, and access to his daughter hinged on that. Now I call that a successful completion, and I don't tell the probation officer exactly how many sessions he's been to, because I don't want to get the probation officer into trouble. I don't know if the probation officer had told his senior what he was doing.

Flexibility, however, did not preclude a robust, pragmatic perspective on enforcement: "I don't see a breach as such a big deal. It's a review, really, of where we [have reached]. It will pull some people back into line, or get them out of my hair. That's good for me, because I'd rather have a space for someone who wants to use the programme rather than fill it up with dead weight."

The contribution to supervision

Substance misuse workers' familiarity with criminal justice issues, and the counsellor's absorption of perspectives observed among probation officers, raised the question whether the partner agency was effectively "colonised" (Abrams 1981) by the probation service, forfeiting its separate identity.

The counsellor distanced himself from the role of supervising officer in his relationship to the courts. He resisted attempts to involve him in reporting to the courts on clients' progress. While a probation officer, in such a position, would be accountable for an objective appraisal, the counsellor identified with his agency's principle of acting only supportively towards clients: "I don't want to set a precedent, because then everybody would ask me to go and talk in glowing terms about them. Because I would not actually say anything bad about someone in court."

Moreover, the counsellor considered that his relationship with clients was privileged. Disclosing information would compromise his position as a confidential counsellor. Thus: he declined a request to attend court for a client who disclosed a relapse during a period of deferment; he refused to attend proceedings concerning the care of a female client's child, believing that his testimony "would ruin our counselling relationship." In a sense, other professionals were themselves protected by the substance misuse agency's principles, consequently failing to appreciate the extent of potentially damaging disclosures by its clientèle.

Unlike probation officers, the counsellor paid little attention to recorded offence histories: "I'm not that interested. I'm only really interested in knowing whether they can get through an order." Nevertheless, he was not spared from incriminating disclosures:

> [V]ery often they haven't told their probation officer the full extent of their offending as it relates to drugs. For example, a lot are dealing, and it's a problem for them, but they are not going to tell their probation officer that. So it doesn't necessarily give me a clear idea of what's going on to get a list of previous convictions, or the probation officer's knowledge.

The counsellor described his role as helping people "to achieve a high quality of life. If that means they are trying to achieve a high quality of life within their drug taking, so be it." Indeed, his counselling drew on insights into clients' predicaments afforded through sensitive information:

> It's purely the knowledge of the drug [issues] which gives me that expertise... It could be in terms of where they raise their money, or their lifestyle. For example, someone was referred for being caught in

possession of speed and cannabis. I couldn't get a hold of this guy, where he was at, what was going on, and he wasn't coming in. So I was telling him I probably wouldn't see him any more. Then he told me that he was a speed dealer who operated out of a particular pub. Suddenly it all fell into place... He had a real drink problem and was trying to cut down by not drinking till after six, when he went to the pub.

There was a guy who had been dealing at a fairly low level and was getting pressure to move up a notch. He was frightened of getting involved with the bigger dealers, shifting larger amounts... So it can be a major part of their lives, such that what else they are talking about doesn't make any sense until you know that.

The counsellor's understanding of his role legitimated his practice within the partnership enterprise:

My main aim is to try to get people through the order. I suppose that's what probation officers want as well. So I guess I'm trying to achieve the same as them, and there may be people who are ready to talk about their drug use at that time. Pursuing a harm reduction policy, if people can change their drug using practices in a way which helps reduce their offending and improve the quality of their lives, then that's a good thing. So I can and do talk about illegal things with them.

Harm reducing interventions were thus significant milestones. Following a client's departure from the agency, the counsellor marvelled: "He told me he's using just two needles a week! So by the end of the week he was really hurting himself. I told him 'We can help you with that! We give needles to people here, that's what we do!' He's been coming here for all these weeks!" Asked if this was a case of naivete, or ignorance of the substance misuse agency's services, he reflected: "Yes, it was naivete. But it was also denial. Because now he's got a supply of clean needles, he will see how much he's using. Now he's got a sharps bin for disposal and it will be there in his bathroom. That will tell him every time he sees it that he's got a drug problem. So it's a big step."

Probation officers reported successes among the counsellor's interventions:

A lot of them really like going there and say they get something out of it. The clients seem to be open about [their drug use]. A few have told me they've reduced. I know one who goes for clean needles regularly.

Very positive. He struck up an instant relationship with [the counsellor] and could identify with a lot of it . . . He got more than half way. That was pretty good quite honestly. He had reduced even though his partner had not.

Probation officers perceived enhancements to their practice, most commonly in terms of expertise in specialised knowledge and therapeutic skills. Other important attributes were the confidential, independent and non-authoritarian status, and "street credibility" of the partner agency. Several officers enjoyed an additional perspective in their own case management:

It's good to have an outside view. Maybe we don't see so clearly if we work with our clients all the time with no external input.

I would not do in-depth drugs work . . . There is a difference between trying to sort out deep personal problems and managing a probation order. It's maybe not possible to do both. It's not always safe for them to talk in probation.

Problems

Problems for Project A were of three types: the move to coercion; the impact on historical relationships; and workload management.

The move to coercion

A review of Project A after six months of operation reassured substance misuse staff that the agency's overall image was unchanged, and that clients who were initially coerced subsequently remained in contact voluntarily. Moreover, coercion was recognised as a more generalised issue in agency practice.

Although I think we crossed a line with the probation partnership work, it is a myth to assume that people contact a service like this on a purely voluntary basis. Most people come here because someone or something is giving them grief. Compulsion is just another step down that line. (Co-ordinator)

We have a contract system for supervising the withdrawal process for people on a script from their GP. We manage the bad stuff for anxious GPs. That's to do with working with unwilling clients, where they have something to lose and we can trigger [its] withdrawal . . . So it's not a new concept, to be working with unwilling clients. (substance misuse worker)

Equally, there were limits to tolerance of coercion. For example, on government proposals to remove the legal requirement for an offender's consent to probation, one substance misuse worker observed: "That's a disaster. If it goes ahead, I think we'll refuse to do partnership work. The whole drugs field will refuse. Because we won't work without consent."

Project A was effectively "quarantined", contained within the role of a specialist counsellor. Thus, coercion of clients subject to legal sanction intruded only indirectly upon the daily practice of other staff.

> I think if I hadn't been in post and it had been [introduced] people would have been really twitchy. But it was brought in on the sly, really...I would like to hope that we could reach a point where partnership work could be devolved throughout the agency. [But] I don't think there's the will, because there are still fears about how it will "contaminate" – that's the word that was used when I came – the other work. (counsellor)

Although quarantine facilitated Project A's successful absorption into the substance misuse agency, it created particular stresses for the counsellor. Firstly, he struggled initially to balance authority and care in his practice. Unlike probation officers, working within an environment in which this focus was constant, the counsellor's terrain did not command much attention from his colleagues:

> I've changed. When I started off I was very clear that the whole issue of compulsion...was not my job. My job was to do counselling. It was the probation officer's job to enforce the order. [My plan was] to play the good guy, they could play the bad guy. [But] when people started not turning up, I was...getting quite heavy with them and giving them a hard time...It was just horrible. I'd fallen into the trap of becoming a pretend probation officer. It was pissing me off, it was pissing them off, and they were getting it from both ends. It was a bloody nightmare! I don't know quite why I fell into it, but I did...I wasn't doing any work with that at all. So after discussing the supervision with various probation officers, I went back to my original tack...It's been working much better since then.

Ironically, then, flexibility was modelled by probation officers, who shared a professional culture based on negotiating resistance, or, perhaps more mundanely, were moulded by long experience of offenders' shortcomings. The counsellor appreciated this common ground: "Drug counselling can be isolating work. I have a kind of colleague if I get on with the probation officer, who I can work alongside. Most of them are really supportive. We work well together." However, it also added complexity:

> The problems, for me as an individual, have been to do with boundaries... I get people to sign contracts to say that they'll attend, and the National [Standards] apply to their attendance here. I was thinking, "I've got clear boundaries. Two misses and you get breached." It hasn't worked like that, and operating far more flexible boundaries for people has caused problems for me in terms of stress, by having to work things out with individuals. Things are far more individually tailored to both individual probation officers and how clients are actually doing.

Concentrated work with offenders was notably stressful and short on rewards. In the case of the client who confessed to relying on two needles per week, the counsellor's sense of achievement was evident. This was not only harm reduction, in terms of safer drug use, but also meaningful progress for a wary client. Reflecting on the counsellor's predicament, others observed:

> He's got a disadvantage with his clients, because they don't turn up in the first place. It's getting hold of them. It can be demoralising working with that kind of resistance all the time. We all like variety. We get bored doing the same thing all the time. [He] is working with resistance all the time. (substance misuse worker)

> A problem for the partnership is the success rate. We only send hardened clients! So it's not a good success rate. I think [he] is used to it now, but it must have been dispiriting at first for him. As probation officers we're used to that... Getting one through must have seemed like a miracle. Our clients aren't easy. (probation officer)

At Project A, then, the move to coercion was managed through mechanisms which protected the partner agency's ethos, revealed similarities with its other services, and protected staff who might oppose direct participation. However, the project's "quarantine" exposed the counsellor to a concentration of resistant clients and an isolated struggle with authority and care.

The impact on historical relationships

Historical relationships between the probation service and the substance misuse agency were affected by three issues: a threat to established links; bureaucratic control; and internal changes in the probation service.

Home Office instructions to withdraw probation service representation from management committees of partner agencies were a severe blow. The voluntary agency owed its existence to pioneer probation officers. The senior probation officer was insulted:

> I dislike the fact intensely that [the partnership] threatened my position in [the substance misuse agency]...I was very angry and very upset and very resentful that the probation service, which I've given twenty years of my life to, would do that to me...All [the probation service] has given us is twenty grand. It spends that on paper clips! That they would then require me to resign and give up ten years of endeavour and investment, just [for] one bloody worker. Had we known that was going to happen, we might have thought twice about taking that particular post in the first place. The four probation officers who are on the committee constitute a large portion of it. Three of us have all the history of [the substance misuse agency].

The Co-ordinator echoed this sentiment:

> Our expertise on our management committee is largely based in probation officers, who originally set up [the agency]. So if we were to lose them, we would lose a lot of our history, continuity and expertise. If that circular had pre-dated the supervision grants budget, we would probably have said, "We don't want the money. We'd rather keep the probation officers, thank you very much."

The probation officers resolved to remain on the committee as private individuals. This move, supported by a sympathetic Assistant Chief Probation Officer, stabilised existing relationships for most practical purposes. However, a question-mark remains over the probation service's involvement after the eventual withdrawal of these pioneer personalities, in the absence of official endorsement for representation on management committees.

Bureaucratic control was somewhat contentious. Notwithstanding the Assistant Chief's enthusiasm for partnership, the probation service's bureaucratic control of Project A aroused irritation.

Most staff come here on a straightforward contract. [The counsellor's] contract is far and away the most rigorous. The probation service has chosen to call it partnership, but I call it purchasing. It's not really different from a health authority purchasing a service from us. But it's very much more rigorous and controlled... [W]e weren't told [by the health authority] to get 500 people through the needle exchange, but [the counsellor] has [a throughput measure] written in [to his contract]. (substance misuse worker)

Echoing the senior probation officer's comments above, irritation was connected to the size of the probation service's investment.

It's a bigger deal to them because they are such a small organisation. If the health authority is spending £25 million on a hospital, they're not worrying about our drugs contract... It's as if they're doing us a favour, when I think it's the other way round. There's no other agency round here to do it anyway. (substance misuse worker)

This interviewee preferred a different approach: "The health service is the major lifeline to the project. There should be more joint funding between the health service, social services and the probation service. They should see that health, social and criminal outcomes aren't separate. They should be more ready to fund core services rather than special services."

Monitoring and evaluation presented particular problems. The probation service adopted a standard monitoring form for all partnerships in which the generic performance indicators were incapable of measuring activities specific to particular services. The counsellor complained: "It's not showing up the work that I'm doing and the work that my clients are doing. Good stuff that's actually [happening]. Because it's the same monitoring that [a motoring project] would get. So there's no mention of drugs in it!"

Recognising this, the probation service agreed that the counsellor develop service-specific performance indicators. However, it was wryly observed that clients who appeared as failures at Project A, usually also failed under probation officers' supervision, but were not so counted.

Internal changes within the probation service rebounded on inter-agency relationships. Following budget cuts, eight posts were deleted within one year and major restructuring of field services ensued. Probation officers were pre-occupied with the implications of these changes. These were inauspicious times for partnership work.

Things are in such a state of flux. People are changing functions, roles, caseloads. I wouldn't be surprised to find that affecting partnership quite negatively. There's a general feeling in the probation service that someone has pushed the pause button. It's about surviving in the service. Referrals to outside agencies have fallen away. (senior probation officer)

The conjunction of establishment shrinkage in the probation service and partnership development was unfortunate:

I really do feel the danger of looking at partnership in isolation from other change. There's the information technology costs, the cash limiting, the National Standards. From probation officers' point of view there's their own incompetent managers! Why can't we protect them from change and maintain their environment as it was? There's a risk of scapegoating partnership, which is only a part and a symptom of other changes. (Assistant Chief Probation Officer)

Notably, no probation officer here blamed the partnership enterprise for the service's plight. However, the probation service's predicament strongly affected the counsellor:

Morale is low, probation officers are very angry and depressed. So that's going to be a problem. But because probation officers' positions are going to change, I'm probably going to have to re-market myself to those people [in the positions] it seems best to speak to.

Workload management

Probation officers most frequently complained that Project A was inadequate to meet demand. The counsellor could not cope with demand for his services.

Certain factors strengthened this issue. Firstly, the counsellor was mandated to offer a county-wide service, increasing both demand and time pressure by necessitating travel to outlying areas. Secondly, the counsellor imposed a ceiling on his caseload: "I know from experience that in order to maintain good links with probation officers, and to do good work with individuals, fifteen is the absolute maximum. We set twelve as a maximum initially, but because I was reacting in a knee-jerk way and couldn't say no to probation officers and couldn't keep a waiting list, I got up to twenty. That was [totally unmanageable]."

Asked how he thought this compared with probation officers' case-loads, the counsellor explained: "Oh, I know. I felt embarrassed about it at first. But I see people weekly for an hour. Sometimes I have days out [for other commitments], but I've still got to see them all on a weekly basis. So I might have to see four in one day. That's four hours pure counselling in one day, if they all turn up. That leaves three hours for all the other [stuff] I have to do, such as assessments and meetings. Probation officers won't see everyone for an hour, or on a weekly basis, and they generally won't be counselling."

How should the project bear the weight of popularity? Three options were under consideration. One was to move to a groupwork structure. An experiment, based on voluntary attendance at a group held in a probation office produced a good response. However, the counsellor foresaw problems which might cancel the apparent cost-effectiveness of shifting to groupwork: "I would have to reduce my client load to eight and then start assessing for the group. To start a group with six or eight people, I will have to assess about twelve. I can't do it all at once... Groupwork was really a response to the pressure of individual work. I was overly enthusiastic as a result of [a good experience]."

Another approach was to suggest that courts defer sentence for three months in cases appearing appropriate for the treatment requirement. During this period, the offender would attend the substance misuse agency's "drop-in" service for support. This strategy offered the dual advantages of reducing pressure on the counsellor and testing offenders' motivation. However, given Project A's continuing popularity, the immediate reduction of pressure on the counsellor would presumably be short-lived; the strategy might instead produce a large "waiting room" of clients requiring entry to the programme after deferment. Effective removal of Project A's "quarantine" might also become controversial, in terms both of probation service "colonisation" of the partner agency's resources and of the requirement to report on attendance at a service based on voluntarism and confidentiality.

A third option was to shift the counsellor's role from direct service delivery to consultancy. The counsellor thought this was a constructive approach: "It would be a waste of the last eighteen months if I wasn't able to pass on what I've learned to other [substance misuse workers], and to other probation officers. I would see my role as more of a consultant at policy and strategic level as well as practitioner. I'd like to see some training on drug issues and ways of working with [users] for probation officers."

Reflecting on the workload predicament, the counsellor observed: "[You get] a taste of what the work is like and what expertise is needed. Then you can't deal with it all, so you start to give it back to [probation officers] and help them." As one probation officer remarked, however, this would be a paradoxical outcome to the partnership enterprise, particularly in the light of the Home Office's declared aim of contracting for supervision services. The counsellor linked this irony to a general issue for service providers: "We've talked about this – protecting funders from the reality. We ran out of needles on the needle exchange because we used too many too soon. And the [issue] became to move budgets around and fill the supplies from another budget. We were asking why did we do this? Why don't we tell the funders we've already used the money?"

Each of these proposals, beyond their specific disadvantages, raised the potential for drift from Project A's original aims. As a programme identified with specific criminal justice provisions, the project risked losing its clarity as a distinct sanction for high tariff offenders. As an exercise in harm minimisation, it risked losing the unique contribution to supervision offered by a drugs counsellor in direct service provision.

Conclusion

Project A illustrates a special form of the probation service's contribution to the wider community, in the pioneering creation of a new agency. The marriage of the primary objectives of both partners was more than a democratic nicety. It legitimated the delivery of harm reduction services to high tariff offenders via an arrangement which protected the professional integrity of two separate organisations.

At Project A, the potential sensitivity of clients' disclosures was a stronger theme than at other case study projects. There may be two reasons for this. Firstly, as will be seen, its distinctive client group indicates a likelihood that significant drug-related offending would emerge in a focused confidential relationship.

Secondly the counsellor's sustained attention was required to manage his obligations towards the substance misuse agency's guarantee of confidentiality while fulfilling a role connecting him to statutory systems of control. The factors underpinning Project A's success testify to the difficulties of maintaining the integrity of structured, high-tariff programmes for vulnerable offenders.

7
The Statutory Team

Project B was an in-house specialisation centring on half-time second-ments of three probation officers to statutory substance misuse teams within the area. Specialists took forensic referrals within the statutory teams, provided training, advice and consultancy to probation officers, and covered substance misuse elements of the service's intensive group-work programmes.

Background to specialisation

Project B originated in 1988 in a "reverse partnership": probation officer secondments were initially funded by the voluntary sector. Charitable funds from a local association for offender resettlement covered salaries for two full-time secondments to statutory multi-disciplinary teams in the county. The project's success brought an extension to a third year's funding.

Pioneer specialists divided their time between different substance misuse teams in the area, undertaking assessment, casework and train-ing. An emphasis on developing work with prisoners was partly a legacy of the project's sponsorship source. Overall, however, seconded officers were absorbed in to the general work of the multi-disciplinary teams.

In 1991, when the probation service resumed responsibility for those salaries, the project's popularity was such that a third secondment was instituted, enabling each specialist to join one statutory team. The charitable organisation continued to fund their clerical support. Resumption of financial responsibility for specialists created direct links between the probation service and the three District Health Authorities operating the host substance misuse services, leading to service level agreements for each secondment.

This process of formalisation clarified relationships between specialists, their host statutory teams and the probation service. One statutory team manager observed "a shift from a sketchy, quite amateurish attempt to define the project to a much clearer sense of mission. Like [the] health [services], probation have to give a much clearer and crisper account of themselves to justify the project."

Several consequences flowed from this. Firstly, the role of secondment was refined, focusing exclusively on forensic referrals. Thus, seconded officers became specialists, not only in substance misuse within the probation service, but also in criminal justice within the multi-disciplinary teams.

Secondly, secondments were reduced to half-time, deploying specialists within probation teams for the remaining time.

Thirdly, a job description was produced, defining expectations of substance misuse specialists in terms of fulfilment of probation service aims and objectives. For example, while earlier documents described a broad contribution to multi-disciplinary substance misuse services, the job description defined the purpose of work in partnership with other agencies as enhancement of supervision programmes. The earlier emphasis on work with prisoners disappeared, although not precluded from specialist duties as generally defined. Instead, the job description emphasised provision of structured groupwork for offenders under supervision.

Finally, clear lines of supervision and management accountability were developed. Specialists belonged to the probation service's "Resources Team", which provided groupwork programmes throughout the area. While senior staff within the multi-disciplinary teams provided casework supervision, primary organisational accountability was managed by the senior probation officer responsible for that team.

> [It's] very important, because a part of the concern was that the probation officers in these secondments might have begun to become... distant from the probation service. Because I am now based for part of the time in the probation office, and because all the people I see are people who have been in trouble with the law, then I am clearly rooted in the probation service. (specialist)

Specialists' professional identification with the probation service was a crucial justification of its continuing investment in the project. The senior probation officer explained that early specialists developed new careers:

Now one of the things the probation service [noticed] was "Oh, dear, we don't get these people back. We train them, we're paying their salaries to be out there and then we lose them." ... [S]o they want to make sure that they're getting their investment back.

Aims and principles of specialisation

Two aims remained constant throughout Project B's history, apparently fundamental to the enterprise: enhancement of specialised provision for offenders with substance misuse problems; and pursuit of effective multi-disciplinary relationships. At all phases of Project B's development, multi-disciplinary work was regarded as crucial to achieving enhanced specialised provision. The pathway to this was routed through secondment to the statutory teams, which combined a range of professional expertise, including psychiatry, psychology, nursing and social work. Secondment thus brought the probation service to the heart of multi-disciplinary endeavour.

> One of the main achievements is being able to use the total knowledge base of the multi-disciplinary team to help the probation officers really increase their understanding of the issues ... The secondary part is building partnerships with people from different disciplines, really working at *how* to work together. (senior probation officer)

Nevertheless, protection of the probation service's professional interests gained importance at both organisational and individual levels, highlighted by the reduction to half-time secondments. At the organisational level, specialists' exclusive focus on forensic referrals, deployment within teams and participation in groupwork programmes provided a visible return on investment.

> The symbolic idea was that the probation service could feel that it still had the resource, that it wasn't losing the resource to a community agency. Also ... if the probation officer were more visible to the probation staff, actually working alongside the court team officers, then the quality of the work and the rate of referral would be high. I've not had any problems with that compromise at all ... I think that's been stunningly effective. (senior probation officer)

At the individual level, specialists endorsed the importance to the project's health of reinforcing their professional identity:

Because we work with offenders and our role is to minimise harm to the offender and to the community, to try to encourage change to reduce the likelihood of offending, it's a very clear brief. I work happily within that. I've always felt comfortable working with that criminal justice structure.

Specialists also believed that their unique contribution to the multi-disciplinary teams was rooted in a distinctive professional identity:

The way in which I work is that I'm a probation officer first and foremost within that team. That's what I offer to that team. Therefore, it makes sense for me to pick somebody up who is involved in the criminal justice system as I have a better understanding of how that operates.

All my work is probation work, but some of it is done via the multi-disciplinary substance misuse team. But all the people I see are people whose use of drugs or alcohol has got them into trouble with the law, which is very important because that's the probation service's justification for being involved in this work.

Thus, in-house specialisation at Project B evolved through pursuit of two aims: the enhancement of specialised services for substance misusing offenders; and effective multi-disciplinary working relationships. Increasingly, the principle guiding achievement of these aims was the protection of the probation service's professional identity.

In this job I'm doing some of the most important work that I have done as a probation officer. Because not only am I able to use the knowledge and expertise from the multi-disciplinary team in dealing with probation clients, I'm also able to pass that on to probation colleagues and act as an important point of liaison between the probation service and [the statutory team]. So, yes, to me it's a very important job. (specialist)

Management

Project B was initially practice-led, by pioneers who developed multi-disciplinary relationships. Later, senior management became proactive in moderating their legacy, roused by resumption of financial responsibility and anxieties about probation service funding.

Although management-inspired change is commonly unpopular, the restructuring of Project B was well received. Not only specialists appreciated their clear professional identity; their presence within probation teams rendered them visible, accessible and responsive to field officers, evidenced by an enthusiastic referral rate. Applying the principle of protecting the probation service's identity, in conditions of economic constraint, thus enriched professional activity.

> Even if the cash limit is better than we are expecting, we face increasing costs and have little money to develop new programmes. When there is a tension between maintaining specialisms and maintaining core work under financial and workload pressures, then it is really important to ensure that the added value of the specialisms is demonstrable. (Assistant Chief Probation Officer)

The Assistant Chief perceived efficiencies in specialisation in a multi-disciplinary context:

> It means we have three probation officers who are very up-to-the-minute in terms of substance misuse, who are likely to be using a level of skills with immediacy. It enables us to refer more swiftly to other agencies – for example, to get a community care assessment – because they are there in the multi-disciplinary team and we don't need a separate protocol for how to access them... *Our* probation officers respond at *our* pace. If we went to partnership [elsewhere], we would have to include a response-time element.

Specialists' role and tasks were clarified in detail: a job description for their posts; a service level agreement with District Health Authorities; and a protocol on disclosure of information by the probation service to linked agencies. Each of these documents defined the probation service's expectations and obligations.

Statutory team managers appreciated this management interest, notwithstanding their disappointment at the reduction of secondments. One team manager, dismayed by the difficulties of many partnerships between probation services and voluntary organisations, identified Project B's success in organisational terms:

> Generating workload, confidentiality and so forth have never been issues [for us]. This is a distinctive aspect of a relationship between two statutory agencies. Many interprofessional issues

don't arise. All of these practical difficulties have never been there for us... We're bound by statutory instruments, so we know clearly where we are, we have a clear service level agreement, we've never had a referral deficit, confidentiality is not an issue. People bring their own professional boundaries to the multi-disciplinary team.

Statutory team managers invested in the success of revisions to the project:

I saw the move as inevitable. Trying to hold on to a generic role was rather naive. If you want to justify the post to the probation service or Home Office, you need to show it has value to them. Equally, it has always been clear that although we are a multi-disciplinary team, we all have our specialist roles also.

Within these arrangements, the senior probation officer's role was vital to the project's health, bridging relationships both between senior management and specialists and between the probation service and statutory teams. This was no mean feat: "The agencies in the three areas are quite different. The three health authorities are quite different" (senior probation officer). To accomplish it, she participated in meetings of area-wide and local multi-agency committees concerned with substance misuse, and some meetings of each statutory team. Resources Team manager was a distinctive role:

In some ways it's quite different really, from, for instance, the Court Team senior's role, which is much more about the monitoring of cases. I have a lot of briefs, but the way I work with them is much more developmental rather than supervision based.

Service level agreements clarified the different and complementary responsibilities of statutory team managers and the senior probation officer.

My supervision of the three workers is not case by case. They have clinical supervision within the multi-disciplinary team. So my supervision with them is much more about management of workload issues rather than case work. Because they work outside here a lot, I spend a lot of time telling them about corporate issues. (senior probation officer)

In assisting specialists to manage their accountability to different agencies, the senior probation officer steered a diplomatic course between uncomfortable considerations. For example:

> We had an instance recently with [one specialist] where I needed to reduce her involvement in the weekly clinical meeting, just because she was so overloaded with referrals that she couldn't see people quickly. At a time when we were trying to evaluate the project in a way that shows its value for the probation service, if one thing had to go it couldn't be her rapid response to referrals, much as I see meetings as important learning. So then I had to negotiate with the multi-disciplinary team to reduce her contact, which didn't go down terribly well. But I do expect that to be part of my role, so I am not complaining about that. That's what I would expect to do.

Judgements could be stressful:

> At times one can feel [anxious about] what is going on with this case? Is there a risk issue? Should I know more about it? That then very much depends on the worker, how much trust you have in the worker, confidence that they're doing the job as you hope they would be.

Nevertheless, statutory team managers appreciated the senior probation officer's handling of tensions:

> The things I see as being in [the specialist's] interests are the same things [the senior probation officer] sees. I suppose there might arise an issue where we don't agree, but it's never happened and I don't know what it would be. The only time I can think of when there was a difficulty was when the probation service told the substance misuse specialists that they had to take on extra court duties to relieve some other probation officers who were going to run a sex offender group. The issue was, *that* time was taken from the time they spent in their substance misuse teams. But that was a dictum from on high. It was never an issue between [the senior probation officer] and me, because we both felt the same way about it.

Significantly, Project B held increasing value for senior management, through its prescient adaptability to policy development. For example, the probation service's endorsement of harm minimisation achieved immediate reality through specialists' presence within multi-disciplinary teams which explicitly pursued such strategies. Later, government requirements for new local Drug Action Teams comprising senior members of relevant agencies necessitated participation by the Assistant Chief, who happily found support in the established representation of the senior probation officer on substance misuse committees in the area, and accumulated specialist expertise. Consequently, he found preparation of the required service strategy document not excessively onerous:

> My discussions with [the] health [authority] suggest that if I go to a Drug Action Team and ask how best to spend this money, I get a lot of support for the arrangement that we have. If I could spend more, I would probably seek to assist to develop other services rather than the specialism. But I can't. My first priority is to maintain the part-time specialist posts.

Service delivery

Service delivery at Project B was characterised by "principled pragmatism", the contribution to multi-disciplinary teams, enhancement of probation officers' practice and public relations.

Principled pragmatism

Unlike the two partnership projects, coercion and confidentiality were not core issues at Project B. Although not unimportant professional considerations, they did not prescribe practice but rather were approached from a perspective of "principled pragmatism".

Offenders under supervision remained the responsibility of the field officer, with whom, therefore, enforcement decisions resided. Forensic clients arriving at the statutory team by alternative routes were treated as self-referrals. Thus, specialists regarded all their clients as voluntary. Coerced co-operation with substance misuse treatment was not popular, although there was no general antipathy to special requirements in probation orders within the area. Indeed, the Resources Team existed to deliver intensive groupwork programmes.

> As a service, we really don't have any problem with the idea of conditions. Virtually all our groupwork is done on conditions...because our experience has been that, within our structured approach to offending behaviour, conditions seem to be more effective than

voluntary. We actually don't get people along if it's voluntary. (senior probation officer)

Nor was there resistance in principle to special requirements for substance misusers. For example: "We have a flourishing drink-drivers' group as a condition of probation...It's usually co-led by one of my substance misuse specialists and a field probation officer. We usually get 85 to 100 per cent completion rate, whereas it's more like 60 to 67 per cent for other groups" (senior probation officer).

Simply, no gain was anticipated from using special requirements in practice with individual clients. If anything, the prospect of specialists' involvement in enforcement was considered counter-productive and more trouble than it was worth.

If you start getting into breach with somebody, based at a drug and alcohol agency, then clients may be more reluctant to approach an agency like that in the future, or other clients may be less likely to approach as well. Also, if you're getting into breach and a client pleads not guilty, then you become almost a prosecuting officer. That's not an appropriate role for a substance misuse worker. (specialist)

Breaching is an enormously bureaucratic process. No one would relish it. Our substance misuse specialists don't get into that. (senior probation officer)

Field officers echoed this "principled pragmatism":

Treatment conditions are difficult to enforce. How do you make them [do it]? It's very difficult. I don't often propose conditions.

I'm against compulsion and conditions, but the reality is sometimes people won't get out on parole without conditions. (The specialist) isn't scared to tackle people who are reluctant.

The people we work with have different needs. We often have the resource available when the client isn't ready. If we can refer when the need is there and the resource is available, that's good. We shouldn't have to wait for the client to offend again and get a probation order with a condition!

Confidentiality was rather more contentious, although this derived almost entirely from the legacy of full-time secondment, which one specialist experienced before being reduced to half-time, with some consequent transitional difficulties. The senior probation officer was emphatic: "I can't see any point in having an internal specialist if you don't feedback and communicate important information, particularly given that the supervising officers rarely have to act in a way that will be unconstructive for the client." Consequently: "I've worked very hard on confidentiality, to ensure that my substance misuse specialists are operating on the same level as all other probation officers. Now they're OK on that. We don't seem to get into the messes that [arose before]."

Indeed, specialists expressed robust views on confidentiality:

> Clients sometimes have less problem with confidentiality than professionals ... I say to them that as I'm a probation officer, if a supervising officer is involved it's helpful that we can discuss some of the work that I'm doing with you so that we can give you the most appropriate service. But I've never had a client who has said that I can't speak to their probation officer.

> I would be much more concerned about the possibility of probation information being passed to other hospital departments, because [my] substance misuse team is a hospital department. I would be much more concerned about, for instance, probation files which revealed previous convictions being passed to gynaecology or maternity. I've instituted checks to make sure that doesn't happen.

Contribution to multi-disciplinary teams

Specialists' sense that they offered a unique professional contribution was endorsed by statutory team managers:

> Probation is a very important contribution, because the training is distinctive, the perspectives are different. It's very measured and balanced. It breaks us from the chains of our health model. For example, bringing the implications of a recognition of the offence to a case.

> Probation officers bring a sense of clarity that we sometimes lack, a sense of boundaries that we sometimes lose sight of. They're very good at the risk aspects of the job – risk to clients, to staff, to families. They're good to consult on criminal justice issues and practice.

Team managers found that the immediacy of this contribution offset the inexperience of newly seconded specialists:

There is a specialist drugs knowledge base and some new skills. In assessing someone for the post, you would see that this is a person with a strong learning curve and commitment. That's borne out by the speed with which they learn once in the post. Also, since the probation officer comes with different skills to contribute, such as group-work, then there is a payback for us while they are developing in post.

We've had three people who have been very gifted, very enthusiastic and contributed to the team in various ways. I see this as a field where people are trained up to a high level of expertise and then take it back to the probation service while another person comes in to do the learning. There's a very steep learning curve. We've never had a problem about it.

They agreed that the project brought new clients into treatment:

It generates an additional workload. People refer here because they know that [the specialist] is a probation officer. But [her] clients may also access parts of treatment by the rest of the team which they wouldn't have reached before.

Common sense dictates that the secondment brings some new peo-ple in. For example, a 13-week waiting list does de-motivate a lot of people. The faster response to forensic cases may keep people moti-vated. So it may engage people in the service who otherwise might drop out. It may also attract probation officers to refer by illuminat-ing the service and making it easier practically and psychologically to refer.

The biggest single asset has been the connection it makes between our service and the probation service. The probation service gets an opportunity for clients coming through the criminal justice system to gain access to treatment. I'm quite confident that those clients were not reaching us previously.

They also agreed that forensic clients presented particular challenges:

[A]lthough we can deal with very difficult people, the probation officer's clients present with greater difficulties generally in terms of complexity, chronicity and severity of problems.

They tend to be more difficult clients. That flows from the first premise that they're forensic clients, and not trivial ones. From that flows the likelihood that they're more entrenched, less controlled users, and more damaged people – more manipulative, argumentative and difficult to engage.

Enhancement of probation officers' practice

Probation staff at Project B repeatedly reported disappointment with local non-statutory substance misuse services. Indeed, specialists withdrew from early attempts to extend into two voluntary agencies, feeling that they, as representatives of a statutory organisation, or their clients, as poorly motivated candidates for treatment, were unwelcome. Field officers were similarly critical:

> I was a volunteer counsellor with [the statutory team] and we saw people who had been to voluntary counselling organisations. They had no boundaries. We want to make them independent, not dependent. I don't think voluntary organisations aim for that quite so early. There's a high level of supervision in [the statutory team] and [the probation service]. Clear boundaries.

> I learned by mistake. A client had a condition of his order to attend [the voluntary agency]. But they said they didn't think he was motivated, although he had been assessed by [the specialist] when she was part of the agency... So now I refer everything to [the specialist].

> The voluntary organisations locally are very reluctant to talk to probation. It's ironic as we place a very high importance on confidentiality... [W]e don't always *want* to know what's going on exactly. It's easier to work with [the specialist]. You don't have to set up new ground rules every time.

By contrast, field officers praised the enhancements offered by specialisation. Firstly, integration of specialists within probation teams promoted access and information exchange:

> There's fast take-up, regular liaison, and he keeps us up to date.

> I always refer to him as a "database". He can direct me to books and so on. He and his colleagues are a real information base.

> I've noticed a big improvement... [since] the job had to be evaluated, reassessed and modified. [The full-time specialist] was at [the statutory team] mostly, inaccessible. He was divorcing himself from the

probation service. So he didn't see himself as dealing with offending and he went at their pace.

Secondly, specialists' mandate to support probation officers encouraged flexible and diverse approaches, including consultancy and joint working:

It led to a series of sessions with [the client] and his wife. [We] met them for a total of seven sessions to explore their co-dependency [on alcohol] and their relationship . . . to strengthen them as individuals as well as a couple.

It runs alongside what we do. We can work together on some things. They have a specialist input on others. Sometimes we see them together, sometimes separately and then discuss it. So it's flexible.

[The specialist] was overloaded so he helped me to help [the client] at first and then came to work with us on anger management.

Thirdly, offenders' access to the range of services offered by the multi-disciplinary teams was facilitated:

They have a foot in the door to other services, it's a speedy way to other agencies. It's useful for child protection too, there are social workers there. So the multi-disciplinary team is good. We can link into other services within the substance misuse team.

The client turned up very much the worse for wear, and a risk to himself. I remember it was good that [the specialist] could ring up and get him admitted to hospital immediately.

[The client] had always resisted groupwork. [The specialist] offered one-to-one work and liaison with the doctor. But now he's committed another offence and he's in crisis. He has said he will go along to the relapse prevention group there.

Fourthly, specialists integrated substance misuse and criminal justice expertise. The quality of assessments and interventions was consequently enriched, boosting confidence in problematic decisions:

He was quite chaotic in the beginning . . . Part of my probation order proposal was for him to see [the specialist] while he was on a reducing methadone prescription. At first he failed appointments. It looked like he'd got his prescription and didn't want to know. So we gave him a breach interview...and said we'd withdraw the prescription. From then on he responded well. Some people need that structure.

The fact that he is a probation officer means that he understands the primary role of the probation service. So he helps to formulate work plans...from the pre-sentence stage...[to] whatever the disposal.

She did work on shoplifting as addiction behaviour with one of my clients.

I wondered what to say to the court. I discussed it with [the specialist]...It clears your head to discuss it and how to get over to the court what the best disposal is. I wanted one-to-one, not the drink-driving group, and it was his second drink-driving offence.

Field officers recalled successful outcomes of specialist intervention, even in entrenched and apparently intractable cases:

Success! He went to a detox twice. The first time was not a success. But the second time...was very successful for him...He finished his order. The last I heard he was doing well.

He spends long abstinent periods and then relapses. It's good for someone who was done for drink-driving and was always five or six times over the limit. His pattern of drinking really has changed.

He has given very positive feedback about contact with [the specialist]. He writes very thoughtful letters to him and to me as well. He has found it hard going, he's highly motivated not to go back [to prison].

He modified his drinking significantly. He got on really well with [the specialist]. He gave me copies of the controlled drinking manual he'd done...He'd modified his drinking so much [the specialist] thought he was cured! But I knew his background.

Field officers appreciated specialists' detailed knowledge, skills and focus on substance misuse:

[The specialist] keeps you to task. Clients can talk you out of it.

Having [the specialist] frees you to do other work with clients... We're both interested in court welfare work, (which) has a knock-on effect on substance misuse in this case, so we work together on both issues.

Specialists also offered formal training. For example, one specialist trained field officers in motivational interviewing.

Few clients were considered unsuitable for referral to Project B. This partly reflected the flexibility of the service, for, as officers pointed out, advice and consultation was available when clients did not meet the specialists. Reasons for not requesting direct contact included considerations of the client's motivation and level of substance use, but were also informed by pragmatism and the need to moderate specialists' workload:

> She has to limit her time, so I couldn't refer all those who have substance misuse problems. So I refer acute clients.

> Only because the length of sentence is too long... I have a lifer at the moment, lots of alcohol-related offending and hospital admissions. But he's just gone inside. It would be useful to have [the specialist's] input into the post-sentence report, but he just hasn't time.

> I have sixty or seventy people in prison. If I referred them all to [the specialist] he would be swamped.

Six clients talked about their experience. All averred that they had not accessed treatment facilities previously, apart from one who recalled an unsatisfactory encounter with a therapeutic community: "I walked out after four days. I couldn't handle all those blokes hugging each other." All spoke with graphic approval of their dealings with the specialists:

> You can't con her. She tells you point blank. I like people telling me straight. The first time I met her I thought she was hell on wheels. She's still hell on wheels, but she's brilliant.

> I haven't been drinking for 67 days! That's down to [the specialist]. It's the first time I've stopped. She's friendly, gives good advice, made me do a drink diary chart and I cut down. Then I just stopped.

> What he's got to offer is what he has offered me. He's given all the help in his power. I never needed anything else more than that.

> It would be useful if the police advertised it. When the police picked me up that night, they could have given me a leaflet. People could

really be thinking "I need help". GPs are useless. They should know about this place, but some don't think it's worth sending [people like] me along.

Public relations

Project B's popularity at the multi-disciplinary teams testifies in itself to a masterly public relations coup. Moreover, as central policy drove inter-agency integration at local level, the Assistant Chief remarked: "You can see a developmental programme opening up. I need to take account of that context. We're working on a wider front, therefore, in terms of inter-agency initiatives."

Public relations, however, had broader significance for the probation service's contribution to the local community. It emerged unprompted in interviews with probation staff, that specialists were appreciably involved in discussions about their work with sentencers and community groups. Such opportunities to raise awareness, not only of substance misuse problems but also of the probation service's contribution to crime prevention were regarded as vital promotion of the service's ethos, goals and achievements.

> It's another value of the service for me that the three workers spend a lot of time speaking to community groups...You've got to look beyond the statutory work they do with high tariff offenders at the public relations and crime prevention work they're doing. At an early stage trying to educate the public, being prepared to go and talk to the public. I'm proud of that, because they've done some good work. (senior probation officer)

> This job enables me...to promote the work of the probation service, which I think is important. I've spoken on quite a few public platforms in the last year – parents' evenings, crime prevention panels, I've spoken to women's groups, I've spoken to a scout group, I've done a radio interview, I've taken part in a Home Office video. I enjoy doing that. I enjoy having the opportunity to promote the work of the probation service in this field. I'm pleased about that. (specialist)

Testimony to the quality of this endeavour was offered, again unprompted, by a field officer:

> I've seen [the specialist] working with magistrates, enlightening them. There is energy running up and down the room from the

input he gives. He makes them think differently, gives them greater insight. He's a good public relations person, for probation and for substance misuse.

Problems

Difficulties for Project B derived from professional allegiance, workload and insecurity.

Professional allegiance

Although the project's health was crucially linked to strong professional identification with the probation service, certain disadvantages were nevertheless connected to this allegiance.

Statutory team managers were aware of tensions which arose uniquely for probation officers within the multi-disciplinary setting. There was a potential for isolation, despite the strong support systems of team meetings and individual supervision within both agencies.

> It's a difficult job to do. I see probation as being quite a tight knit community. It's hard for a probation officer to be isolated from their internal professional support. The probation officer is the only one in the multi-disciplinary team whose profession is represented only by them. (statutory team manager)

> It's potentially quite isolating being the only probation officer in the team. (specialist)

Notwithstanding the general agreement of professional perspectives on confidentiality, one team manager acknowledged unease:

> Both social workers and probation officers that come to this team seem to have to grapple with issues of confidentiality. In nursing and health care we have very strict rules of confidentiality, but there's a looser approach by social workers and probation officers. I would never phone up the police or probation about a client who disclosed an offence. But the probation officers feel compelled to make contact. That's some sensibility that they bring with them [about their professional identity]. They remain feeling very connected to that. I have raised this … that I'm not happy about a probation officer sitting in our multi-disciplinary team meetings and hearing names and information which they then feel compelled to pass on.

Measured against the standard of principled pragmatism, specialists were not indiscriminate in their disclosures to probation service colleagues.

> I've never had a refusal. They see it as in their best interests. I don't give every detail of what they say to me. I give information that the probation officer needs to know to be able to plan work with the client. So I don't go into every detail about what they're using. I don't give irrelevant information such as what contraceptives they use. (specialist)

Nevertheless, choices had to be made. One specialist acknowledged a pragmatic dimension to the issue:

> There is a difference between the "independent" drug counsellor and a probation officer. A confidentiality which I lack to some degree. I have to tell my clients that there are no real secrets. That has occasionally presented a stumbling block. But the downside of the independent arrangement seems to me to be an inferior referral rate, because the probation officer lacks confidence because he or she isn't receiving feedback.

Specialists' professional allegiance also influenced their working priorities. It was difficult to disappoint the expectations of their colleagues in the field:

> Saying no is something that doesn't come easy. Saying "That is a piece of work I cannot undertake." I find that hard.

> One of the most difficult things to do within a job like this is to say to probation officers "I'm a limited resource"... I can't see every client that's referred because of resource implications.

The predicament resulted in prioritisation of probation service referrals over other forensic cases, an uneasy accommodation carrying certain disadvantages. Potentially satisfying opportunities for effective intervention were missed.

> How do you prioritise a referral? That's quite a difficult one. My standard, stock response when [a specialist] asked me this was [that] we have to deal with statutory ones as priority. So someone about to come to court, [that's] fairly urgent, that's got to be first priority.

Second priority needs to be people on supervision. The third priority probably needs to be resettlement cases...The fourth and least priority should be people who are referred voluntarily...But then, of course, [the specialist] turned that on its head by saying "Yes, I know that's our standard response, but the voluntary clients...are by far the most satisfying to work with because they're motivated." He does a small piece of work with them and its really satisfying for both parties. So this might be the statutory priority list, but it's not necessarily the workers' satisfaction priority list. (senior probation officer)

Prioritisation thus resulted in a concentration of relatively intractable cases.

When I first started I accepted anyone who had any forensic at all, but then I came under pressure with probation officers making referrals, so I realised that I needed to give priority to those first...Both I myself and my agency are moving to time limited work, but the ones I tend to take on are the more entrenched, more difficult-to-manage clients who need the multi-disciplinary team. (specialist)

Workload

The exclusive focus on forensic cases meant that specialists did not participate in multi-disciplinary allocation, carrying their own waiting lists within the statutory teams. Nevertheless, probation service clients enjoyed a "fast track" into all services. The specialists' faster response, in accordance with probation service expectations, effectively increased the speed of client access to the multi-disciplinary team. As one team manager remarked: "The pay-off for keeping the probation service was a kind of fast track access to substance misuse services via the probation officer. But that does have a systemic impact on the team."

Field officers did not fully recognise this. One team manager recalled the impact of a gap between one specialist's departure and another's arrival: "Probation officers were ringing up and asking us to see someone. They were *amazed* to be told it would take 12 weeks, and also that they would have to work ongoing cases." Such encounters with the general waiting lists led to diminishing referrals to the statutory teams during absences of specialists.

Field officers' appetites for their specialists' services seemed insatiable:

If we refer...we hope that they will do that particular piece of work. But sometimes...all they do is come back with suggestions for us to do it. It's a selfish way of looking at it, as they do get lots of referrals. But we have heavy workloads too!

I'm not satisfied, really. Generally, it's inaccessible because of over-load. One has to assume it's resources. You get back the waiting list answer. Maybe they've by now rationalised that as a good thing! But it's a serious point of resistance to working with people. She has to spread herself too thinly.

A specialist recalled needless anxiety on arrival in post:

The post had been vacant for eight months when I took it up, so my initial concern was that I might not get any referrals...I've had 131 referrals in the [first] year, spread evenly over the year. I'm faced with the fact that I've been too successful. I've had too many referrals, because I've currently got more than I can deal with.

Workload prioritisation, in these circumstances, went beyond accommodating professional allegiance and job satisfaction, to hard decisions about time management.

I could fill every working week three or four times over. So the frustration is deciding what to do and what to leave. That's one of the most difficult parts of the job. (specialist)

The pressure of work, because you've got so many people who have expectations of you. You want to deliver...The job could be enormous...Where do you have the cut-off line, because you can't keep taking on huge numbers of clients. You can't have a caseload of a hundred. (specialist)

They've had to work incredibly hard since they've been in post... They're working absolutely to capacity. They have to prioritise constantly how many multi-disciplinary meetings they can go to and how much groupwork they can assist with here. That's why most of our supervision time is spent in managing those priorities...It's all about management at the boundaries. They are working very hard. (senior probation officer)

Insecurity

The Assistant Chief was cautiously optimistic about Project B's survival, at least in the short term: "The great problem is the cost. This has been brought down by making [the specialists] half-time. As long as the relationship with the field teams is maintained at a high level, it is manageable." Nevertheless, financial constraints resulted in perpetual insecurity.

> My Assistant Chief is very supportive of the project. I've tried to give a lot of information to show its value. I don't think anyone queries its qualitative and its practice value . . . It's purely and simply a cash issue. A probation cut in cash limits. At the very heart of it, it is more important for someone to be writing pre-sentence reports for the court than to be making assessments on substance misuse . . . I have to accept that. That is the core of the service. (senior probation officer)

This plausible argument might be challenged. For example, specialists were required to prioritise their contribution to pre-sentence report preparation, presumably because their assessments were considered vital to effective proposals. Set against a general waiting list of three months within statutory teams which did not prioritise courtroom deadlines, Project B offered a means to achieving a core task. The alternative was to default on an integral aspect of that task, as defined by the probation service itself.

This argument turns on the definition of a "core" task, and whether substance misuse assessment is integral to effective pre-sentence investigations, or an optional enhancement. Similar questions may be raised about "core" supervision tasks, in the light of the "fast track" into treatment of high need and high risk offenders via specialisation. As one statutory team manager impatiently remarked:

> I have heard [the Chief Probation Officer] say "We're really over-stretched with community supervision and we've lost three members of staff to the substance misuse teams." I said "Actually, you've gained three multi-disciplinary teams to help you with your clients."

This problem concerns the visibility of specialisation in the accomplishment of high priority duties. The project's recent heightened visibility to *management*, in terms of its value in fulfilling government policy objectives, was thus instrumental in shifting its defence from qualitative practice enhancements towards accomplishment of service responsibilities.

> I've done four years in this job . . . In every year there's always been this issue about the future of the specialism. But we've worked so *hard*

on this over the last two years, to make the substance misuse specialists integral to their probation teams. We've been helped by the
White Paper and its emphasis on multi-disciplinary work on substance misuse and targetting drug-related crime. The Assistant Chief
Probation Officer is sitting on the multi-disciplinary committee. He
needs the substance misuse specialists now to implement the initiatives. (senior probation officer)

Project B also produced direct savings for the probation service. For
example, one specialist was trained in motivational interviewing,
funded by the health authority as a member of the statutory team.
Subsequently, the specialist offered training to field officers: "When I
worked as a field probation officer, the majority of my clients were pre-
contemplative or contemplative. So motivational interviewing is the
most useful skill any probation officer can have."

These observations add irony to Project B's precarious position: while
contributing directly to the fulfilment of government drug policy, it was
still thwarted by restrictive definitions of task accomplishment which
regulated the cash limited funding formula of the probation service.

The strain of perpetual insecurity was more than an organisational
issue. It was an individual burden for specialists.

To cope with the possibility of it being limited, reduced, axed. To try
and prepare the three workers for that. Because I feel passionately
about the secondments, but it's also about these three individuals'
career paths. It's the uncertainty and how to prepare for that. (senior
probation officer)

It's not just the uncertainty, but also the devaluing of the person.
You're not just saying that the secondment isn't important. You're
saying the person isn't important and the specialism isn't important.
Which is patent nonsense when you look at all the research. (statutory team manager)

Conclusion

Project B illustrates the value attached to, and benefits derived from the
probation service's active contribution to local communities. It also
demonstrates mechanisms through which the probation service not
only protected its professional identity but clawed back its investment
by re-distributing specialist expertise. Despite the periodic resurgence of

insecurity, Project B represented a cost-effective mechanism for accessing and delivering substance misuse treatment services to probation service clients. It will be seen later that the case file survey confirmed an exceptionally high throughput of clients at Project B.

The enthusiastic endorsement of proactive management to define and regulate the terms of the project underlines the significance of complaints about the quality of management at problematic partnerships. Moreover, at Project B, senior management was rewarded for its efforts, not only by staff appreciation, but by substantial advantages in responding to policy development and enhanced inter-agency standing.

Project B arose in a context of dissatisfaction with the quality of local voluntary substance misuse services, coinciding with the existence of highly professional statutory multi-disciplinary teams. It successfully capitalised on a local opportunity to maximise the probation service's access to high quality treatment for its clients. In this environment, partnership development for substance misuse services would have been a misdirected investment.

8
Social Crime Prevention

Project C was a financial partnership established in a large rural area to provide outreach workers who offered a confidential, open access service of advice, counselling and support on drug related problems to the community.

Background to the partnership

The substance misuse agency at Project C had a complex history. Established in 1986, it was based within the substance misuse department of a hospital. Its budget, controlled by the Health Authority, was almost entirely dedicated to training volunteer counsellors, whose main role was to offer free confidential advice to individuals and families and to operate a telephone contact line. The agency's ambiguous status and poor visibility, resulting from its funding arrangement and location, contributed to inadequate use of its services and consequent wastage of trained volunteers.

In 1992, responding to growing prevalence of street drugs and recognition of a number of injecting users in a particular locality, one volunteer began to offer information, advice and opportunities for needle exchange on an outreach basis. This initiative heralded a major shift in the agency's role towards specialised provision for street drug users. Increasingly regarded as a main provider of substance misuse services in the county, and promoted as such by the area's multi-agency forum on drug issues, the organisation achieved independent agency status in 1994, using its new budgetary control to appoint a Development Officer and obtain community based premises which promoted its public visibility and accessibility.

Project C was rooted in an eruption, in 1993, of local concern in one town about heroin use. Following a public meeting at which the scale of the problem, and fears of a drug-related crime wave were hotly debated, the Chief Probation Officer used probation service funds to create a temporary outreach post, to which the pioneer volunteer was appointed. During the three months of his appointment, this worker contacted some 40 active users in the town. Thereafter, expansion of outreach became a popular theme in county-wide multi-agency planning for drug misuse services, and first priority in the development plans of the newly independent voluntary agency.

However, notwithstanding temporary support from the Health Authority and Social Services Department, financing the enterprise remained problematic until the opportunity arose for Home Office funding via the SUGS scheme. Home Office grants permitted employment for two years of two full-time outreach workers, continuing the original post and creating another in a second location. The success of outreach in these areas encouraged the Health Authority to agree the appointment of a worker for a third location.

Project C is thus an example of networking in partnership development. It origins lay in the multi-agency deliberations taking place in the wake of local alarm about drug problems, which endorsed a volunteer's pioneering initiative.

> The post came into being because people in the local community had got together. Social services, probation, health, teachers, police had got together because of a concern...I was on one of the working parties, which was looking at drug misuse issues. I sent a note to the senior probation officer, [which] he received at the same time that a circular came round from the Home Office about funding for particular projects. Because, in our experience, most of the people that come our way have got problems with drink or drugs, we thought if there was any chance of getting funding for an outreach worker, then that was good. That was in the interests of our probation clients and would help others in the community as well. (probation officer)

Viewed retrospectively, the project's development appears a logical, stepwise process. However, the extent to which its evolution derived from coincidence and opportunism was not lost on those involved.

> It's a shame that it was such a hit and miss thing. If I hadn't gone to this particular meeting and forwarded the minutes to [the senior probation officer], and if this circular from the Home Office hadn't happened to be going round, and the two [joined up], then we

wouldn't have put in an application, we wouldn't have got the funding and we wouldn't have this post and all the work that [the outreach worker] is doing, nobody would be doing that. (probation officer)

Aims and principles of partnership

Project C was regarded within the probation service as a substantial contribution to social crime prevention. The Chief Probation Officer's swift initial action, followed by the opportunity for Home Office support, placed the probation service at the heart of a response to a local problem. Moreover, the initiative supported a fledgeling independent voluntary organisation, in a form which matched both that agency's particular priorities and local multi-agency policy for the provision of drug misuse services. The substance misuse agency thus moved centre-stage to provide a specialised service within the county.

The vision of partnership thus emerging at Project C is one of collaborative community involvement, in which the specific needs of offenders may be met through provision of broader services adapted to meet local problems. The essence of outreach lay in full-blooded embracement of principles of open access, voluntarism and confidentiality. The probation service allied itself to these fundamental principles of the substance misuse agency's endeavour.

The service is offered to everyone because that is the principle on which [the agency] operates. They wouldn't be there just to offer a service to offenders... The whole benefit of outreach is that it's a free confidential service and that users must feel able to approach the service. If they started putting obstacles in the way as to who could and who couldn't use it, then the basis on which they operate would be undermined. So it's a very important principle. I believe it's what makes the work effective. If they started to offer a particular service to a limited group, they would actually lose their appeal to [that group]. That's probably particularly true in a rural area where people tend to know one another. So word gets round very quickly as to what sort of service is being offered. I think if it was felt that a service was being offered purely for offenders with a substance misuse problem that would deter some of them from using it because they would see that as an additional stigma within the local community. Whereas if they see other people, other users they know, using the service, they will also be willing to use it. (senior probation officer)

One outreach worker summed up the arrangement more succinctly: "*I* agree to see people from probation, and *they* agree not to hassle me about it."

Project C's aims were therefore twofold: to respond to a locally identified crime-related need in the community; and to enable a local voluntary organisation to develop the capacity to provide the service required. The service which grew from those aims embraced three fundamental principles: open access; voluntarism; and absolute confidentiality.

Management

The senior probation officer who held responsibility for partnership development was trained in community work and skilled in inter-agency collaboration. The Chief Probation Officer capitalised on this individual's enthusiasm and ability, allowing him a high degree of autonomy in performing his role: "When we set out to develop partnerships, we viewed it as critical that we had someone in the service who played a key role at management level. So our restructuring included freeing up [the senior probation officer's] time... He has a free hand to call meetings, liaise and deal... It's very important that he has a free hand, so when he's out there talking to agencies he knows he can take decisions with them."

The senior probation officer's role, then, was explicitly that of champion to the service's partnerships, and he enjoyed management recognition for this. Accordingly, there was a considerable thrust towards partnership development in the county, Project C being one of several initiatives. The senior probation officer saw himself performing "a dual role: to develop and monitor the probation service part of the partnership; and to assist the partner agency itself to develop and grow." One aspect of the former part of the role, thus defined, was to encourage probation officers to use partnership opportunities: all staff involved in criminal work used the outreach service on their clients' behalf. With regard to the latter part, the senior probation officer assisted several small local agencies to access resources and improve their status or functioning.

A rural area offered certain advantages for this approach, particularly the relative ease of inter-agency communication by virtue of familiarity between personnel of different organisations. Nevertheless, the senior probation officer considered that recognition of the necessary painstaking investment was the crucial factor in the success of his developmental approach:

I could deliver this model elsewhere if I had sufficient time. One forgets partnership is a long term enterprise. I would have to get into the probation service and then set up the networks with community agencies. So I couldn't just set it up in a year or two. The contract culture doesn't recognise this: partnership is a long term enterprise. You can't successfully get in and out of partnerships in a year or two. Probation officers are very suspicious people. They wouldn't take very readily to some whizz kid coming in and setting it up straight away. I was a practitioner here for several years first.

Coincidentally, this senior probation officer also held responsibility for substance misuse, attending the multi-agency forum which advised on policy for the county. He was an active member of the partner agency's committee until, following Home Office advice against this, the organisation conferred observer status on him.

The senior probation officer and Chief Probation Officer were in frequent communication, assisted by their location in the same building. The Chief Probation Officer also took active part in partnership strategy meetings. However, the senior probation officer summed up his situation thus:

I'm very fortunate in having a fairly free hand and a fair amount of independence. Fortunate in having a Chief Probation Officer... who allows me to get on with things in terms of general direction... I'm not saying that I'm not accountable to the probation service for everything that I do, but I feel I sometimes have more freedom than some of my colleagues in other areas to develop things in the way they *can* be developed.

For his part, the Chief Probation Officer adopted a robust interpretation of recent changes in management emphasis from process to outcome accountability: "How do I know what [the senior probation officer] is doing? I don't care. I want to know that probation officers are referring, the partners are happy and the clients aren't re-offending."

Service delivery

Project C may best be considered from two perspectives: the overall approach to outreach; and the specific response to probation service referrals.

Outreach

Outreach was fundamental to the policy goal of reducing drug-related harm in a rural area in which fear of public exposure within small communities deterred users from seeking help.

> [I]n an area like this, if you set up an office and expect people to come, they won't, because it's there, everyone knows what it is and knows if you're going there. (Also), there are people who know me and will talk to me in the pub, but would flip if I visited them at home. Their home is their space, people are very guarded about that. It's much easier to talk in a space where there's people around. Once I go to their house it's personal to them. (outreach worker)

Making contact with a concealed population of drug users depended largely on outreach workers' initiative. Moreover, each outreach worker's practice was shaped by the contingencies of geographic location, which included both physical resources and the nature of the local problem. For example, one outreach worker, with a target client group of young "party drug" users, explained:

> All I use the office for is phone messages. The rest of the time I spend out and about in public places, for example outside the supermarket here, where kids gather. They know who I am. I sit here with my paper and my fags…My work could change dramatically, for example if there was a big police raid, then there would be a lot of people with legal problems. Or if the fashion changed and the main drug of use changed from speed to opiates. Opiate users aren't sociable, they're not going to parties and getting out, so then I'd be working more by way of home visiting.

Another outreach worker was based in a close-knit community in which there was a culture of greater openness about problems, including drugs. This worker was able to obtain two rooms in a building occupied by the Citizens Advice Bureau, and to develop a team of volunteers. Many local clients used this facility on a "drop in" basis, giving it the flavour of a small street agency, while "traditional" outreach continued, often by home visiting, in surrounding villages. This outreach worker reflected on the implications of the direction of his practice:

> I'm doing things now I never even thought about – using a computer, managing a group of volunteers. I had some problems with that at

first. I'd never managed people before. I made some mistakes. I found it hard at first to delegate clients to the volunteers. I was protective about the clients and didn't like to let them go. Now I'd like to be able to leave the office in the hands of other people and get out more again, making the outreach contacts. That's what I like best.

The ability to perceive, exploit and adapt to local opportunities was an impressive skill which these workers elevated to an art form. All three were candid about their personal histories as former users, regarding their experiences as a formative source of the knowledge and skills upon which they now relied professionally:

This is the kind of job you're really suited for if you've spent the last few years bumming around and scoring. Transferable social skills – that's exactly what it is. The kind of social skills you need to lead that kind of life are exactly the ones you need to do this job. I was never anxious about meeting the clients when I came.

The hazards of outreach work had little to do with failure to make contact, but concerned the need to calibrate intervention to the receptivity of potential clients:

It takes a certain amount of discreetness, to do this work. A problem I found initially was I forgot to take into account the claustrophobic atmosphere of rural life. That's where I made a lot of mistakes. Generally, I can identify people who use without actually knowing them. So I sat around here and saw people in groups who I could tell were using. I made it obvious I knew and what I did for my job. Some people got very paranoid about being exposed like that in front of others.

The method which transformed contact into effective, harm reducing help was explained simply enough by one worker: "The whole point about outreach is to respond immediately. If someone says they've got a problem, you help to solve it *now*. You don't say you'll think it over for a week, because you won't get the chance to do anything in a week's time." What this actually meant in practical terms is best illuminated by examples.

1. Outreach workers regularly attended raves, where they attempted to alleviate situational drug-related problems. At one such event, the mains supply of water was turned off; expensive bottled water

was the only available means of cooling down, in conditions of excessive heat conducive to dehydration, potentially exacerbated by dance drugs. The outreach worker persuaded the organisers to re-connect the supply, and spent much of the night distributing water to ravers.

2. A known client was given a large supply of injecting equipment, for distribution among users who were geographically isolated, unable or unwilling to approach the agency themselves: "We use several people as "satellite distributors'; others can get "works' at their houses rather than having to come to the project." Interestingly, therefore, numbers of dirty needles returned each month were not widely discrepant from those issued, according to figures provided by the outreach workers.

3. An outreach worker was permitted by a school to run a weekly drop-in advice facility with a volunteer. This was considered a remarkable advance. As another outreach worker explained: "I envy [that] good relationship with the school, although the problem there is so bad they can't ignore it. If schools invite me in it's like admitting they have a problem. They won't admit it here." Following this introduction through the school, a number of young females contacted the outreach service, bringing to light a hitherto unidentified group of vulnerable users.

4. An outreach worker was asked by a local rave organiser to provide drug awareness training for the bouncers. He was attempting to interest a nightclub owner in similar training. As he saw it, statutory agencies could provide training for their staff using professional networks, but local businesses lacked such a culture of opportunities.

5. An outreach worker had occasion to telephone a GP, with whom he had no previous contact, twice in one day. The GP reacted with some vehemence, asserting that he "never had patients with drug problems, and now you're on to me all the time!" The worker managed to turn this exchange into an opportunity to meet with the group practice, exchange perspectives and develop co-operative relationships. He was considering whether to ask a sympathetic GP to come periodically to the drop-in, since some clients were reluctant to attend surgeries.

Probation referrals

Outreach workers were responsive to requests from probation officers for advice or to make contact with particular clients, and became familiar figures in their local probation offices. Indeed, one probation officer, who used a room in a leisure club as a "satellite" reporting office, shared it with the most recently appointed outreach worker, who made it his base. Nevertheless, probation officers understood that the service was a community resource, considering it a strength of the project: "It's better that they are there for the community. They are reaching a much wider client group. It is less stigmatising for our clients."

The project's success derived substantially from probation officers' ready acceptance of the principles of open access, voluntarism and confidentiality. The open access policy was interpreted literally by probation officers: only one could identify a known client who was deemed unsuitable to refer, for reasons concerning a specific personality disturbance. Psychiatric disturbance was also a general potential ground for non-referral for another officer.

An informal referral system operated in which probation officers would "advertise" the project's existence to clients and encourage contact, but did not themselves approach outreach workers unless requested. Thus, introductions could take a variety of forms:

It's part of my repertoire. I say the outreach worker is available, and ask them if they want to [meet]. If they say no, as time goes on I might mention it again. There's no one on my caseload that I'd think it inappropriate to talk to about the outreach workers and their service.

He referred himself in a way. I told him [the outreach worker] existed. An interesting case, five pages of pre-cons, gets pulled pretty regularly. He comes in on time and says "No problems" and leaves. I said I'd never recommend another probation order, but I got him again last year. It was the same "No problems" up until Easter. Then he got quite depressed. He came in and talked quite a lot then. I showed him the leaflets and told him about [the outreach worker]. He made contact. He's kept quite close contact with [the outreach worker].

I did a drink-drive group and we had different speakers. [The outreach worker] was really good. The clients met him and he left his cards. Some of them followed it up of their own accord. So he's working with people who we might not have referred ourselves... One guy approached him and [the outreach worker] became the primary worker rather than me. He chose to work with him rather than being on probation. We got the court order discharged. He saw the order as a stigma, but he was very comfortable with [the outreach worker] and did lots of work with him.

Probation officers were convinced that voluntarism was crucial to the project's success:

> It's got to be voluntary, otherwise people won't be motivated. It's important for the clients and the workers not to feel compromised.

> It's very important really. These are age old arguments, but the people we work with have to come and see us or go back to court, so that affects their motivation and what they tell us. But if they choose to go to [the outreach worker], their motivation is different. They will tell him different things. It would be counterproductive for him to become part of the sanction process. People have a lot to lose by disclosing.

Not surprisingly, given the principles of open access and voluntarism, and frequently indirect methods of referral, probation officers did not feel a responsibility to know whether contact with the project was established, but to respect what they saw as their clients' right to confidentiality. On several occasions probation officers appeared unaware of a client's contact with the service. Officers explained:

> If I refer, I don't necessarily know what's going on. Some may go because they think it might help with a court case. Some are "sussing it out". They probably wouldn't go [to the service] just about smoking some dope. So, if they've told me they only smoke, they're probably not going to tell me they've seen [the outreach worker]!

> He will talk to [the outreach worker] more about his drug use than to me. He tries to minimise it, but when there's a problem he asks to be referred to [the outreach worker] again. But it won't be in the files. I don't put it all in, partly for confidentiality, but also because there is quite a lot of contact with [the substance misuse agency]. I can't write it *all* down.

> I don't question people about what they do with [the outreach worker]. That would destroy it.

On the other hand, communication between probation officers and outreach workers was open and sometimes frequent in cases where mutual contact was known, which was more often the case when it persisted over time. Information exchange was regarded as helpful to inter-professional relationships, and mutually facilitative. One outreach worker participated in a local co-operative multi-professional group:

We've got a substance misuse care team which is specific to [this town]. [The probation officer], a community psychiatric nurse, me, and sometimes a social worker. There's really good, active co-operation there. Within it there's a sharing of information which allows us to get an angle on what's happening generally and in relation to certain individuals. So I could say "Does anyone know this individual?" and "What's been your experience?" But the information doesn't go any further.

Another outreach worker commented: "A lot of work I do with probation is almost unofficial in a way because I think I have good relationships with probation. So I know that I can and often do have totally 'off the record' discussions with them." The general criterion for information sharing was a perceived "need to know" in order to work more effectively with a client.

I don't tell [the outreach worker] anything that isn't relevant to what he is doing. I don't sit down and have a good yack and tell him the ins and outs of everybody's life. If it's an issue that needs sorting out, if it's a task, then that's what we're trying to resolve. (probation officer)

Equally, outreach workers saw themselves bound to honour privileged relationships with their clients: "I'm privileged really. I'm not accountable to anyone except myself, [the substance misuse agency], and the client. So I will only say things that are helpful to the client. I won't lie, but if it's not helpful then I won't say it."

Probation officers perceived enhancements to their work through the confidence of knowing that a specialist resource was available, or that their knowledge was supported and expanded through contact with outreach workers.

If I go for advice or information, it gives me more confidence to say to someone [that what they are telling me] doesn't add up.

It's added another dimension. It's nice to have someone else involved who cares. It's more rounded, having another perspective.

He can react quicker in a crisis. Also he has specialist knowledge: I have to look it up, but he has it in his head. The clients know he has been in their situation. I haven't.

Problems

There were three problematic issues at Project C: accountability to the probation service; inter-agency relationships; and financial insecurity.

Accountability to the probation service

Home Office expectations for partnerships to be assessed in terms of value for money have generally encouraged establishment of performance indicators involving, for example, throughput and duration of client contact. While the value of outreach within a large rural area with a scattered population appears indisputable, nevertheless, there are several aspects to the probation service's justification for funding an independent community resource.

Firstly, when effective social crime prevention is seen to require open access, voluntarism and complete confidentiality, what measures could be applied without distorting the project's fundamental philosophy?

The Chief Probation Officer elaborated a further perspective on this issue: "The cash limit formula for the probation service contains a perverse incentive. Commencements of new orders are the largest factor in the cash formula. So when outreach is successful, for example in increasing the willingness of the police to divert offenders from prosecution straight into counselling, I don't get cash for the prosecution, the pre-sentence report, or the case."

Secondly, outreach concerned not only prevention of crime, but also of drug-related health and social problems. While the probation service supported these goals in principle, it is nonetheless debatable whether an agency which derives its purpose and function from the criminal justice system should provide primary financial support to a project embracing alternative allegiances to health and social services, and seeking, accordingly, a diverse clientele within the community.

The Home Office Inspectorate of Probation raised these challenges during an examination of the service's partnership activity, exerting pressure both to exact greater accountability for work undertaken on its behalf by partner agencies, and to distance itself from underwriting the costs of services for other organisations.

Inter-agency relationships

Project C demonstrated commendable inter-professional co-operation, collaboration and good will. Nevertheless, delicate inter-agency relationships held potentially large significance for the project's survival.

In the field of illicit drug involvement, relations between substance misuse workers and police are critical. One outreach worker, arriving in post at a time of intensive police activity against drug users in his location, found himself targeted as an informant: "I was getting threatening phone calls, but I just kept on doing the work. I couldn't disappear off the scene as that would have looked suspicious. I was scared, but I kept going. I kept stressing to people that I would have been suspicious if I had been them."

While this experience was ascribed to unfortunate timing, occasional problems occurred when police officers confused their priorities with those of the substance misuse agency.

> Someone knocked on my office door. I opened it. It was a guy from the drug squad! Luckily there were no clients around at that point. But I told him to go and said "For God's sake, if you want to talk to me about anything, I'll come down to the station to talk to you. Don't come here!" It could have been over a year's hard work down the drain. (outreach worker)

The establishment of an arrest-referral scheme, whereby individuals found in possession of drugs for personal use were cautioned following an introduction to an outreach worker, was instrumental in fostering better relationships. Outreach workers were generally sympathetic to police dilemmas: "They're into harm reduction themselves, I think. They've got daft laws to deal with, just like I have and the users have."

The substance misuse agency's independence raised its profile in the multi-disciplinary network of services within the community. One outreach worker reflected that this was a sensitive transition: "Greater independence has helped [the substance misuse agency] in some ways, but it's made it more vulnerable in others. Statutory workers see it as more of a threat to their own jobs now it has independent status."

Increased interaction with statutory organisations also had implications for the substance misuse agency's relationship to its clientele. Co-operation with other professionals and protection of privileged relationships with drug users required a careful balance. One probation officer observed: "It's a double-edged sword. Raising the profile of the substance misuse agency means [the outreach worker] has to be careful. Clients may become suspicious that he's one of us. His low profile is very important." An outreach worker explained:

> By a million miles its the most strange and stressful job I've ever had, but not overwhelming. You just have to sort out your priorities. My

first priority is to the client, and however I can help the client. If there's anything I can do to help the other agencies, then I'll do it. I can see those two things might conflict, but I have to make it clear that my priority is confidentiality to the client.

Professional roles were clarified and relationships strengthened through mutual involvement in particular cases. For example, one outreach worker sought to involve a community psychiatric nurse with an adolescent, in an attempt to clarify the balance between psychological problems and substance misuse. Some delicacy was reported in these relationships, arising from the initial suspicion of community psychiatric nurses that the outreach project would usurp part of their role. Yet relationships with health personnel were important to outreach workers. Clients quite often approached them in acute emotional or physical difficulty. Relationships with local GPs and other health workers therefore provided clients with access to medical treatment, and could be a vital source of support to an outreach worker faced with crisis. One client approached an outreach worker in a condition of severe shock and grief, following his mother's death on the previous night. The outreach worker offered a calming response, and ensured the continuous presence of a volunteer while he sought medical assistance for the client's escalating hyperventilation and disorientation.

Thus, as an open resource for individuals often with multiple or crisis problems, Project C required the respect and co-operation of the range of statutory services. This was not only an issue for the quality of its service delivery, but might have significance for its financial support.

Financial insecurity

Continuation of funding was a besetting problem. The impact of the project's insecurity was apparent to probation officers who in interview raised their concern: "Short term contracts are pernicious, bad for [the outreach worker] and bad for the service."

The probation service had exploited the opportunities of the Home Office SUGS scheme. Project C was only one enterprise generated within the county from this source. As the centralised scheme closed, the probation service could not sustain the level of investment in partnerships from the 5 per cent minimum expenditure required by the Home Office. Moreover, in 1995, its budget was severely cut.

Project C thus crucially exposed local contention surrounding the proper source of funding for initiatives designed as services for the full community, rather than reserved for a particular group within it.

Notwithstanding its pioneering provision for a previously concealed or unresponsive, yet vulnerable population, and its multi-agency popularity, there was a dearth of financial backing for the project.

Both the Home Office and the probation service deserve tribute for their efforts to support Project C in these circumstances. The Home Office extended funding for several months after the official closure of the SUGS scheme, given indications of possible support from other agencies. The probation service devoted enormous energy to establishing a charitable trust fund, which it was hoped would be capable not only of maintaining, but in the longer term expanding support for voluntary organisations involved in offender rehabilitation. The service meanwhile offered a reduced contribution to the substance misuse agency, falling far short of the cost of outreach appointments. The senior probation officer was closely involved with the partner agency's application for expanded Health Authority funding to absorb the outreach workers' posts.

The extent to which expectations were raised by the project's successful innovation perhaps sharpened disappointment and frustration during a protracted period of insecurity.

> I find it tedious having to justify what I consider is a very good project to people who basically just want to keep the status quo. They don't want to see things move forward...I dislike the fact that we have to go round cap in hand to other people asking for funding for it...I find that extremely galling because we're not talking about huge sums of money when you look at the budgets of some agencies. (senior probation officer)

Following the final closure of Home Office funding, the project secured further temporary financial survival through the social services department and health authority. The multi-agency substance misuse forum was disbanded, and a new body established, following government recommendations on the formation of local action teams. This group held a broader brief, covering both strategy and commissioning. In its representations, therefore, the substance misuse agency sought a sympathetic and enabling approach to its services within the area.

Conclusion

Project C demonstrates the frequently declared aim of partnership to support and empower local voluntary organisations. The undertaking, however, required a framework for its accomplishment to be first established within the organisation of the probation service itself. Significantly, the skills and enthusiasm of a senior probation officer were strategically deployed and supported, in contrast to the time-honoured tradition among welfare agencies of reliance on pioneers to make their own headway. Thus, the championship role was crafted into the structure of the partnership enterprise by the Chief Probation Officer.

The excellence of inter-professional relationships between field probation officers and outreach workers at Project C, appearing to spring from good will alone, can obscure this point. While good will undoubtedly flourished, Project C showed its development and sustenance at an organisational level. It also, however, demonstrated the tenuousness of inter-agency good will as a basis for financial security.

9
The Projects Compared

The case file survey covered all 55 referrals to Project A since its inception, a sample of 84 referrals to Project B during the previous year, and 56 referrals to Project C who were known by outreach workers to be mutual clients of the probation service. The data will be presented with little comment in the first instance, leading to a broader discussion later. Some issues in data collection first need explanation.

It was necessary to sample files at Project B due to the high rate of forensic referrals.

At Project C it was impossible in all but a few cases, to determine the point of referral to, or first contact with the outreach service from probation files, and individual case files were not kept at the substance misuse agency. Recording probably reflected the informal methods of encouraging contact and the agency's confidential, open access style. However, it posed a problem for collecting data which, at Projects A and B, related to the point of referral. At Project C the same information was collected as it related to the last recorded conviction. The one item of information which could not be collected from probation files in this way was the referral route to Project C, and the recourse here was to information provided by the outreach workers.

Corroborative or additional information was sought from substance misuse agency records where possible: at Project A case files retained minimal information, such as correspondence; at Project B full records were maintained; at Project C the substance misuse agency did not keep files for individual clients.

Demographic characteristics

Table 9.1 shows the ages of clients at the time of referral to the substance misuse project. Project A attracted the youngest age group, with 51 per cent of probation clients being aged under 25 years. Project B attracted an older group, with 51 per cent of its clients being aged between 25 and 39 years. Project C's probation clients were more evenly distributed, with 46 per cent aged under 25 and 45 per cent aged between 25 and 39 years.

Table 9.2 shows the gender of clients referred to each project. There was a heavy preponderance of males at each project, particularly at Project C. Table 9.3 shows a predominance of white clients at all three projects.

Table 9.1   Age of clients at referral to substance misuse projects (*n* in brackets)

Years	Project A	Project B	Project C	All Projects
>20	12.73% (7)	7.14 % (6)	10.71% (6)	9.74% (19)
20–24	38.18% (21)	23.81% (20)	35.71% (20)	31.28% (61)
25–29	25.45% (14)	29.77% (25)	21.44% (12)	26.15% (51)
30–39	18.18% (10)	21.43% (18)	23.21% (13)	21.03% (41)
40–49	3.64% (2)	11.90% (10)	7.14% (4)	8.21% (16)
50 >	1.82% (1)	5.95% (5)	1.79% (1)	3.59% (7)
Total	100% (55)	100% (84)	100% (56)	100% (195)
Mean	26.255 yrs	30.274 yrs	27.143 yrs	28.241 yrs
Mode	20 yrs	29 yrs	30 yrs	22 yrs

Table 9.2   Gender of clients referred to substance misuse projects (*n* in brackets)

Sex	Project A	Project B	Project C	All Projects
Female	14.5% (8)	16.7% (14)	7.1% (4)	13.3% (26)
Male	85.5% (47)	83.3% (70)	92.9% (52)	86.7% (169)
Total	100% (55)	100% (84)	100% (56)	100% (195)

Table 9.3   Ethnicity of clients referred to substance misuse projects (*n* in brackets)

Ethnicity	Project A	Project B	Project C	All Projects
White: UK	50.9% (28)	65.5% (55)	57.1% (32)	59.0% (115)
Black: Afro-Caribbean	7.3% (4)	–	–	2.1% (4)
Black: Other	–	–	1.8% (1)	0.5% (1)
Asian	–	1.2% (1)	–	0.5% (1)
Unavailable	41.8% (23)	33.3% (28)	41.1% (23)	37.9% (74)
Total	100% (55)	100% (84)	100% (56)	100% (195)

Criminal histories

Immediate offences

The sentencing court provides a general indication of the seriousness of offences. Table 9.4 shows that 35 percent of Project A's clients were sentenced in the Crown Court, as compared with 26 per cent at Project B and 20 per cent at Project C.

At the time of their conviction immediately prior to referral to the project, the 55 Project A clients were sentenced for a total of 253 offences. The 69 Project B clients for whom data was available were sentenced for a total of 159 offences. At Project C, where the best available data was the last recorded conviction, 56 clients were sentenced for a total of 159 offences. This is summarised in Figures 9.1 to 9.3, which also break the data into offence types. The lower proportion of violence at Project A may be linked to the higher rate of offending overall in this group.

This is borne out in Figures 9.4 to 9.6. Taking the main offence for each client only, the proportion of violent offences committed by the client group at Project A (25 per cent) slightly exceeds that in Projects B (22 per cent) and C (24 per cent). More broadly, 78 per cent of referrals to Project A were sentenced for violence, burglary or theft, compared to 57 per cent of referrals to Project B and 51 per cent of referrals to Project C. Indeed, higher proportions of referrals to Project A were represented in each of these categories.

Twenty-three per cent of clients at Project B and 16 per cent at Project C were sentenced for driving while intoxicated, while this offence accounted for only 2 per cent of Project A's referrals.

Table 9.4   Sentencing court at time of referral to substance misuse projects (Projects A & B) or at last recorded conviction (Project C) (*n* in brackets)

Court	Project A	Project B	Project C	All Projects
Crown	34.5% (19)	26.2% (22)	19.6% (11)	26.7% (52)
Magistrates	58.2% (32)	54.8% (46)	75.0% (42)	67.8% (120)
Youth	5.5% (3)	1.2% (1)	1.8% (1)	2.3% (5)
Unavailable	1.8% (1)	17.9% (15)	3.6% (2)	9.2% (18)
Total	100% (55)	100% (84)	100% (84)	100% (195)

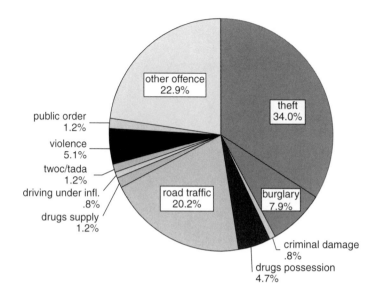

Figure 9.1 Offences prior to referral – Project A (where 55 clients committed 253 offences)

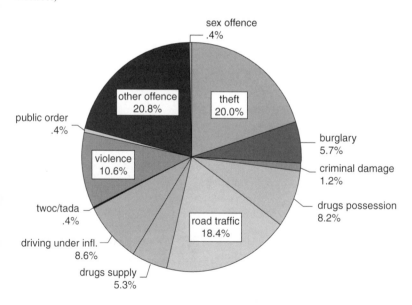

Figure 9.2 Offences prior to referral – Project B (where 69 clients committed 159 offences)

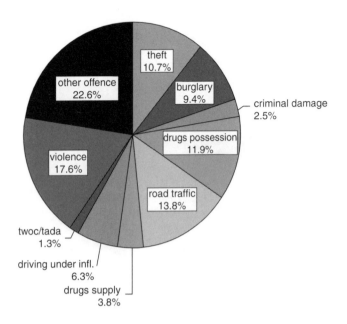

Figure 9.3 Last recorded offences – Project C (where 56 clients committed 159 offences)

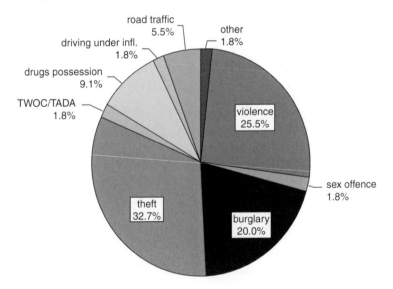

Figure 9.4 Main offence prior to referral – Project A (*n* = 55)

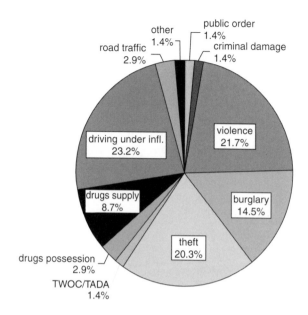

Figure 9.5 Main offence prior to referral – Project B (*n* = 69)

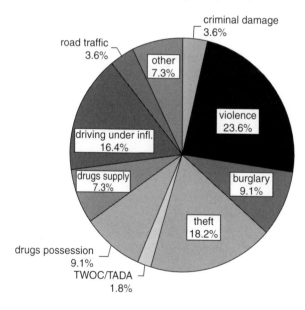

Figure 9.6 Last recorded main offence – Project C (*n* = 56)

Previous convictions

Table 9.5 shows the average number of previous convictions for clients at each project. All projects attracted offenders with an appreciable prior criminal history. However, Project A clients were heavily convicted in comparison with Projects B and C. Few clients at any project were previously unconvicted, but rather fewer clients at Project A had no previous convictions. The range of previous convictions represents the extremes, but Project A received a client with the greatest number of previous convictions by a considerable margin, despite the group's relative youth.

At each project, previous criminal histories, as summarised in Figures 9.7 to 9.9, included appreciable involvement in the most serious

Table 9.5   Previous convictions of clients referred to substance misuse projects

	Project A	Project B	Project C	All Projects
Mean	37.54	15.88	19.65	23.73
Range	137	106	122	137
No Prev. Conv.	3	6	5	14
Valid n	54	68	52	174

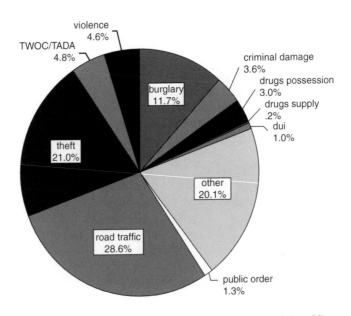

Figure 9.7   Previous convictions of clients referred to Project A (*n* = 55)

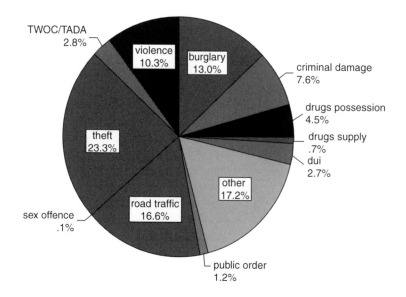

Figure 9.8 Previous convictions of clients referred to Project B ($n = 69$)

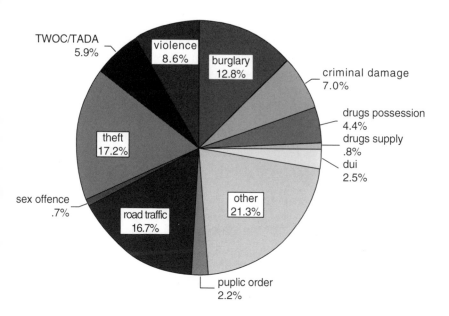

Figure 9.9 Previous convictions of clients referred to Project C ($n = 56$)

Table 9.6   Previous experience of community penalties and custody of all clients referred to substance misuse projects

	Project A	Project B	Project C	All Projects
Probation Orders				
– Standard	32	39	19	90
– Treatment condition	1	5	8	14
– Other condition	13	8	3	24
Community Service	31	23	19	73
Combination order	4	2	6	12
Custody	35	31	19	85

offences of violence, burglary and theft. These offences are particularly heavily represented in the previous convictions of clients at Project B. The high level of previous offending by clients at Project A is again connected to lower proportions of the most serious offence types.

Finally, criminal histories were examined for previous experience of higher tariff community penalties and custody. Table 9.6 details numbers of clients at each project known to have previous experience of standard probation, probation with a substance misuse treatment condition, probation with any other additional requirement, community service, combination order and custody. Requirements for substance misuse treatment were quite few, particularly at Project A. However, at Project A, 35 of the 55 clients had previously experienced custody, 32 had prior experience of probation, and 31 had previously been the subject of community service orders. Also at Project A there was greater previous experience of extra requirements in probation orders.

The immediate sentence

Figures 9.10 to 9.12 show sentences for the main offences immediately prior to referral at Projects A and B, and for the last recorded conviction at Project C.

Nearly 76 per cent of referrals to Project A were made the subject of a probation order with a requirement for drug treatment. Probation orders with additional requirements were made in 19 per cent (15 cases of 69 with available data) and 21 per cent (11 cases of 55) of clients referred to Projects B and C respectively. For Project B, these additional requirements for the most part directed attendance at the probation service's intensive groupwork programme, only two requirements for substance misuse treatment being imposed. For Project C, additional requirements almost entirely concerned attendance at the probation

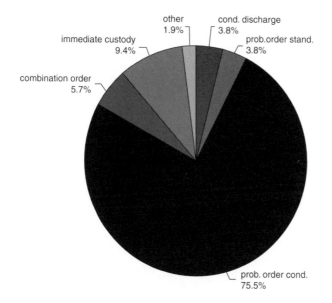

Figure 9.10 Sentence for main offence prior to referral – Project A (*n* = 55)

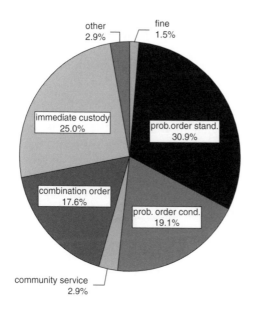

Figure 9.11 Sentence for main offence prior to referral – Project B (*n* = 69)

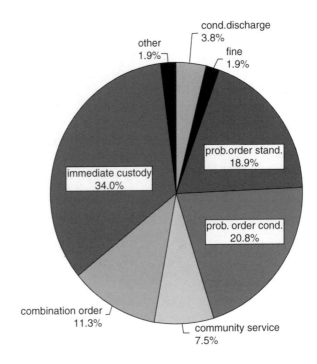

Figure 9.12   Sentence for last recorded main offence – Project C (*n* = 55)

service's drink-driver's programme; no requirements for substance misuse treatment were imposed.

Notably, only 15 per cent of Project A's referrals received a higher tariff disposal than the probation order with treatment requirement, i.e. custody or a combination order, although these were the two most frequent other disposals. At Project B, nearly 43 per cent received either custody or a combination order, and this was also the case for 45 per cent of referrals to Project C at their last recorded conviction. However, higher numbers of clients referred to Projects B and C received standard probation orders without additional requirements, about 31 and 19 per cent respectively.

How did these disposals compare with the proposals of probation officers? Figures 9.13 to 9.15 show the proposals in pre-sentence reports prior to referral for Projects A and B, and for the last recorded offence at Project C. For clients at Project A, the probation order with a condition of substance misuse treatement was an extremely popular proposal. At Projects B and C there was a broader spread of proposals across the range

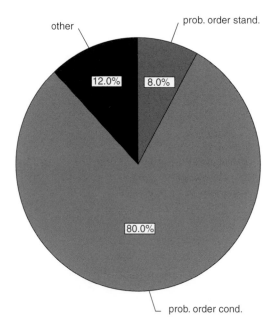

Figure 9.13 Proposals in pre-sentence reports prior to referral – Project A (*n* = 55)

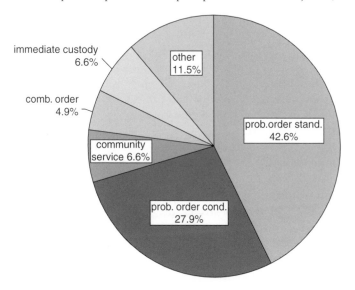

Figure 9.14 Proposals in pre-sentence reports prior to referral – Project B (*n* = 69)

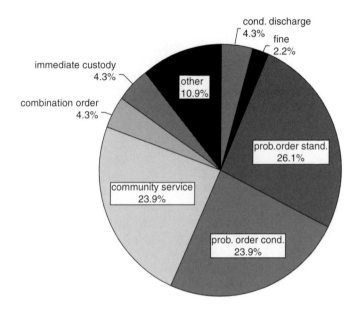

Figure 9.15   Proposals in pre-sentence reports for last recorded offence – Project C
($n = 56$)

of probation service administered disposals. There is a notable discrepancy between the relative popularity of proposals for standard probation orders without additional requirements and for community service orders at Projects B and C, which is not obviously explained by the data on the clients in itself. Taken together with the relatively high numbers of custodial sentences at project C, this may be better explained by more general local differences in sentencing and proposals in pre-sentence reports.

Levels of concordance between probation officer's proposals and actual outcomes at court were examined. At Project A the majority of proposals (40) were for a probation order with a requirement for substance misuse treatment, and these were successful in most cases (34). At Projects B and C there was a greater spread of proposals across the range of alternatives, with emphasis on standard probation and probation with an additional requirement, which was rarely for substance misuse treatment at Project B and never at Project C. Proposals for any disposal at Projects B and C did not achieve the concordance rate of the proposals for probation with a substance misuse treatment requirement at Project A, although they were generally more successful than not.

Substance misuse

Figures 9.16 to 9.20 show the main drug of concern for clients referred to each project. For Projects A and B it was possible to collect this information for each client from both probation and substance misuse files, and both sources are presented here as being of some interest. At Project C, information on individual clients was not available within the substance misuse agency, and therefore only probation file information is presented.

At the time of referral to Project A, the main drug of concern to probation officers for nearly 51 per cent of clients was an opiate, followed by cocaine or crack (about 16 percent) and amphetamines (about 15 per cent). Alcohol was the main concern for only 6 per cent of referrals. At the substance misuse agency, these figures altered somewhat. In particular, multiple use increased from 4 per cent, in the probation files, to 15 per cent, and alcohol as the main drug of concern declined to 1 per cent. Opiates remained the primary focus of concern, although at a reduced level.

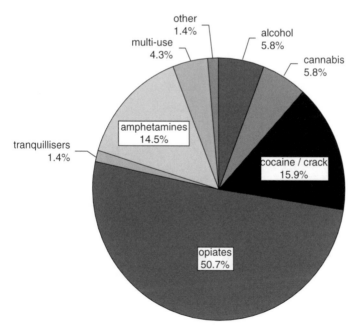

Figure 9.16 Drug of concern for clients at Project A (*n* = 55); source: probation files

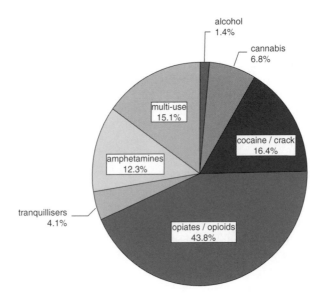

Figure 9.17 Drug of concern for clients at Project A (*n* = 54) source: Substance Misuse Project

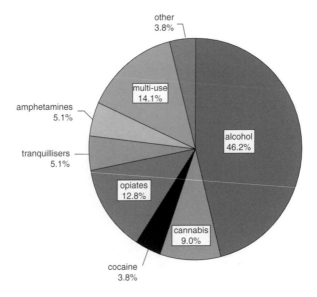

Figure 9.18 Drug of concern for clients at Project B (*n* = 55); source: probation files

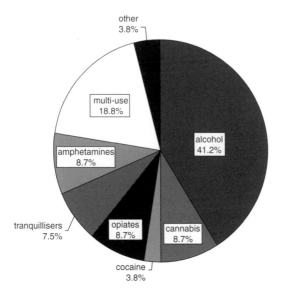

Figure 9.19   Drug of concern for clients at project B ($n = 83$); source: Substance Misuse Project

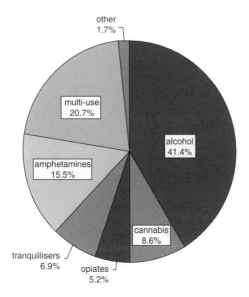

Figure 9.20   Drug of concern for clients at Project C ($n = 56$); source: probation files

At Project B, alcohol was the main concern of probation officers at referral for 46 per cent of referrals, followed by multiple use (14 per cent) and opiates (about 13 per cent). Again, these figures were somewhat revised in specialists' records. Alcohol remained the primary focus of concern, but at a reduced level of 41 per cent. Again, multiple use increased, although less dramatically than at Project A. Opiates as the main drug of concern declined to about 9 per cent.

At Project C, alcohol again appeared to be the main concern of probation officers for 41 per cent of probation clients, followed by multiple use (about 21 per cent) and amphetamines (about 16 per cent).

Referral route

Referral routes to the projects are summarised in Figures 9.21 to 9.23. Nearly 24 per cent of clients self-referred to Project C, compared with about two per cent at Project A and about five per cent at Project B.

Conclusion

Although the three projects showed differences between themselves in the age ranges and main drugs of concern of the probation service clients, these differences appear to reflect, at least in part, the areas of

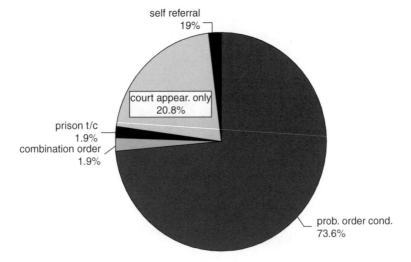

Figure 9.21   Referral routes to Project A (*n* = 55); source: probation files

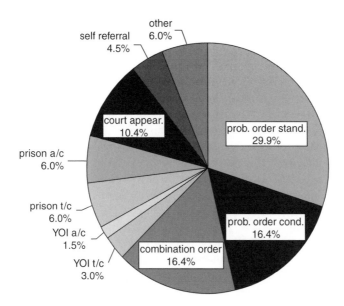

Figure 9.22   Referral routes to Project B ($n = 69$); source: probation files

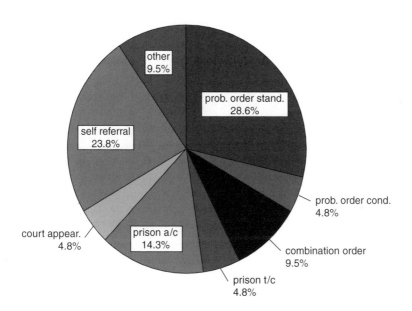

Figure 9.23   Referral routes to Project C ($n = 56$); source: Substance Misuse Project

greatest activity of the different partner agencies: a voluntary street agency attracting young opiate, crack/cocaine and amphetamine users; a group of statutory agencies servicing predominantly older, chronic users; and an outreach project which, in a rural area with few substance misuse resources, contacted users across the spectrum of age and use.

Comprehensive comparison between probation service and other clientele of the partner agencies was not attempted. However, substance misuse managers were invited to compare the profile of probation service referrals with the characteristics generally of their clientele. There was general agreement that each probation client group was broadly similar to overall clientele of their receiving agencies. The most notable difference was the preponderance of male referrals from the probation service.

At Projects B and C the preponderance of white clients reflected predominantly white areas, but at Project A there was concern about poor attraction of black clients. This was generally thought to result from the location of the substance misuse agency in a large urban area, with probation teams in districts with concentrations of black clients preferring to use nearer drug and alcohol teams. However, the substance misuse manager was more cautious, observing that ethnic differences in drug use patterns, particularly a higher level of crack-cocaine involvement, combined with differences in their treatment by the criminal justice system might present considerable difficulties for probation officers trying to make effective contact with black clients. By contrast, at Project B, despite the paucity of ethnic minority clients forthcoming from the probation service, numbers over time were greater than referrals from any other source. It was believed at the statutory teams that the criminal justice system provided the main point of entry to substance misuse treatment for minority clients, even though numbers were so small.

Although caution is needed, given the well known hazards of case recording, there was an indication that while field probation officers were reasonably accurate in their assessments, substance misuse workers were able to identify more problems, particularly in terms of multiple, rather than single use. This "added value" is the product of concentrated exposure, facilitating recognition and confidence in dealing with particular varieties of problems. It supports probation officers' identification of focus, awareness and confidence as essential enhancements of an expert resource.

An accumulation of evidence from the case file data suggested that Project A achieved its aim of attracting high tariff offenders to a non-custodial alternative. Referrals to Project A appeared to be a young group offending rapidly, repeatedly and seriously, as judged by their number of offences, prior convictions and disposals, the sentencing court and sentences received.

The impressive level of concordance between probation officers' proposals and sentencing outcomes at Project A requires some caution. When comparing this with the levels of concordance achieved at Projects B and C, it must be remembered that Project A data concerns a group which had already been selected as appropriate for the treatment programme in tariff terms. For the other two projects, this was not an issue. It cannot, therefore, be claimed from this data that probation officers at Project A were *generally* more successful in their proposals. What can be said, however, is that at Project A the availability of the treatment programme offered a viable sentencing alternative, particularly for a group of young, criminally active men with highly problematic drug involvement. Project A, therefore, performed very well according to the aims which it set itself of extending a harm reduction service within the context of a high tariff sentencing framework.

However, this is not to say that Project A was performing *better* than Projects B and C, since these were established within quite different conceptual frameworks. Such a conclusion would therefore derive from an inappropriate comparison. Both these latter projects were able to attract high tariff and chronic offenders, if rather less distinctively so than Project A, but preferred a voluntary approach and also offered a service across the range of probation service involvement with offenders. For example, the relatively high rate of self-referrals to Project C suggests that it provided a valued service to a group which is notoriously hard to reach, prompted by informal advertising and encouragement by probation officers. The price for Project A's success in targeting a highly problematic group, in both criminal and substance misuse terms, was the programme's restriction to clients at the point of sentence. Nevertheless, the concentration of multiple difficulties presented by that targetted group might be justified as a price worth paying, in terms of focusing attention and activity on high need.

Project B demonstrated the effectiveness of in-house specialisation in accessing treatment services for offenders. Indeed, throughput of clients at Project B was extensive. In sheer numerical terms, it outperformed other projects in terms of contacts with probation service clients (or, at least, *known* probation clients in the case of Project C). Again, differences between the projects' conceptualisations must be considered when evaluating this point. Project C, as an open access service, was not confined to probation clients. Indeed, prior to the project's birth, there was no such service at all within the community. To create an exclusive programme for offenders in the absence of a needed service in the community would be anomalous, if not ridiculous. Project A, on the other hand, might justify a lower throughput in terms of the sentencing prospects and concentration of high needs among its targetted client group.

These findings raise complex questions about the structures for programmes for substance misusing offenders, and in particular their relationship to the sentencing tariff. It is, for example, tempting to conclude from the relatively high numbers of custodial sentences received by clients at Project C that a high tariff opportunity such as that provided at Project A might make a useful impact on local use of imprisonment. However, Project A built upon a history of development at the substance misuse agency, and long collaboration with the probation service. At Project C, the agency's expansion emanated from the partnership itself. Provision for substance misusing offenders is thus closely connected to opportunities for treatment existing to serve the wider community. They cannot develop in isolation from such broader local provision and indeed would make little coherent sense if they did so develop. A similar point arises at Project B, where extensive use of substance misuse services was facilitated through successful development of a particular type of opportunity. It is precisely because the programmes for offenders at each of the three case study projects made sense within the broader framework of local services that probation officers in each location approved so highly of their innovation and perceived their value so clearly.

10
Learning from Experience

What lessons did probation and substance misuse staff take from their experiences in partnership and specialisation? Their accounts shed further light on the interprofessional issues underpinning the partnership enterprise.

The most difficult action in individual experience

Interviewees were asked what was the most difficult thing that they had to do in their work in relation to the project. Responses at partnership projects are summarised in Table 10.1.

Table 10.1 The most difficult action in the experience of probation and substance misuse staff at successful and problematic partnerships

Interviewees	Probation		Substance misuse		
Partnership	Successful	Problematic	Successful	Problematic	Total
Manage conflict	3	3	2	9	17
Manage new culture	1	1	4	1	7
Imposition	2	–	1	2	5
Formalise/monitor	2	1	1	1	5
Bureaucracy	2	2	–	–	4
Find time	2	1	–	–	3
Cover all aspects	1	–	2	–	3
Start from cold	–	–	2	–	2
Find new funding	–	1	1	–	2
Establish boundaries	–	–	1	1	2
Cope with custody	–	–	1	–	1
Identify client need	1	–	–	–	1
No answer/uncoded	3	3	1	2	9
Total	17	12	16	16	61

By far the most difficult thing was to manage conflict, particularly for substance misuse staff at problematic projects, who also emphasised the hostility of conflict:

> Going into ... probation teams and having to deal with the hostility, which was directed, not at me, but at partnership and management. I found that demoralising. I felt that I was inadequately prepared by for that, both by my own management and the probation management ... I had not worked in this field before. I was taken aback by that hostility.

> Trying to get anywhere. Trying to get some sort of response. Bashing my head against a brick wall. That is how it feels.

Also at problematic partnerships, substance misuse workers sometimes found the working styles of probation officers difficult to tolerate:

> Put up with probation officers. Really. Maybe I'm being somewhat dogmatic, but I just get irritated. Is it me being big headed? But when probation officers talk at cross purposes to me in the group, that's very irritating for me, it doesn't help the group, and it means that I'm trying to look after the probation officer as well as the group. Trying to shut them up, or encourage them to say something different, as well as thinking about all the other group members. So the hard thing is acting as a team.

> Dealing with that probation officer. I found myself getting extremely angry. This particular guy whose mother had died and his father had committed suicide. It did affect me ... the damage he's caused. I felt strongly about that ... when the probation officer was rubbishing his feelings. I did find that the most difficult thing, and dealing with that probation officer since.

There were only two problematic partnerships where managing conflict was not raised by at least one substance misuse interviewee. Two substance misuse workers at successful partnerships mentioned conflict management. For one, probation officers' hostility was skilfully defused:

> Going to an office where I knew there was incredible hostility to the partnership. I did find that very hard, but it was OK because [the Assistant Chief Probation Officer] had talked to me about it

beforehand. I felt totally supported and validated ... at first the meeting was very uncomfortable but then it [turned out all right].

For the other, conflict arose at committee level over his appointment, although he developed the project proposal. He felt no animosity towards probation officers: "The most difficult part was keeping my head together when all that stuff was going on at the very outset. Apart from that ... things have just come together."

Managing conflict was also difficult for probation staff. For one unfortunate senior probation officer, both internal and external conflicts arose:

Getting concrete information from [probation officers] as to what isn't working well with the partnership and making sure that it is real, because they will personalise [issues] ... To try to get across to [the substance misuse agency] that we're both in this partnership and we want the partnership now that we've got it! We want to make best use of it and not undermine their agency in any way. That's probably the most difficult.

At one successful partnership, the probation officer found dealing with the substance misuse agency's director difficult. Elsewhere, probation officers recounted attempts to protect the feelings of substance misuse colleagues:

The programme was specifically designed for Asian drinkers, to conduct the groups in Asian language. On this occasion it had to be Punjabi. One of the group leaders clearly didn't have this language ... It was difficult for me to discuss this about another colleague. In some way it was a bit personal as well ... But I had to use my professional judgement and [explain] the reasons for doing it. At the end it was resolved adequately and to everyone's satisfaction.

I copped out of doing the most difficult thing I've come across ... A drinker and his wife told me that the drinker needed a drink before he went to see [the substance misuse worker] because [he] was so confrontational ... This man was a terrible liar who had huge mood swings ... He died recently. I did not pass this information on to [the substance misuse worker] as it is irrelevant now and would be distressing for him. I'm not blaming [him]. He *should* be challenging and confrontational, that's what he was there for. But I don't see any point in upsetting him.

Grappling with a new culture was particularly difficult for substance misuse workers at successful partnerships.

> Grasping all the legislation the affects the client group in order to make some real response. I have a responsibility to do that. That increases my workload, because that's the sort of work I do at home. I choose to do it because it helps me to clarify things, and I've produced something which is, I hope, of benefit to the client group. That was the big thing. (substance misuse manager)

> It's unusual for a partnership worker to have come from probation and gone into a voluntary agency. The difficulty is getting my colleagues in the probation service, where I always worked, to understand that I'm going to be doing different work. That I am not just a probation officer who now works in [a substance misuse agency]. That I have become a [substance misuse agency] employee. That's also been hard for me to see, too. It's losing your previous identity and yet keeping it as well. It's hard. (substance misuse worker)

> The most sensitive issue was about people bringing needles and syringes into the building, when we talked about having a sharps box in the [substance misuse worker's] room. It wasn't so much probation officers, but secretaries and people who weren't actually supervising the offenders who felt uncomfortable about that. It was calming their fears... There was a minority who felt this was perhaps going too far. (senior probation officer)

Two probation officers mildly felt that an imposition had been made upon them, relieved, in one case, by the substance misuse worker's assistance:

> A colleague went on holiday having arranged for somebody to go to a rehabilitation centre, but for some reason the referral hadn't gone through. I got involved in picking up someone else's work... But [the substance misuse worker]... did a piece of work that was really outside her remit, and made the referral.

> Paradoxically, although I enjoyed it, it was an imposition. You get time off in lieu for running the group, but it's not easy to take. I feel vaguely – but only vaguely – resentful. That's just a reflection of the increased managerialism of the probation service.

For substance misuse staff, impositions comprised inappropriate requests:

> The group that I was invited to talk to, which was a group of young men. The two probation officers were young women. They were completely out of control. It was an ineffective use of my time to try to talk about alcohol problems... I would be very chary of getting involved in a group like that again.

> Some probation officers would really like to hand responsibility over to me. Perhaps they're very hard pressed... For example, if a long term residential place is required... I do know of some, so I make suggestions. But in one case the probation officer wanted to leave it to me to make all the arrangements, but I can't do that... This probation officer assumed I had set it all up and took the client down cold... They were out in fifteen minutes!

> Speaking in a seminar, with no form of training. Coming to terms with the fact that what I expected the job to be, which was secretarial, was really a high level co-ordinator's role.

Formalising and monitoring the partnership arrangement was also difficult: "Working out what the probation expectations were going to be of this particular post and how to measure the realisation of those expectations. That was a puzzle" (substance misuse worker). Similarly, bureaucracy was a problem: "Were the stats right? Were some things not counted as partnership, when really they were? If another substance misuse worker was dealing with a probation client, could we make sure we got it on the stats form?" (probation officer). Simply finding time for the partnership was hard: "It's been time consuming, to be on this working group. Because I do like to keep on with things, I don't like to let people down... But there have been a lot of meetings and we don't get anything back for that" (probation officer). Covering a complex set of tasks was an issue: "The nature of the post, physically being half at one project and half at another one. Where do I keep my information? Where do I keep my stats?" (substance misuse worker).

Finance was the problem for one substance misuse manager seeking to extend the agency's projects generally, and one senior probation officer at a partnership from which funding was being withdrawn:

> It's the most difficult period now... I feel unhappy about what is happening. That's to do with the loss of a useful resource, but it's

also uncomfortable that the project was set up to deal with offenders and neither the Home Office nor the probation service are going to pay for it ... We have people who are [in contact] with the scheme now. What about someone who is referred next week? Who is going to fund that?

Three different responses concerned the quality of service:

[To be clear] that we are not involved in the process of offending, but purely the substance use ... That is our role, and not being drawn into problems and boundaries beyond that ... From my perspective it's irrelevant that the client is an offender. Maintaining that boundary is difficult. Sometimes I feel I'm being obstructive, or [that] I'm seen to be obstructive and that's been difficult. (substance misuse manager)

That somebody ends up going back to court for not coming to us and ends up in prison. Or that we've gone to a prison to see a person who is going to court, and we know we can work with that person ... and the judge says "No, you're not getting an opportunity." It's very hard to know that they've got [a prison sentence]. (substance misuse manager)

You've got to assess the person first of all before you make a referral, because if a client doesn't perceive that he has a problem ... then it's pointless. So that's been the hardest thing for me. Identifying the need. It's not just how *I* see the need. The person has to see the need as well. (probation officer)

Responses of interviewees at in-house specialist projects are summarised in Table 10.2. Managing conflict was mentioned only once, by a substance misuse manager who was uncomfortably caught up in an internal matter for the probation service:

To deal with a very distraught probation officer ... when we were told at the last hour, literally, that he was being moved. He didn't know. I didn't know. He was on holiday when the decision was made. It was pretty poor, difficult and unpleasant ... It made me wonder if I do that to my staff.

One specialist, half joking, disliked supervising urine tests. Curiously, three specialists, rather than substance misuse workers at any type of project, found confronting unco-operative clients difficult:

Table 10.2   The most difficult action in the experience of probation and substance misuse staff at in-house specialist projects

Interviewees	Probation	Substance misuse
Manage the work	3	–
Confront client	3	–
Change culture	2	–
Acquire new skills	2	–
Clarify objectives	1	–
Monitor	1	–
Train colleagues	1	–
Manage restructure	1	–
Cope with insecurity	1	–
Supervise urine	1	–
Manage conflict	–	1
Cope with specialist change	–	1
Absorb unique post	–	1
No answer	2	–
Total = 21*	18	3

* 4 probation interviewees offered 2 answers

I find it very difficult when we eject people ... That's difficult. A messy ending. I don't like messy endings. I'm an optimist with people. I think that everyone deserves a chance. Sometimes I see people leaving here with their whole world in a black plastic bag and they're going off to drink ... That I find very difficult to cope with.

Otherwise, comments were largely directed at organisational concerns. Managing the workload was difficult: "Time. You have to work lots of long hours. I don't get home until quarter to ten after the group and getting time off is difficult. That's hard. That's the hardest thing." For both managers at residential projects, changing an earlier professional culture was most difficult:

It's a clear shift from the illness point of view. Getting the management committee to understand that and to agree to that and support me on it. There was [also] one staff member here who clearly did not accept my point of view ... with the result that she left. So the issues of philosophy.

The culture shift. I really thought the team was open to the changes. But there's been lots of subtle resistance. I feel as though we're over the worst now and that people are really starting to make the place work. But there was resistance...We had a couple of staff changes and the effect was immediate. But it surprised me that the resistance was there.

Acquiring new skills was hard: "The organisational issues...Those were skills that I had to develop myself. They were difficult...You've got to suck and see and learn." At the most recently established project, clarifying objectives was most difficult thus far. One senior probation officer affirmed: "Information, evaluation. Because I'm not a statistician. I'm not trained in that." A specialist remarked: "The difficult challenge has been training my colleagues in probation...because of the relationship I already have with them." A senior probation officer felt responsible for supporting specialist officers during a period of insecurity for the project's future.

One substance misuse worker had difficulty coping with changes in specialist officers: "The most difficult thing is getting to know them again. You get used to one person and then they leave, then you get used to another person and they get promotion, then another one comes along and it all starts again." At the youngest specialist project, the substance misuse manager grappled with a unique arrangement: "The fact that the probation officer came with a caseload of people on probation means that it set different boundaries. None of [the rest of] us came with a caseload."

Thus, organisational issues were difficult at both partnership and in-house specialist projects. The most striking difference was the conflict described at partnership projects, particularly where they were problematic. It is not wholly satisfactory to attribute this difference to the age of the specialist projects, enabling "teething troubles" to be long forgotten. Although both residential projects were the scenes of conflict in recent years, this was described primarily as a problem of theoretical approach. At problematic partnerships, conflict became personalised. Equally, no specialist complained of imposition, although all were stretched to manage their obligations to the project. Specialists defined their difficulties in terms of achieving quality services, rather than personalised conflict or resentment. Probation staff at problematic partnerships, however, were less concerned by conflict than their substance misuse colleagues. This again reflects their detachment from the enterprise.

The benefits of hindsight

Interviewees were asked what they would do differently, were they starting the project over again knowing what they now knew, with the benefit of their experience. Their responses are summarised in Tables 10.3 and 10.4.

At partnership projects, the most frequently advocated change was the service to clients, despite the earlier endorsements of benefits already gained. A successful experience encouraged probation staff to consider expansion or refinement: "I'd like to have someone of [the substance misuse worker's] calibre who was available for ongoing work with clients". At the only problematic partnership where the probation

Table 10.3 Changes advocated with the benefit of hindsight by probation and substance misuse staff at successful and problematic partnerships

Interviewees Partnership	Probation		Substance misuse		
	Successful	Problematic	Successful	Problematic	Total
The service	5	1	4	4	14
Prepare probation officers	2	1	3	7	13
More business like	6	3	2	1	12
More time to develop	3	2	1	4	10
Clarify roles	3	2	2	1	8
Evaluation	1	2	–	3	6
More structure	1	2	–	2	5
More space	1	1	–	3	5
Prepare sentencers	1	1	1	1	4
More resources	2	1	1	–	4
Have confidence	2	–	1	–	3
Understand workload implications	3	–	–	–	3
Control probation officer involvement	–	–	–	3	3
High level decisions	–	–	2	–	2
Refuse	–	–	–	2	2
Involve probation officers in plan	–	1	–	1	2
Access probation resources	–	–	1	1	2
Synchronise	–	–	1	–	1
Not to overinvest	–	–	1	–	1
Pro-active referral	–	1	–	–	1
Pay fares	–	1	–	–	1
Total	30	19	20	33	102
Percentage of total comments	29	19	20	32	100

Table 10.4 Changes advocated with the benefit of hindsight by probation and substance misuse staff at in-house specialist projects

Interviewees	Probation	Substance misuse	Total
Clear agreement	3	2	5
Service	3	–	3
Space	3	–	3
Publicity	2	–	2
Select staff	1	–	1
Follow-up provision	1	–	1
Monitoring	1	–	1
Protect identity	1	–	1
Involve management	1	–	1
Review best approach	1	–	1
Supervision	–	1	1
Specialist rotation	–	1	1
More specialists	–	1	1
Total	17	5	22

interviewee mentioned altering the service, the issue was indulgence of wayward clients: "I like the idea of some of the different groups they run, but being stricter". Substance misuse staff at both successful and problematic partnerships wanted to improve the quality of service: "It would be great if there was a reporting centre at [the probation office] which clients could use as a drop-in ... I could be around within that." Three substance misuse workers wanted the programme to address more personal issues: "It doesn't get as deep as I would wish it to. I would like it to be a deeper, more self-awareness oriented group than it is." For one probation officer, change in the service was not required, but more pro active encouragement to use it: "It's asking a lot to expect someone to turn up to a new group ... [We should expect] probation officers to bring their client along."

Over half the responses concerned planning and preparation for partnership. Preparing probation officers was mentioned frequently, particularly by substance misuse workers at problematic partnerships:

I would like to be assured that [the Assistant Chief Probation Officer] carried the staff with him, because that has caused us quite a few problems ... It's important that whoever negotiates on behalf of the probation service makes sure that the basic grade officers feel consulted.

[I should] have gone to probation management and said that they needed to explain the partnership properly to the team. I didn't get feedback from the consultation with the probation officers...I could have gone in with a ready made package and asked for comments and made changes as I went along.

Two interviewees at problematic partnerships wanted to include field probation officers in "ground up" development: "Passing this to our headquarters and letting them get on with it was a mistake. We can't really expect headquarters to be aware of local issues" (senior probation officer). By contrast, three disenchanted substance misuse workers preferred to control probation officers' involvement in the project: "Probation officers don't have the same training that I've had and the same outlook on clients...That for me causes problems, because we're not always working in unison in the group...That kind of friction I would try to avoid another time, maybe by interviewing probation officers or asking for someone who shares my views." Four interviewees mentioned preparatory work with sentencers: "If you've got those people on your side, you've got the whole system on your side" (substance misuse worker).

Probation staff, especially at successful partnerships, wanted to become more business like in negotiations, setting clearer objectives and task specifications at the outset.

It would have to relate more clearly to the objectives of the supervision of probation. How it met those objectives. Whether the [substance misuse agency] had the skills to deliver that. (senior probation officer)

The logic behind funding is service delivery. That's a priority...So we wanted to make sure that the direct service delivery recommendations were the ones which were prioritised. Perhaps that could have been clearer right at the outset in the job description. (senior probation officer)

It should be appropriately funded. I'm not asking for a luxury. I'm asking for funding for success...You can't do this kind of work on low paid, unskilled, untrained workers. You can't do it in an unpleasant, degrading environment. You can't do it without equipment...I do believe...that in statutory agencies people are unaware of this. They are frightened of big figures. We in the independent sector are encouraged to be entrepreneurial and to develop things, but in the statutory sector people are under confident about that, because they are unfamiliar with it. (substance misuse worker)

Ten interviewees wanted more time for early development.

> The initial stages seemed to be rushed. I wasn't involved in that, it was senior management. That may have had to do with time scales on partnership schemes and moves in our senior management... It was a tight time scale. They did well to secure the funding for this year, but in an ideal situation there could have been better preparation by both agencies (senior probation officer)

> I would want more development time. More lead time... In any major development like this, lead time is very important. (substance misuse manager)

Another theme was clarification of roles and relationships.

> I would have a clearer statement in terms of how we recruit workers, what is our role as a probation service – who aren't the employing body – in the recruitment process, from shortlisting right down to interview. (senior probation officer)

> It's too complicated. Certainly, if I was being paid by both [substance misuse agencies] it would be better than [being employed by] one and being expected to work in the other. That's difficult for the other agency as well... It's a very wide remit for one person to manage. (substance misuse worker)

More structure would improve inter-agency communication and collaboration. Evaluation was a concern.

Several interviewees requested specific resources, including physical space: "When I started, I didn't have a desk to work from, and when I did have a desk, it was in what was affectionately known as Hitler's bunker!" (substance misuse worker). One probation officer wanted to pay clients' fares to a rather distant project. Others were concerned more broadly with resources: "People don't lack the enthusiasm or commitment, but just the resources to do it properly" (probation officer). Three probation interviewees at successful partnerships failed to anticipate the projects' demands on time and attention: "I just thought it would be lovely working in partnership. I wasn't thinking that it would require me to supervise an additional person regularly." Two substance misuse workers wanted partner agencies to be linked to probation service resources: "I would like to have met with the information service at probation...to find out how I could disseminate the information quicker through them, rather than posting it out from here." One also saw advantages in synchronising partnership and probation service activities: "It's important to look at the people coming in and out of the probation centre. To get the van there at the times when probation officers feel that most clients will use it." Adequate resources required high level decision making: "It's all right to identify gaps and respond with a facility to meet the needs of those people, but that should be dealt with at a higher level, whereby the people with power, the real decision makers, look at it and cost it out" (substance misuse manager).

A few responses were personal. At three successful partnerships, interviewees advocated greater confidence in potential achievement: "Think big [in order] to be bigger. It worries me that drugs projects hide away in little back alleys. They're actually keeping their clients down and they're perpetuating that stigma" (substance misuse worker). One substance misuse worker would conserve energy: "Knowing how the time scales work, I wouldn't have tied up so much time in it as I have done over the past couple of years." Two disappointed substance misuse workers thought that they might refuse to participate: "I'm not sure I would want to be involved with it, quite frankly."

At in-house projects, the desire for clear agreement on the scope of the enterprise reflected a potentially overwhelming demand for specialists' services:

I would try to make clear to our bosses what time was involved and what were the aims. There seemed to be a problem that it said in policy documents that we should be working in a multi-faceted way. We shouldn't restrict ourselves to working only with offenders when it comes to drugs and alcohol. We have a wider range of responsibilities, like education, going into schools [and so on]. [But] when it comes to resources, we're very limited...That tends to lead us into a bit of a mess...But I have tried to get as clear a remit as possible.

Two substance misuse managers would be clearer about the relationship between the specialist and the host agency: "We would be in a better position to identify what exactly would be the commitment of the probation officer...What kind of input she would have within [the agency] other than clients."

Three specialists would modify their service:

I'd get in a community psychiatric nurse at the start to provide clinical input. I'd like a director who was able to bring together all the aspects of the programme...I'd put the real focus on the assessment period...and individual supervision plans built around the core programme.

Two specialists would publicise the service, outside the probation service itself: "Publicity is the important key. I would try to have as big a publicity drive as I possibly could...to make sure as many people knew about the groups as possible, and particularly the family support group." A specialist at a residential project wanted better after-care provision.

Three specialists wanted more physical space: "I'd like a place which gave us two more groupwork rooms, so that we have greater flexibility."

Remaining comments primarily concerned project management. One seconded specialist thought that managers at both agencies should exchange views more frequently. Getting the right people for the task was important: "We need expertise. It's not enough just to have good will, you've got to have the knowledge and the ability to use that knowledge." Improved monitoring systems and mechanisms to protect the professional identity of specialists were required, as was a review of the best approach for service delivery: "Whether secondment is the best way to do it. Is everybody getting value for money? Could it be done more effectively in other ways?"

Substance misuse staff were also concerned with project management, although with different emphases. One manager would improve supervision for seconded specialists: "That wasn't apparent five or six years ago, but I would definitely bring it in if it was starting tomorrow. The access to support, to supervision, both from our service and from probation." Rotating the specialist post struck one manager as a good innovation:

I like the new idea of eighteen months' rotation...More probation officers should feel able to deal with drug using offenders. Increasing the rotation will help that. I've no doubt about that. That's a positive move by the probation service. They need to be applauded. When I first heard about it I felt it was negative, because I thought they were taking away. But they're not. They very much want to continue and I can see the benefits behind what they're doing.

A substance misuse worker wanted more specialists: "It would be beneficial if there were two people...That would allocate more time.

There could be more in-depth work done and the opportunity for the other person to concentrate on the groupwork."

Recommendations from in-house specialist projects did not include mechanisms to reduce conflict. At partnership projects, recommendations focused heavily on effective preparation and structures to reduce confusion and conflict. Most striking was the concentration of such responses among substance misuse staff at problematic partnerships, particularly regarding involvement of field probation officers. Paradoxically, probation staff at successful partnerships made many suggestions for improving their projects, while at problematic partnerships they offered relatively little. Again, this reflects the strong investment of probation staff at successful projects, and their detachment elsewhere. That substance misuse staff at successful projects also made fewer recommendations for change, and were less troubled by deficiencies in preparation, may testify to the support which they encountered from the outset.

Professional satisfaction

The energy that probation officers dedicated to preserving their casework activity, and the gloom with which many forecast their transformation into enforcement agents suggested that they perhaps envied substance misuse workers their continuing, and even expanding, professional role. Would they wish to swop places? The answer was overwhelmingly negative. One consideration was their superior conditions of employment:

> I have thought about it, because, when the [partnership] post came up, I did consider it. But [the substance misuse agency] is appallingly badly funded, pays appallingly badly and doesn't have a pension scheme, so that's it!

> Not likely!... Tremendous pressure on them. The problems of day by day having to justify your existence in the job. [Here], funding is reasonably secure, the role and functions are reasonably secure ...I've got a team of ten probation officers. If one person goes sick, it doesn't cause major problems in the short term. If you've [only] got two members of staff, you're knackered, aren't you?

> I would not want to swop places with somebody in that position, working for a small organisation with low job security. I have worked for some voluntary organisations before entering the probation

service and those issues are at the top of the agenda for staff all of the time. They are way down the agenda when you work for a big organisation. Also... there is more security of employment working for a large organisation which is less hampered by personality.

Another popular explanation was the variety of probation work:

I would hate to swop jobs. I couldn't think of anything worse. It would drive me mad, talking to incessant drinkers all day and every day.

I'm very happy with the job I've got because it's so varied. Drugs work would be depressing. Although you see people at their lowest ebb in this job [too], to me that's different.

I wouldn't expect it to give me the variety that I've got in probation... There are other choices in probation – hostel work, court work.

Contact with offenders and the criminal justice system was an important aspect of job satisfaction:

I would find it difficult to do that, because [the substance misuse worker] has told me that whereas the people we get to the group are people who have offended, for the people he counsels during the rest of the week, it is very unusual for their misuse of alcohol to have caused them to offend. So, if I was to swop, I'd have to think very hard, because the crime element doesn't feature in the sort of people that they counsel on a regular basis.

Six probation staff might change places, usually subject to certain conditions:

Well, I think they're not very professional. I wouldn't mind running an agency like that provided I had the resources... It's quite an exciting prospect, but they should be developing a lot more with other agencies.

There are things about the voluntary sector which grab me. It's quite exciting, there's a lot of innovative work... It would get away from a lot of the bureaucracy that is inherent in the probation service... [But] voluntary sector agencies vary so much. Some seem to be just fighting for survival. That insecurity, and having to dance to different tunes, would bother me...The answer's no. Not unless it was the right job, in the right voluntary agency, in the right part of the country.

There were only five clearly positive responses:

I wouldn't have any problems at all. I expect I'd enjoy it. I think the voluntary sector is the main growth area in this field. The statutory sector is increasingly limited and increasingly required to spend its money in the voluntary sector, so there's very little opportunity for growth. The voluntary sector provides more potential...Also a lot of voluntary organisations...make us look rather institutionalised. So I think I'd be happy to work for a good voluntary sector organisation.

Occasionally I have thought it would be nice to get away from the compulsive [sic] element of probation work, and not to have to send out constant letters saying you haven't kept you're appointment, and to be involved in the different atmosphere that there is in voluntary agencies where clients are coming because they want to. You're not seen quite so much as a threat or an upholder of law and order.

These responses were not influenced by the quality of partnership in interviewees' experience. Nor were the predominantly negative reactions of substance misuse workers to this question. While probation officers at this point acknowledged stability and security in their agency, they had apparently convinced their partners that they were severely threatened:

I wouldn't, because I think probation is going to be cut, to have part of its functions contracted out in a number of years. There's a very dissatisfied group of probation officers, who have often been in the service for a long time, who came into the service because they wanted to do hands-on work with individuals, [but] the emphasis is now very much on quantity, not quality. Managing that kind of discontent is hard, particularly since probation has always been a fairly flat organisation, and individuals have had a lot of responsibility and control over their own work. Taking that back, which is what the changes mean, is hard.

[The probation service] has been dictated to by the Home Office and government as to how to work with people. It's now more about punishment in the community. Probation officers have been put into that soft policing role, which doesn't lie comfortably with me.

Substance misuse staff were deterred by the criminal justice environment:

> I have big problems with the criminal justice system, personally. It's just scandalous that you take drug addicts and lock them up. That's absurd and inhuman. You don't do it to an alcoholic ... you don't do it to a cigarette smoker. These are better analogies for me than criminal behaviour ... These are personal views, but they would make it very difficult for me to work in the criminal justice system.

> I wouldn't be able to breach somebody, and I wouldn't be able to lay the law down. It just isn't me ... Because I'm youth work trained, so I would be looking at the informal approaches. Looking at the motivational opportunities I see.

Several interviewees based their conclusion on direct experience:

> I did my social work placement in probation, so it is not an alien area to me ... It sounds too much like hard work to me, to be perfectly honest. Also it is moving and changing towards the more controlling aspects. I like to dress like this. I couldn't do that in a straight agency. But I am also very committed to working with drug users.

> Well, I still am a probation officer one day a week! I've always worked in the probation service before now. I don't really want to go back ... I'm going to start trying to work in a counselling practice ... trying to do some training.

A striking aspect of these responses was the admiration sometimes expressed for probation officers:

> I don't think so, because I think their work is appallingly hard. I think that it's one of the toughest jobs in the universe, from what I've seen of it ... They are in a very horrible position, because sometimes they are having to work within very limited resources ... They have to work with desperately undesirable people and they have got no choice about whether they will work with them or not. They can't say "My agency doesn't handle you." They have to go with it, and communicate with them. That is very, very hard, because some of the people are just dead nasty people.

No. I don't have any kind of social work background, I'm not social work focused, and I have a cynical point of view. I'm a counsellor, not a rescuer.

It's something I've thought about... I admire what they do. It's just unfortunate that they're misconstrued by the public and by the people they minister to. Although they are court officers, they are a lot more friendly and a lot more understanding.

No! I would not! Good God, they've got their work cut out for them! No, I love alcies. They're the nicest bunch of people you could hope to meet, when they're sober. I love seeing the changes that they go through, I love seeing them get well... I wouldn't swop with a probation officer for the world. They've got a terrible job!

Three interviewees thought it might be an interesting job: "I would question their last restructuring and the way it was handled, and the money spent on it... But before I was here, I worked for a beer importer, and it's the other side of the coin. I was bringing the beer in and now I'm trying to save them from it! The service has a purpose to it and I like that." Two would like to change places, apparently thinking they could do a better job than some already in post: "I have seen this lack of communication, lack of understanding. Obviously they have their rules and procedures, but there must be a degree of flexibility within that. I like to think I'm fairly good at communication... So, yes, I would be delighted to change places."

For specialist staff at in-house projects, the attraction of substance misuse work lay in the distinctive nature of their particular roles:

The reason I took on this post was because I was very interested in the developmental side of it. I didn't want to come here just as a substance misuse worker or just as a probation officer.

I have tremendous regard for the manager of the drugs project here... Would I like to step into his shoes? No. He's so profoundly non-judgemental. I think that's really cool at times, but I've got this moral righteousness that I'm always trying to shake off. I've still got this belief that it's probably easier to give up using a drug altogether than to try to cut it down. You're talking to an ex-smoker, and harm reduction didn't work for me!... Most of the people we deal with here are not recreational users. These are people who will tell you that they have do a lot of burglaries every day just to break even with their debts...I'm certain that without a place like [this] these problems will continue...I want to see [this project] get its own act together, and I'll leave other people to run their own agencies.

I don't have the particular drive to work in the substance misuse field. I'm a probation service manager. I'm not driven by any other peculiar commitment to drug and alcohol work. It's just a job that should be done as well as possible.

The social worker was on the verge of leaving about twelve months ago. I thought that would be quite nice, to be a social worker in the clinic. But then, now I've been there a year, I don't fancy it, because that's got political problems. The social worker role in the clinic isn't very [exciting]. He gets landed with all the housing problems, all the welfare problems, the benefit problems or the community care assessments...So he's very limited in what he can achieve.

Three specialists thought, doubtfully, that they might make the change: "I did begin to wonder if I would like to do a course in counselling skills and work in the field of alcohol...But I now wonder if you could get stale with it and feel that you're dealing with the same stuff a lot of the time...I'm probably very steeped in the probation mould by now and would have to change very drastically to fit in to some of my perceptions of substance misuse agencies." Three were attracted: "In some ways I wouldn't mind, because it seems to be a freer way of working, not worrying about National Standards so much. Working for a voluntary agency has lots of attractions...Yes, yes, that's a yes!"

One substance misuse manager at a specialist project did not find the prospect of working for the probation service compatible with personal attitudes: "I come from a [particular cultural] background. I believe in custodial sentences, I believe in forced labour. I come from a country where we have forced labour...I do not feel these people should evade custodial sentences because of a drug or alcohol problem." Another liked the challenge: "As a lot of drug using clients have also got probation backgrounds there's a lot of similarities, but at the same time there's a lot of newness...I would like to feel that might be an exciting thing to get involved with, like this was when I first came into it." A substance misuse worker offered a compromise: "What I would consider is [to work for probation] as long as I could keep this role. A specialist role. That does appeal to me."

Conclusion

While probation officers and substance misuse workers perceived their jobs to be distinct, this was not apparently because of a widening gap between the roles of case management and service delivery. Probation officers saw breadth and variety in their work unavailable in the drugs field. Indeed, we saw earlier that substance misuse staff valued the additional variety which their involvement in partnership offered. Even for probation specialists, interest in substance misuse was rooted in the distinctiveness of their projects, rather than a general attraction to the field. This was, certainly, clear in the experience of specialists at Project B. Despite anxieties for their professional future, probation officers found much to claim their continuing allegiance to their agency. The unhappy experiences at many problematic partnerships reveal that the nature of that allegiance must be understood and harnessed if the partnership enterprise is to succeed.

11
Pathways to Partnership

This study began at a time of upheaval in the planning and delivery of public welfare services. A series of complex, interconnected transitions were taking place as the partnership enterprise began, involving statutory organisations and the voluntary sector in transforming the structure of health and social care arrangements. The probation service itself was experiencing the early stages of alterations to its funding, allied to expectations of a wide-ranging shift in its approach to the supervision of offenders, in which the partnership initiative played a part. Thereafter, however, the imperatives of penal policy and associated arrangements for the delivery of penal sanctions developed in unanticipated directions, with renewed emphasis during the 1990s on incarceration supported by tough, enforcement oriented community penalties. There seems no end to the flux of penal innovation and no relief from the pace of change. This unstable state of affairs increases, rather than diminishes, the relevance of studies such as this. Research output cannot keep pace with the penal tide. Yet studies such as this reveal lessons about the ways in which organisations, and individuals within them, define change in terms of insecurity and threat or opportunity and challenge, and respond accordingly. At times of rapid and complex refigurations of the penal environment, such lessons can be applied to new situations, in order to achieve footholds of stability of purpose and strategy amidst the queasy anticipation of impending chaos.

Who needs partnership?

The lack of concern expressed at substance misuse agencies about the material consequences of losing partnership with the probation service was initially considered in terms of the limited opportunities which it brought. However, a broader perspective may be derived from literature concerned with the voluntary sector's experience of the "contract culture" in the aftermath of the NHS and Community Care Act in 1990. Voluntary organisations have demonstrated their ability not merely to survive, but to flourish in the developing market for health and social care services (Johnson, Jenkinson, Kendall, Bradshaw and Blackmore 1998; Ware 1990). A number of reasons have been suggested for this.

Firstly, accepting funding from government sources to provide particular forms of care was not the new experience for voluntary organisations that purchasing such services was for statutory agencies such as the probation service (Kendall and Knapp 1996; Taylor and Lewis 1997). An undertanding of the partnership experience which is predominantly coloured by the probation service's perspective risks obscuring this point. Billis (1993) also points to the relatively recent rapid expansion of agencies which look primarily to government both for resources and direction, by virtue of the centralised concern for the problems with which they deal. Many voluntary substance misuse agencies serve as examples of this phenomenon, not least due to their direct involvement in health promotion among client groups which are hard to reach. These agencies increasingly number among the key players in the pursuit of a co-ordinated drugs policy (Lord President of the Council and Leader of the House of Commons et al. 1995; President of the Council 1998).

Moreover, the scarcity of voluntary sector providers at local level, and particularly of those, such as substance misuse agencies, which offer highly specialised services, strengthens the position of those which do exist (Forder, Knapp and Wistow 1996; Johnson, Jenkinson, Kendall, Bradshaw and Blackmore 1998). Indeed, the more stigmatised and unattractive the client goup, the more likely it is that provision will be, partly or substantially, located in the voluntary sector (Billis and Glennerster 1998), thus again underlining the mutual interdependence of statutory and non-statutory agencies for the achievement of policy objectives in certain spheres. Finally, loss of agency autonomy in the world of contracted care services has perhaps been more feared than actual (Kendall and Knapp 1996).

Thus, substance misuse agencies were relatively free to view potential loss of partnership in terms of its qualitative impoverishment of services for a vulnerable client group. Indeed, recognition of otherwise unmet need may be one of the strongest "barriers to exit" (Forder, Knapp and Wistow 1996) from contractual care arrangements. In contrast to this relative security, the probation service has found itself under mounting pressure to re-define its mission in terms of correctional enforcement (Brownlee 1998; Worrall 1997). In stark opposition to the enthusiasm of probation officers for proactive contribution to the health of local communities revealed in this study, the service's role in the community is increasingly discussed in the negative sense of enforcing those punishments which are not custodial (Crawford 1997).

This study reveals the depth of resistance within the probation service to such an impoverished delineation of its mission. In these circumstances, the service needs strong alliances with partners willing to assist it to reassert its connections with care, rehabilitation and reintegration within the community. Partnership may thus, paradoxically, be seen as vital to the endorsement and preservation of a tradition of care seen to be properly located within and expressed by an agency of government.

Partners in punishment

As has been noted also in the development of community care contracting (Johnson, Jenkinson, Kendall, Bradshaw and Blackmore 1998), the haste with which the partnership initiative was contrived forced probation services to rely on historical and informal connections. Yet in many areas it was assumed, however reluctantly, that open competitive tendering would become the predominant mechanism of partner selection. The practice of reliance on traditional relationships might, therefore, be expected to change as the partnership enterprise gathers momentum and probation services gain experience.

Yet, on reflection, why should it change? Notwithstanding discomfort with the terminology and methods of the market place, which may lessen over time, there are several deeper reasons to question a major shift towards open competitive tendering. First, in this context, it may be noted that the experience of the "contract culture" in community care does not clearly predict the growth of a competitive market for probation service partnerships. The findings of one recently reported study of community care contracting offer several grounds for scepticism: contracts were awarded predominantly to known providers; open competitive tendering was used only for the largest contracts; "managed competition" occurred within a relatively small field of players; and competition declined, rather than accelerated over time, with increasing bias towards the "resident" contract holders (Johnson, Jenkinson, Kendall, Bradshaw and Blackmore 1998).

A second reason requires us to take seriously the vision of partnership expressed in partnership plans and frequently endorsed by telephone survey respondents. While it is tempting to attribute reliance on historical and informal connections to circumstantial expedience, which clearly *was* a factor in selection, partnership development on this basis produced examples of projects which were entirely compatible with ideologies of sharing, support and empowerment. The emphasis on local initiatives in substance misuse workers' accounts of the origins of their agencies complemented the importance which partnership plans and probation staff attributed to neighbourhood relationships.

Moreover, in terms of their theoretical orientations, partner agencies were apparently well chosen, whether by accident or design. Theoretical approaches described by substance misuse staff were familiar and acceptable to most probation officers. Their diversity complemented the broad, pragmatic notions of harm reduction expressed by telephone survey respondents. Most particularly, the tolerance and flexibility shown at partner agencies towards the fallibility of their clients, and in particular the non-judgemental, pragmatic responses to continuing or resumed substance misuse, offered a crucial lifeline to wayward offenders, enabling a path to be steered between accountability for service and sympathy for personal vulnerability.

These partner agency perspectives were clearly instrumental in enabling probation officers to avoid entrapment in narrow roles of correctional enforcement. The evidence of previous chapters strongly suggests that the areas of real contention between probation officers and substance misuse workers were rarely connected with the allegedly sensitive issue of coercion in treatment. The general resistance of probation officers to coercive intervention and the consensus between probation and substance misuse staff as to the important characteristics of meaningful engagement with clients reveal clear complementarity in approach.

Problematic partnerships foundered on quite different rocks: failure, particularly by probation staff, to invest in the partnership enterprise; failure to identify enhancements to professional practice; concern to protect the quality of professional life in the probation service; deficiencies in the organisation of partnership; and failure to derive personal gains from the partnership experience. These are not ideological divergences *between* organisations, but structural faults embedded *within* them. Moreover, the evidence from successful partnerships and in-house specialisations tells us that they are not inevitable and irremovable flaws, but may be overcome through positive leadership and management.

Minimising harms

Probation services and their partners *could* elect to make their alliance of perspectives explicit in future projects, openly challenging presumptions of their complicity in coercion. Again, it is the relative strength of the position of *voluntary* partners which makes this possible. Substance misuse agencies are becoming vital players in the delivery of penal sanctions, as problems of drug abuse command the attention of policy makers and practitioners in the criminal justice system. In such a climate of "criminalisation of social policy" (Crawford 1997), it does not follow that the contribution of these agencies must pursue the objectives of surveillance and law enforcement. Imaginative partnerships may yet exploit the opportunities of criminal justice funding to enhance social provision for the disadvantaged, marginalised and stigmatised populations common among the caseloads of probation officers and substance misuse workers (Crawford 1997).

The manner in which probation officers articulated the importance of meaningful engagement with clients and of professional discretion in complex judgements of individual accountability and vulnerability reveal an intuitive awareness that the penal sanctions which they administered were capable of delivering varieties of harm to offenders which brought no countervailing benefit to other members of society. In this sense, probation officers were daily engaged in efforts to reduce experiences of "penal harm" (Clear 1994). They were thus no strangers to harm minimisation, although the specific terminology and techniques of drug interventions might have been unfamiliar to some.

The reactions of probation officers and substance misuse staff to the invitation to consider drug testing as part of offender supervision exposes a strong differentiation between treatment and enforcement. It was their common view that drug testing of offenders under supervision confused these two separate issues by implementing a treatment activity *as if* it were an enforcement activity. The consequences of such conflation of objectives in threatening an otherwise promising project have emerged in one recent report (Barton 1999). The issue remains to be resolved, while experimentation with new forms of court mandated drug treatment presses on.

This is not to argue against coercion in treatment in itself. The experience at Project A demonstrates that coercion can play a useful part in attracting into treatment groups which are otherwise hard to engage, within both the community and the criminal justice system. However, the use of coercion to construct treatment opportunities for otherwise unreachable groups does not imply that the *activities* of treatment and enforcement are the same. To equate such disparate activities raises the prospect that the technologies for reduction of drug-related harm will yield increases in penal harm. This phenomenon has been well established in American research into the effects of intensive supervision programmes in which enforcement dominates over treatment in professional activity (Clear and Hardyman 1990; Petersilia and Turner 1990). The effect will be strengthened when the pace of development of drug treatment resources fails to match that of enforcement processes (Erwin 1990).

Yet these consequences do not have to flow inevitably from closer alliances between probation services and drug treatment agencies. This study shows the creativity with which probation officers and substance misuse workers approached their tasks. However, without explicitness in defining the harm reducing enterprise in which both are engaged, the mutuality of objectives, the complementarity of tasks, and the strategies of leadership, management and support, those creative energies will be misdirected, counterproductive and disappointing for both parties.

These observations have strong implications for the quality of the relationship to be understood by the term "partnership". Explorations of the so-called "contract culture" of community care suggest that narrow, legalistic definitions of the contracting relationship between statutory and voluntary organisations neglect the value-based, informal and creatively collusive inter-agency negotiations which contribute to the delivery of health and social care (Batsleer and Paton 1997). In a field of endeavour in which complex needs are necessarily treated holistically, and "quality of life" evaluations impede concrete measurements of effectiveness (Flynn, Pickard and Williams 1995), it is overly simplistic to view the contractual relationship merely as one in which a weaker voluntary agency yields degrees of autonomy to, and fulfils only those tasks which are determined by a more powerful statutory one (Batsleer and Paton 1997). More sophisticated and helpful analyses appeal to the interdependence of different organisations, embedded within a network of relationships which *necessarily* involve mutual alliance, reciprocity, assistance and trust (Batsleer and Paton 1997; Flynn, Pickard and Williams 1995; Johnson, Jenkinson, Kendall, Bradshaw and Blackmore 1998).

The partnership mission

Predictions that partnerships for the delivery of programmes for substance misusing offenders would founder on ideological differences lack a full appreciation of the probation service as an agency within the criminal justice system. They signally fail to comprehend the breadth of the probation service's vision of its role in the community, which this research has revealed most clearly in the examination of in-house specialist projects, but is also apparent in the extraordinary diversity of inter-agency activities which were found in the partnership plans. In-house specialist projects, and successful partnerships capitalised upon this vision of the probation service as an active contributor to the health of local communities. The belief that they were fulfilling some part of this role fuelled the energies and commitment of probation officers at these projects. It is this larger organisational enterprise which is truly at stake in the partnership initiative, rather than the narrow individualism which resistance so often appears to represent. While some probation officers at problematic partnerships acquitted themselves poorly, there were also structural reasons for their failure to identify enhancements which were rooted in the inadequate design and management of their projects. A more telling and poignant indicator of the source of their resentment can be seen in the lack of personal investment in the health of problematic projects, where officers were unable to fulfil their ambitions for the mission of the probation service through the partnership enterprise.

The true vision of partnership, then, concerns the fulfilment of the probation service's broad professional mission through inter-agency activities. It is not merely a matter of contracting for isolated elements of supervision programmes. The apparently inspirational initiatives at in-house specialist projects and successful partnerships testify to the capture of this vision within the realities of local constraints and opportunities, but this is an achievement which is not easily accomplished, and most certainly cannot be left to chance and goodwill. These projects' experiences present the strongest justification for the argument that there is no formula for an inter-agency project which guarantees success, but rather success derives from the injection of certain types of effort into locally defined opportunities.

The varied local environments of community care arrangements, organisational structures, the nature and quality of substance misuse services and existing inter-agency relationships cannot be accomodated by a prescription for a single type of arrangement for the development of special programmes for offenders. Indeed, such programmes make no coherent sense unless they are embedded within the local framework of services to the wider community. This was the backdrop to Project A's successful innovation of a targetted programme for offenders, to Project

B's effective integration into multi-disciplinary statutory teams, and to Project C's empowerment of a fledgling voluntary agency.

This point should not be confused with the noted tendency of probation officers to laud diversity for its own sake (Mair 1996). It promotes a practice which is quite the antithesis of indiscriminate, albeit well-intentioned and energetic, activity, but which instead hones service development to respond to identified local needs, constraints and opportunities (Petersilia 1990). Moreover, the emergent locally defined arrangements require the infusion of the ingredients of success, which are not matters of chance or goodwill, but which can indeed be identified and deliberately structured into the enterprise (Petersilia 1990). The evidence of this study indicates that those ingredients of success include effective championship, the delivery of recognised enhancements, and proactive management in the design and promotion of the partnership venture.

References

Abrams, P. (1981) *Action for Care: a Review of Good Neighbour Schemes in England and Wales*. Berkhamsted, The Volunteer Centre.

Advisory Council on the Misuse of Drugs (1982) *Treatment and Rehabilitation*. London, HMSO.

Advisory Council on the Misuse of Drugs (1988) *AIDS and Drug Misuse: Part 1*. London, HMSO.

Advisory Council on the Misuse of Drugs (1991) *Drug Misusers and the Criminal Justice System. Part 1: Community Resources and the Probation Service*. London, HMSO.

Barton, A. (1999) "Breaking the Crime/Drugs Cycle: the Birth of a New Approach?" *The Howard Journal of Criminal Justice*, 38 (2): 144–57.

Batsleer, J. and Paton, R. (1997) "Managing Voluntary Organisations in the Contract Culture: Continuity or Change?" pp. 47–56 in Perri 6 [*sic*] and J. Kendall (eds) *The Contract Culture in Public Services: Studies from Britain, Europe and the USA*. Aldershot, Arena.

Billis, D. (1993) *Organising Public and Voluntary Agencies*. London, Routledge.

Billis, D. and Glennerster, H. (1998) "Human Services and the Voluntary Sector: Towards a Theory of Comparative Advantage." *Journal of Social Policy*, 27 (1): 79–98.

Blagg, H., Pearson, G., Sampson, A., Smith, D., and Stubbs, P. (1998) "Inter-agency Co-ordination: Rhetoric and Reality." In T. Hope and M. Shaw (eds) *Communities and Crime Reduction*, pp. 204–20. London, HMSO.

Brain Committee (1965) *Drug Addiction*. Second Report of the Interdepartmental Committee. London, HMSO.

Broad, B. (1991) *Punishment under Pressure: the Probation Service in the Inner City*. London, Jessica Kingsley.

Brownlee, I. (1998) *Community Punishment: a Critical Introduction*. Harlow, Addison-Wesley Longman.

Clear, T.R. (1994) *Harm in American Penology*. Albany, NY, State University of New York Press.

Clear, T.R. and Hardyman, P.L. (1990) "The New Intensive Supervision Movement." *Crime and Delinquency*, 36 (1): 42–60.

Clear, T.R. and Rumgay, J. (1992) "Divided by a Common Language: British and American Probation Cultures." *Federal Probation*, 56 (3): 3–11.

Crawford, A. (1997) *The Local Governance of Crime: Appeals to Community and Partnerships*. Oxford, Oxford University Press.

Crawford, A. and Jones, M. (1995) "Inter-agency Co-operation and Community Based Crime Prevention." *British Journal of Criminology*, 35 (1): 17–33.

Department of Health (1989) *Caring for People: Community Care in the Next Decade and Beyond*. London, HMSO.

Department of Health and Social Security (1981) *Drinking Sensibly*. London, HMSO.

Dorn, N. (1990) "Substance Abuse and Prevention Strategies," pp. 232–43 in H. Ghodse and D. Maxwell (eds) *Substance Abuse and Dependence: an Introduction for the Caring Professions*. Basingstoke, Macmillan.

Dorn, N. and South, N. (1985) *Helping Drug Users*. Aldershot, Gower.

Erwin, B.S. (1990) "Old and New Tools for the Modern Probation Officer." *Crime and Delinquency*, 36 (1): 60–74.

Fielder, M. (1992) "Purchasing and Providing Services for Offenders: Lessons from America," pp. 163–72 in R. Statham and P. Whitehead (eds) *Managing the Probation Service: Issues for the 1990s*. Harlow, Longman.

Flynn, N. and Hurley, D. (1993) *The Market for Care*. London, Public Sector Management, London School of Economics.

Flynn, R., Pickard, S. and Williams, G. (1995) "Contracts and Quasi-market in Community Health Services." *Journal of Social Policy*, 24 (4): 529–50.

Forder, J., Knapp, M. and Wistow, G. (1996) "Competition in the Mixed Economy of Care." *Journal of Social Policy*, 25 (2): 201–21.

Goodsir, J. (1992) "A Strategic Approach to the Criminal Justice Act." *Druglink*, Sept./Oct., pp. 12–14.

Haynes, P. (1990) "Sentenced to get Better." *Druglink*, Jan./Feb., pp. 8–10.

HM Inspectorate of Probation (1993) *Offenders Who Use Drugs: The Probation Service Response. Report of a Thematic Inspection*. London, HM Inspectorate of Probation.

Home Office (1988) *Punishment, Custody and the Community*. London, Home Office.

Home Office (1990a) "*Crime, Justice and Protecting the Public.*" Cm 965. London, HMSO.

Home Office (1990b) "*Supervision and Punishment in the Community: a Framework for Action.*" Cm 966. London, HMSO.

Home Office (1990c) "*Partnership in Dealing with Offenders in the Community.*" London, Home Office.

Home Office (1992) *Partnership in Dealing with Offenders in the Community: a Decision Document*. London, Home Office.

Home Office (1993a) *CPO 23/1993: "Probation Service Partnership Policy: Submission of Partnership Plans 1993–1994."* London, Home Office.

Home Office (1993b) *PC 16/1993: "Probation Supervision Grants Scheme: Arrangements for Grants to Local Projects 1994–1995."* London, Home Office.

Home Office (1993c) *PC 17/1993: "Partnership in Dealing with Offenders in the Community: Submission of Partnership Plans 1994–1997."* London, Home Office.

Home Office (1993d) *Probation Circular No. 6/1993: Probation Services and the Management of Voluntary Sector Organisations*. London, Home Office.

Home Office (1995) *Addressing the Problems of Drug and Alcohol Misuse Among Offenders: Guidance for Probation Service Management*. London, Home Office.

Johnson, N., Jenkinson, S., Kendall, I., Bradshaw, Y. and Blackmore, M. (1998) "Regulating for Quality in the Voluntary Sector." *Journal of Social Policy*, 27 (3): 307–28.

Kendall, J. and Knapp, M. (1996) *The Voluntary Sector in the United Kingdom*. Manchester, Manchester University Press.

Lee, M. and Mainwaring, S. (1995) "No Big Deal: Court-ordered Treatment in Practice." *Druglink*, Jan./Feb., pp. 14–15.

Lipsky, M. (1980) *Street-level Bureaucracy: Dilemmas of the Individual in Public Services*. New York, Russell Sage.

Lord President of the Council and Leader of the House Commons, Secretary of State for the Home Department, Secretary of State for Health, Secretary of State for Education and the Paymaster General (1995) *Tackling Drugs Together: a Strategy for England 1995–98*. Cm 2846. London, HMSO.

Maguire, M., Peroud, B. and Raynor, P., (1996) *Automatic Conditional Release: the First Two Years*. Home Office Research Study 156. London, Home Office.

Mair, G. (1996) "Developments in Probation in England and Wales 1984–1993," pp. 25–38 in G. McIvor (ed.) *Working with Offenders*. London, Jessica Kingsley.

McWilliams, W. (1983) "The Mission to the English Police Courts, 1876–1936." *The Howard Journal*, 22: 129–47.

O'Hare, P.A., Newcombe, R., Matthews, A., Buning, E.C. and Drucker, E. (eds) (1992) *The Reduction of Drug-related Harm*. London, Routledge.

Padel, U. (1990) "Fair Trial for Justice Proposals." *Druglink*, Sept./Oct., pp. 6–7.

Petersilia, J. (1990) "Conditions that Permit Intensive Supervision Programmes to Survive." *Crime and Delinquency*, 36 (1): 126–45.

Petersilia, J. and Turner, S. (1990) "Comparing Intensive and Regular Supervision for High-risk Probationers: Early Results from an Experiment in California." *Crime and Delinquency*, 36 (1): 87–111.

President of the Council (1998) *Tackling Drugs to Build a Better Britain: the Government's Ten-year Strategy for Tackling Drugs Misuse*. Cm 3945. London, HMSO.

Prochaska, J. and Diclemente, C. (1986) "Toward a Comprehensive Model of Change," pp. 3–27 in W.R. Miller and N. Heather (eds) *Treating Addictive Behaviors: Processes of Change*. New York, Plenum Press.

Raynor, P. (1985) *Social Work, Justice and Control*. Oxford, Blackwell.

Rumgay, J. (1994) *Drug and Alcohol Treatment Requirements in Probation Orders: a Survey of Developments since October 1992*. Report to the Home Office Research and Planning Unit (unpublished).

Rumgay, J. (1998) *Crime, Punishment and the Drinking Offender*. Basingstoke, Macmillan.

Rumgay, J. and Brewster, M. (1996) "Restructuring Probation in England and Wales: Lessons from an American Experience." *The Prison Journal*, 76 (3): 331–47.

Ryan, M. and Ward, T. (1989) *Privatization and the Penal System: the American Experience and the Debate in Britain*. Milton Keynes, Open University Press.

Taylor, M. and Lewis, J. (1997) "Contracting: What does it do to Voluntary and Non-profit Organisations?" pp. 27–45 in Perri 6 [sic] and J. Kendall (eds) *The Contract Culture in Public Services: Studies from Britain, Europe and the USA*. Aldershot, Arena.

Vanstone, M. (1993) "A 'Missed Opportunity' Re-assessed: the influence of the Day Training Centre Experiment on the Criminal Justice System and Probation Policy and Practice." *British Journal of Social Work*, 23 (3): 213–29.

Ware, A. (1990) "Meeting Needs Through Voluntary Action: Does Market Society Corrode Altruism?" pp. 185–207 in A. Ware and R.E. Goodin (eds) *Needs and Welfare*. London, Sage.

Weisner, C. and Room, R. (1984) "Financing and Ideology in Alcohol Treatment." *Social Problems*, 32 (2): 167–84.

Wistow, G., Knapp, M., Hardy, B. and Allen, C. (1994) *Social Care in a Mixed Economy*. Buckingham, Open University Press.

Worrall, A. (1997) *Punishment in the Community: the Future of Criminal Justice*. Harlow, Addison-Wesley Longman.

Index

Page numbers in bold type refer to tables and figures